MW00826118

Dave Chermanski has more than 50 years of fly fishing experience and he has caught more than 450 marine and freshwater species in North American waters on his own fly designs. He is internationally known for his fishing exploits, which include more than 70 world records. More than 50 of these world records are International Game Fish Association catches on fly fishing tackle. He has also set fly fishing records for the largest fish of 20 species caught in the State of Florida and he has received many other awards for his angling achievements over the past 40 years.

Dave Chermanski is a former freelance outdoor writer and photographer. From 1971 to 1986, he penned scores of how-to articles to various regional and national publications on the subjects of fly fishing, fly casting and fly tying. He is also a lecturer and instructor, who has conducted hundreds of fly fishing programs, fly casting clinics and fly tying workshops for more than 25 years. Since 1971, he has served as consultant to various U.S. and foreign

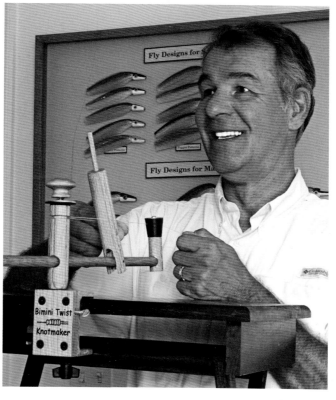

fishing tackle companies in the design and development of various products including fly lines, fly reels, fly rods, rod guides and other fishing tackle.

Professionally, Dave Chermanski has been employed as a scientist/engineer on the Space Shuttle program with Rockwell International and Boeing since 1979 and academically, he holds Bachelor of Science degrees in oceanography and electrical engineering, a Master of Science degree in computer science and an Associate of Science degree in marine biology.

Born in the coal-mining region of St. Clair, Pennsylvania, Dave Chermanski honed his fly-fishing skills primarily on coldwater trout streams and smallmouth bass rivers prior to moving to Melbourne, Florida in 1967. He lives in Merritt Island, Florida with his wife and childhood sweetheart, Carol. They have two sons and two granddaughters. Their younger son, Willie, is a licensed captain who has guided Dave to many of his world record catches.

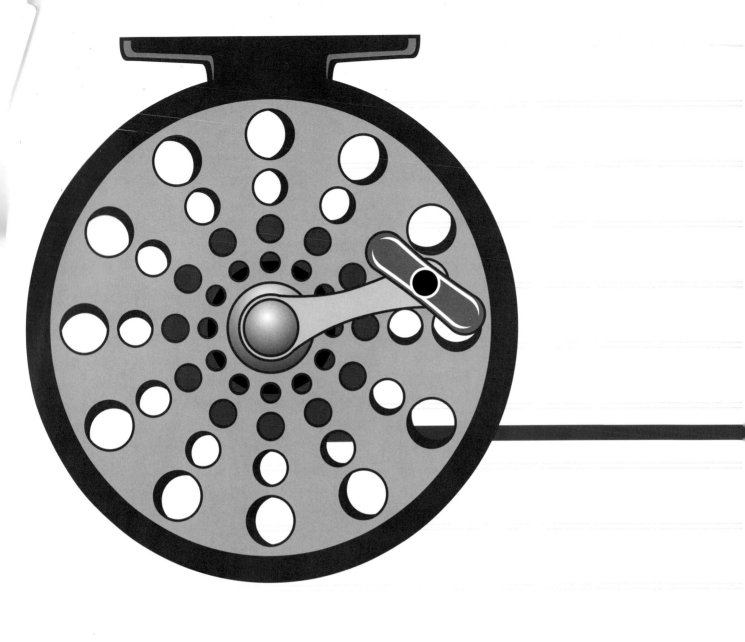

Flyfishing
Knots & Leader Systems

by Dave Chermanski

Frank
Amato
PUBLICATIONS, INC.

Dedication

To my parents, Bill and Dot, for their unwavering love, support, reassurance and confidence in every endeavor I attempted. They exposed me to the wonderment of fishing and the fragile beauty of our natural ecosystems with an independence to explore, experiment and enjoy on my own terms.

To my great uncle, Andy Cremi, for his saintly patience in teaching me how to tie knots and for exposing me to the fly fishing scrutiny of the curmudgeons of the Belmont Minnow Club.

To the love of my life and soul mate, Carol, whose love, assistance, encouragement and understanding helped to make the completion of this book a reality.

©2008 Dave Chermanski

All rights reserved. No part of this book may be reproduced without the express written sonsent of the publisher, except in the case of brief excerpts in critical reviews and articles

Published by:

Frank Amato Publication, Inc. • PO Box 82112
Portland, Oregon, 87282
503-653-8108

Photographs: David Chermanski
Illustrations: David Chermanski & Craig Wann
Layout: Craig Wann

UPC: 0-81127-00258-0
ISBN 13: 978-1-57188-424-4

Printed in Hong Kong
1 3 5 7 9 10 8 6 4 2

Chapter 7: Nylon Monofilament as a Leader & Tippet Material 83-90

Chapter 8: The Advantages of Fluorocarbon Line 91-97

Chapter 9: General Freshwater & Saltwater Leader Systems 98-115

Chapter 10: Specialty Leader System Configurations 116-127

Tables & Charts

Introduction

Fly fishing is a sport of observations and subtleties. It is a game of observation within a game of nuances in which every facet of the sport, from the dynamics of the casting stroke to the number of feathers on a fly, is a factor that can play a pivotal role in angling success. It is challenging, exhilarating, frustrating, exciting and humbling, often seemingly all at the same time. The intrinsic beauty of fly fishing as an artistic sport is not in the cast, or the strike, or the ensuing battle that defines this sport, but in the subtleties of the details and the seemingly endless array of new challenges to master. No truer is this statement than when it is applied to knots, leaders and connections. The subtlety of a properly tied knot, a correctly secured connection, and a befittingly tapered leader are constantly tested with every cast. There are no second chances when one of these elements fail. The problem is fixed, a lesson is learned and the process starts anew on the next cast.

Regardless of our level of skill, the fish species we pursue or our degree of passion and dedication to the sport, we all start essentially in the same manner; that is, having a matched and balanced fly outfit rigged and ready to do battle. We are all somewhere between bluegills and billfish in our fly fishing prowess and endeavors. In the vastly diverse world of fly fishing, we need to know more about how to tie knots and the varied methods to rigging our tackle than anglers of other fishing tackle disciplines. The degree of complexity to preparing and rigging fly tackle is significantly more involved, but these nuances to the sport can still be relatively simple and easy to accomplish.

To be a competent, productive and successful fly fisher, there are many things to master. The most basic of these things is learning how to tie the essential knots and make the necessary connections required to be successful in this sport. In addition to greatly increasing success and pleasure, there is a certain degree of enjoyment and satisfaction in knowing how to do these tasks well. It is as much part of the sport as the fish we pursue and these preparations can consume more of our time than necessary if our approach is not simple, concise and straightforward.

The tasks of rigging a fly fishing outfit, even for a specific pursuit or specialized fishing situation, do not have to be overly complicated. Regardless of the intent, a basic simplicity prevails; that is, a leader is attached to the end of a fly line, to which is attached a tippet followed by a fly. The complexity of the tasks stem from the fact these fly line-leader, leader-tippet and tippet-fly connections can be constructed in many different ways. In addition, there are many variables dictating how these riggings should be made such as the weight, density and size of the fly line, the length and stiffness of the leader, the breaking strength of the tippet, and the size or bulkiness of the fly. It is obvious, for example, a leader system designed to properly present a small dry fly fastened to a fragile, semi-limp tippet would greatly differ from one connecting a large saltwater fly to a heavy shock trace.

With regard to tying knots and rigging tackle, I learned at a very young age that it is not knowing how many knots to tie, but knowing how to tie the essential knots well. As a result, I am a confirmed minimalist. I strive to use the most practical, simplest, easiest and quickest means to achieving a goal or accomplishing a task. With regard to the education about these things, however, I am a firm believer that knowledge is power and the more you know about a subject, its insights and its subtleties, the more opportunities for creativity and innovation, not to mention enhanced pleasure, success and appreciation.

In recent years, most books dealing with this subject have been published as pocket-sized guides or handbooks. The premise to this trend I suspect is to have the laminated guide available on the water as an aid to tying a knot. A real-time fishing situation is not the time or place to tie any knot for the first time or without the trained dexterity that comes with practice. It is a potential disaster waiting to happen and, unfortunately, I have seen the negative side of this mentality too many times in fishing situations and they have always resulted in anguish and lost fish.

This book was developed to provide the angler with a comprehensive insight to knots, leader systems, fly lines and leader system materials. It focuses upon major types of leader systems, which encompass both general and specialized fly fishing situations for all freshwater and marine fish species. In addition to information concerning leader principles and varied leader system materials, the guide provides step-by-step instructions to rigging each integral connection in the construction of a leader system. It also provides step-by-step instructions to tying the 6 essential knots and one alternate that you need to know to catch fish from bluegills to billfish, and from trout to tuna.

This book was designed to provide a cross-reference of all the major components of a fly fishing outfit, such as a specific knot referenced to a certain connection or rigging task. At first glance, all this detailed information about these knots, riggings and connections may seem confusing and overwhelming, but the process to prepare and rig these major elements of a fly fishing outfit is really quite straightforward and relatively simple. It will require some practice, of course, to develop the dexterity to accomplish these tasks, but the time invested will be well spent and it will enhance your fly fishing success and pleasure. To further assist you in understanding the concepts, tying techniques and rigging methods for fly lines, knots and leader systems, the book

Overview Map

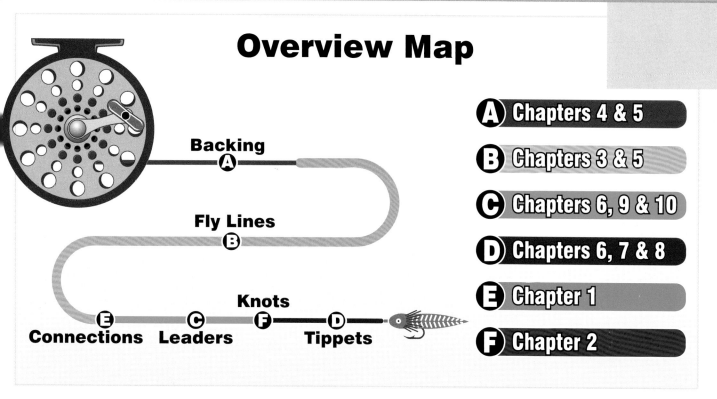

Backing
(A)

Fly Lines
(B)

Knots

(E) (C) (F) (D)
Connections Leaders Tippets

(A) Chapters 4 & 5

(B) Chapters 3 & 5

(C) Chapters 6, 9 & 10

(D) Chapters 6, 7 & 8

(E) Chapter 1

(F) Chapter 2

is richly illustrated with 35 drawings, 30 tables and more than 200 photographs, including some interesting and revealing photographs taken with a Scalar digital microscope. In addition, the book features a comprehensive Glossary of Terms & Definitions, which will help you to understand the meaning of certain words and phrases commonly used in fly fishing. Finally, in order to get a better perspective of how all these key elements fit together, refer to the overview map above. Use it to navigate through the book to specific major topics of interest. The chapter headings in the Table of Contents are color-coded to match the color code of the Overview Map for easier navigation and cross-referencing to the topics most important to you.

So, if you want to learn how to tie a Arbor Jam knot, a Spider hitch or scores of other hawser concoctions, many of which you probably will never use or may use only once or twice in a lifetime, this book does not speculate on the need or usefulness of these things. You also will not find 50 leader formulas for trout in this book either. On the other hand, if you are interested in a dependable, quick-change and interlocking loop system of fly line, leader, tippet and shock trace riggings for all fish species and fishing situations, using only 6 essential knots and one alternate, then welcome aboard and good fishing!

Personally, I would prefer to spend as much of my time on the water actually fishing than hurriedly trying to tie a knot or to rig a leader unless it is absolutely necessary. You may want to ask my wife, Carol, about her opinions on this philosophy. When she first became interested in fly fishing, I introduced her to my interchangeable loop system so she could concentrate her efforts on more important facets of the sport, such as casting mechanics. Once she became more confident and efficient as a caster, I withdrew the system and I forced her to learn to tie the essential knots and to rig her own leader systems. The training went well for the most part until her first fishing trip to the mountains for wild trout in canopied freestone streams. These unique ecosys-

tems test the mettle of an angler's resolve in many ways. Two of her biggest challenges was to change a size 18 or 20 dry fly on a 6X tippet multiple times a day as depicted in the photo below, and to frequently replace a tippet section, under low-light conditions. Needless to say, Carol became a true believer in my system and its chief advocate.

I hope my system of knots and interlocking loops, as well as all the other information contained in this book, will help to make your angling pursuits more successful and pleasurable.

—*Dave Chermanski*

Carol Chermanski

Glossary of Terms & Definitions

AFTMA - The acronym for the American Fishing Tackle Manufacturer's Association, now known as ASA (which see), that developed fly line standards to help fly fishing tackle manufacturers create a system that would match fly line weight to fly rod performance.

Arbor - The axle between the sides of a reel spool.

ASA - The acronym for the American Sportfishing Association, formerly AFTMA, (which see) that safeguards and promotes the social, economic and conservation values of sportfishing in America as the trade association for the sportfishing industry.

Backing - The small diameter line attached to the rear of a fly line, allowing a fish to run a long distance beyond the length of the fly line and leader system.

Barrel Knot - Another name for the blood knot, (which see).

Bimini Twist - A specialized knot for creating a double line from a single strand whose breaking strength is 100% to the rating of the line.

Body - This part of a fly line design is located between the front taper, (which see) and rear taper, (which see). It is the longest portion of the head, (which see) with the largest diameter and where most of the weight of a fly line is concentrated and where the momentum of a cast is generated. See page 38 for an illustration.

Braided Leader Material - A hollow-core line constructed from strands of nylon monofilament that are braided together. It can be used as a shooting line (SL) system, (which see) for a shooting taper (ST), system (which see). It is also commonly used to form loops that attach butt sections of leaders to fly lines, and for other connections.

Breaking Strength - The amount of force, in pounds or kilograms, needed to break a single strand of unknotted monofilament or braided line. See Tensile Strength.

Butt Section - The thickest section of a leader that is attached to the front end of a fly line at one end and the remaining sections of a leader including the tippet at the other end. It is more commonly referred to as the Leader Butt.

Compound Tapered Leader - A type of leader constructed by knotting sections of different diameter leader material to each other to produce a line tapering from a large diameter butt section, (which see) to a small diameter tippet, (which see). Most commonly used knot to construct such a leader is the blood knot, which is illustrated on pages 25-26.

Copolymers - A mixture of various nylons and plastics that are formulated with ultraviolet (UV) light inhibitors to produce a tippet material with exceptionally high breaking strength, (which see). Copolymer line is not as abrasion resistant as nylon monofilament, but its breaking strength is 2 to 4 times stronger.

Core - The internal material of a fly line, which provides the strength and consists of various materials such as single strand nylon monofilament, braided nylon monofilament, braided Dacron or Kevlar.

Cyanoacrylate (CA) Glue - A family of extremely strong and quick drying adhesives that are marketed under various names including Super Glue and Krazy Glue.

Dacron - A special type of braided fishing line with a hollow core that has poor knot strength but high tensile strength (which see). It is stored on a reel and connected to the rear section of a fly line to serve as the backing, (which see).

Dead Drift - A tactic used primarily in trout fishing in which a dry fly, nymph, larvae or pupae imitation will travel at the same speed as the current in a manner similar to the natural insect being imitated. It is most effective to emulate with a slack fly line, leader and tippet section.

Double Line - This term refers to folding a line end over itself to create two strands or the results of using a specialized knot such as the Bimini Twist, (which see).

Double Taper (DT) Fly Line - A fly line featuring a long level body, (which see) and the same taper configuration on each end, which makes it reversible when one end begins to wear. This taper design is ideal for short to moderate range casts, line mending and roll casting. See page 39 for an illustration.

Drag-Free Drift - see Dead Drift.

Dual-Density (F/S) Fly Line - A specialized variation of a weight-forward (WF) fly line, (which see) featuring a sinking front section typically of 6 to 15 feet that transitions to a full-length floating fly line. This type of line density is commonly called a sink tip (F/S). The benefit of a dual-density line is the ability to present a fly deeper in the water column and still being able to watch the floating portion of the line on the surface of the water for improved strike detection. The floating section of the line can also be mended on the water to reposition it during a drift or a retrieve.

End - A loop is a closed curved line, formed by bringing the tag end, (which see) back and alongside the standing part, (which see) or a knot that creates a loop.

False Casting - A standard casting technique in which a fly line is kept airborne in a repeated backward and forward motion without touching the surface of the water or the ground. It is used to lengthen or shorten the length of an airborne line, to change casting direction, or to remove water absorbed by the fly dressings.

Fluorocarbon - A leader, tippet and shock trace material featuring an extremely low visibility when submerged in water. It has very little stretch and a hard, smooth finish that is extremely abrasion resistant to withstand the abuse of obstructions and the raspy jaws, gill plates and scales of certain game fish. Fluorocarbon does not absorb water, it will not weaken or increase in stretch like nylon fishing line. Minimal stretch enhances strike detection and promotes positive hook sets.

Fly Line - A specialized line whose weight beyond the rod tip of a fly rod during a cast is used to propel a virtually weightless fly to a target.

Forceps - A hand-operated medical instrument widely used in fly fishing to remove flies from the jaws of a hooked fish or holding the tag end of a line when closing a knot as described on page 22. Forceps have pliers-like jaws with locking clips that will remain clamped to a hook or line until they are released. In medical terms, forceps are referred to as a hemostat for preventing the flow of blood from an open blood vessel by compression of the vessel.

Front Taper - This section of a fly line taper design determines how delicately or powerfully the fly is delivered onto the water. Its length typically ranges from 4 to 8 feet long as it decreases in diameter from the body, (which see) to the tip. This graduation of mass (weight) along the length of the front taper affects the transfer of casting energy to the fly. The length of the front taper, combined with the diameter of the tip, ultimately determines how delicately or powerfully a fly will land in the target area. See page 38 for an illustration.

Gel-Spun Polyethylene (GSP) - A synthetic fiber that is extremely strong, thin, supple, slippery and very abrasion resistant. It is used as a fly line backing where large amounts of line are required and space on the reel spool is limited.

Head - This part of a fly line design describes the combination of the front taper, (which see) the body, (which see) and the rear taper, (which see) of a weight-forward (WF) fly line, (which see). See page 38 for an illustration.

IGFA - The acronym for the International Game Fish Association, which is a nonprofit organization committed to the conservation of game fish and the promotion of responsible, ethical angling practices through science, education, rule making and record keeping. The IGFA maintains and publishes angling world records including fly fishing.

Interlocking Loops - A term used to describe connecting two loops together as demonstrated on page 18.

Knotless Tapered Leader - A type of leader constructed entirely from a single piece of nylon, (which see) or fluorocarbon, (which see) monofilament, (which see) that has been tapered from a large diameter butt section, (which see) to a small diameter tippet, (which see) through extrusion or acid immersion.

Knotted Tapered Leader - see Compound Tapered Leader.

Leader - A leader can consist of a single piece, a braided segment, multiple knotted sections or an extruded tapered line of nylon, (which see) or fluorocarbon, (which see). It is attached to the end of a fly line, (which see) to which is connected a tippet, (which see) and, optionally, a shock trace, (which see) followed by the fly. There are three basic types of leader systems: level, (which see), knotless tapered, (which see) and compound tapered, (which see).

Leader Butt - see Butt Section.

Level (L) Fly Line - A type of floating fly line that features an uniform diameter throughout its entire length.

Level Leader - A leader consisting of a single continuous strand or diameter of nylon or fluorocarbon, (which see) monofilament material.

Loop - In knot tying, this term refers to the shape produced by a curve in a line that bends and crosses itself. In fly casting, this term refers to the shape of a fly line during a casting cycle that is folded back parallel to itself forming an open loop similar to a candy cane or a capital J on its side.

Loop-to-Loop Connection - see Interlocking Loops.

Memory Set - When nylon monofilament or plastic-coated fly line, (which see) is confined to a relatively small diameter, it will retain the constrained shape and resist returning to its previous state. This condition can usually be removed by stretching the line.

Micron - A braided, hollow-core Dacron, (which see) line manufactured by the Cortland Line Company with a slightly smaller diameter than standard Dacron. It is used as a fly line backing, (which see).

Midsection - This term refers to the middle portion of a leader system that serves as the transitional area between the stiff butt section, (which see) and the semi-limp tippet, (which see).

Monofilament - Also referred to as "mono", it is a single strand of extruded synthetic fiber such as nylon or fluorocarbon, (which see).

Nylon Monofilament - A single-component product that is formed through an extrusion process in which molten plastic is formed into a strand through a die. It is generically referred to as "mono".

Overhand Knot - This is one of the fundamental knots, and forms the basis of many others including the simple noose, blood knot and Chermanski loop knot. The overhand knot is very secure, to the point of over jamming, which makes it difficult to untie if it is cinched tightly. It is also known as the thumb knot because it is formed by creating a loop and pushing the working end, (which see) through the loop with the thumb of a hand.

Overhang - A term used in fly casting to describe the amount of small diameter running line, (which see) or shooting line (SL), (which see) extended beyond the rod tip during the casting cycle. In general fishing, this term refers to structure, typically tree limbs and vegetation, which protrude from the land in a low profile over the water.

Pliobond - A commercial brand name for a rubber-based glue that is used to coat knots and connections.

Presentation - A term used in fly fishing to describe the act of placing or settling a fly on the water in a manner similar to the natural insect or food form being imitated.

Rear Taper - This part of a fly line design is the transitional area between the small diameter running line, (which see) and the large diameter body, (which see). The length of the rear taper affects the degree of control in managing the head, (which see) and therefore provides smooth casts beyond 35 feet. See page 38 for an illustration.

Running Line - The small diameter portion behind the head, (which see) of a weight-forward (WF) fly line, (which see) that can comprise 40% to 60% of its overall length. When extended beyond the rod tip during a casting cycle, the heavier head of the WF line can pull the smaller diameter running line for long distances.

Shock Leader or **Tippet** - see Shock Trace.

Shock Trace - A short length of leader material connected between the fly and tippet that safeguards the tippet from being abraded or severed by sharp teeth, gill plates or other body parts of certain fish species as well as from rough structure and sharp objects on or in the water.

Shooting Head (SH) - A common name for a shooting taper (ST) fly line, (which see) to which a shooting line (SL), (which see) is attached. The standard length of a SH is typically 30 feet.

Shooting Line (SL) - A thin diameter line, which is attached between a shooting head (SH), (which see) and fly line backing, (which see) of a shooting taper (ST) system, (which see).

Shooting Taper (ST) Fly Line - Commonly called a shooting head (SH), this fly line design features a body, (which see) of uniform diameter and a short taper at one end. The standard length of a ST line is 30 feet and it is attached to a small diameter shooting line (SL), (which see) for optimum casting distance. See pages 38-39 for an illustration.

Splicing Needle - A device for creating a loop in braided nylon monofilament. The needle is threaded through the hollow core of the braided monofilament and pushed out one side. The tag end, (which see) is then held at the end of the special needle and pulled back through the core, forming a loop as illustrated on pages 19-20.

Spool - Part of a fly reel that stores the backing, (which see) and fly line, (which see).

Standing End - The short area at the end of the standing part, (which see).

Standing Part - The main part or portion of a line that is fixed and under tension on which a knot is constructed, as shown on page 13.

Strike Indicator - A floating object placed on the leader, (which see) or at end of a fly line, (which see) to indicate a subtle strike or the path of the drift of a fly particularly when fishing a nymph, larvae or pupae imitation with a slack line.

Tag or Tag End - This refers to the end of a line being used to construct a knot. It also refers to the excess line that remains after a knot is tied.

Taper - The shape or profile of a fly line, (which see) or a leader, (which see) comprising of a gradual transition from a large diameter to a much smaller diameter, which is essential for a proper presentation of a fly.

Tapered Leader - A leader constructed of varying diameters of nylon, (which see) or fluorocarbon, (which see) materials. It is thickest where it is connected to the fly line, (which see) and gradually diminishes in diameter along its length to where it is connected to a fly. For the two primary types of tapered leaders, see "Knotless Tapered Leader" and "Compound Tapered Leader".

Tensile Strength - It is a measurement, in pounds per square inch (psi), of the force required to break a line and it is based on the line diameter and break strength of the line.

Tippet - This is the weakest and most supple section of a leader system, (which see) to which the fly is usually attached.

Turn - One revolution of the tag end, (which see) around the standing part, (which see) of a line during the tying of a knot.

Turn Over - A term in fly casting to describe how the fly line, (which see) and leader, (which see) straighten out at the completion of a cast. The length and taper of a leader as well as the size and weight of a fly are important factors affecting how the kinetic energy transferred from the fly line is used to unroll and straighten the leader for a proper presentation. The heavier or more wind resistant the fly, the shorter and thicker the leader must be to keep control of a fly during a cast. The lighter and more streamlined the fly, the longer and thinner the leader can be.

Ultraviolet (UV) - Invisible light rays of a very short wavelength that are emitted by the sun. UV radiation can cause plastics, such as fly line coatings and nylon monofilament lines, to deteriorate and weaken from prolonged exposure.

Weight-Forward (WF) Fly Line - A weight-forward (WF) fly line is designed for easier casting at longer distances than can be made with a double taper (DT) fly line, (which see). Most of the weight of the line is in its forward section nearest to the leader, (which see) and fly. The WF profile typically comprises a short section tapering from the leader, a belly section of uniform diameter, and another short section tapering to a small diameter running line for about 40% of its length. Manufacturers vary the length of these sections to enhance either long distance casting or gentler presentations. See pages 39-40 for an illustration.

Wind Knot - A tangle or overhand knot formed in a leader, (which see) or fly line, (which see) by poor casting mechanics, primarily by overpowering the cast or applying the power stroke for too long in the casting arc. An overhand knot will reduce the breaking strength of the affected line by at least 50%.

Wire (Braided) - Very small strands of wire, usually stainless steel, that are twisted into a braid and used as a shock trace, (which see).

Working End - The part of a line used actively in tying a knot. The opposite of the standing end, (which see).

Wrap - See Turn.

Wire (Solid) - Solid stainless steel leader wire, which is used as a shock trace, (which see) material primarily for fish with razor-sharp teeth.

Chapter 1
Knots & Connections

Knots are one of the oldest inventions. People have used them to tie arrowheads to their shafts, and to tie strings to their bows. Other early uses of knots included making clothes and fishing nets, and binding wood together to make shelters. The ancient Inca Indians of Peru used knots to keep records of sums and figures. One of the most famous knots is the Gordian knot, mentioned in Greek mythology and associated in legend with Alexander the Great. The knot was made by Gordias. It was further prophesied by an oracle that whoever could untie the knot would become the king of Asia. In 333 BC, Alexander attempted to untie the knot. When he could find no end to the knot, he sliced it in half with a stroke of his sword, the so-called "Alexandrian solution". It is often used as a metaphor for an intractable problem, solved by a bold stroke as "cutting the Gordian knot".

Knots have been studied extensively by mathematicians for hundreds of years. More recently, the study of knots has proved to be of great interest to theoretical physicists and molecular biologists. One of the most peculiar things which emerge in studying knots is how a category of objects as simple as a knot could be so rich in profound mathematical connections.

The language of knots was originally developed to name the various parts of a line or rope and the simple shapes into which they can be formed. The **tag end** of a line is the part with which knots are tied. The remainder, or main portion, of the line is called the **standing part**. The simple shapes that can be made with rope form the basis for all knots. A bight is formed by placing the end of the rope alongside the standing part to form a loop. In an overhand loop, the end of the rope is crossed over the standing part. An underhand loop is the opposite of an overhand loop. It is formed by placing the end of the rope beneath the standing part. An overhand knot is simply a loop through which an end has been passed.

In terms of knots and connections as applied to fly fishing, there is no such thing as a second chance and there are many powerful fish species ready to challenge the weakest link in the system. Most knots are actually some form of a clinch knot with the line crossing over and under itself at moderate angles. Knots never break until they start to slip and the actual breakage will never occur within the knot itself. A slip-proof knot will be roughly as strong as the line from which it was constructed. Therefore, a knot should be drawn as tight as possible with a slow, steady pull.

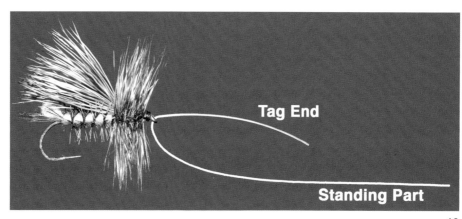

Tag End

Standing Part

Common Causes of Knot Failures

There are good and bad knots. An inferior knot is one that is not suited to the situation, is improperly drawn tight, is incorrectly trimmed, or is simply inefficient for the task. Even the best knot for the task will fail if it is not tied properly. The best and most reliable leader system, for example, will use knots that are stronger than the breaking strength of the tippet, which is, by definition, the weakest section of a leader. A study of the common failures in knots reveals a breakdown that follows a pattern and it is usually traceable to four potential flaws; namely, improper technique, slippage, internal twists and insufficient tightening.

Even when an appropriate knot is selected and tied accurately, improper technique can result in reduced strength or even breakage. Overlapping wraps around the standing part of a line can cause an abrading action by one of the buried turns, resulting in a failure. A remedy is to close knots slowly and to insure their turns are separated until tightened. Some knots like the improved clinch knot and the blood knot, which depend on the cushioning effect of multiple turns to be secured by its jamming action, are most vulnerable to this problem. The photos below show the cushioning effect of multiple turns of 4 pound-test lines connected to size 10 hooks using an improved clinch knot of 3-1/2 and 6 turns. The 6-turn knot is more than 25% stronger because the added wraps cushioned the standing part of the line from the frictional heat generated during the tightening of the knot. The photos were taken with a digital microscope at a magnification of 100 times the normal size of the knots.

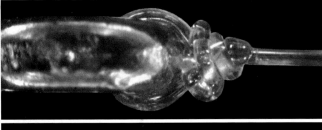

Selection of the wrong knot for a specific line diameter can also cause slippage and inevitable failure. Knots in nylon or fluorocarbon monofilament lines with multiple turns hold the most securely in the lower breaking strength sizes. Less turns are needed in the larger diameters to secure the knot from slipping and it is more difficult to draw multiple turns tightly. The improved clinch knot, for example, has considerably less efficiency when tied in lines stronger than approximately 15 pounds or .018 inches in diameter. Of course, there are always exceptions to every rule when it applies to knots. An 8-turn nail knot tied in a 20 pound-test line, for instance, will cinch tighter and more evenly than a knot with less turns. The photo on the above right shows the scoring effects of cinching non-lubricated strands of

20- and 25-pound lines in a blood knot using 3-1/2 turns of each line size. The frictional heat generated during the tightening of the non-lubricated knot frayed the surface of the lines in multiple areas as indicated by the arrows. The photo was taken with a digital microscope at a magnification of 50 times the normal size of the knot.

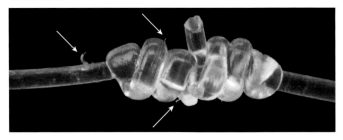

Any line twists within a knot can cause an area of stress, abrasion and eventual failure if slippage occurs. This phenomenon usually happens when dealing with double strands of line or using the Bimini Twist to create a double line. The photo below shows a flawed strand of 12-pound line that is connected to 80-pound line using a 7-turn Albright Special knot. The photo was taken with a digital microscope at a magnification of 30 times the normal size of the knot. The strand was weakened by the frictional heat generated during the tightening of the Albright Special. The solution is to keep these doubled lines parallel each other when tying a knot, such as the Albright Special and Bimini Twist, and to keep twists to a minimum when pulling them tight. Twisted line loses a considerable amount of its elasticity, which is important in buffering the line and its knots from sudden and rapid shock, especially during a strike or setting the hook.

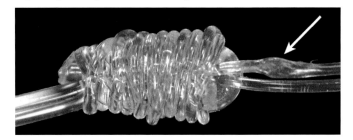

Insufficient tightening of a knot after it is tied can cause failure from ensuing slippage particularly under the stressful loads of setting the hook on a violent strike and battling a powerful fish. The best prevention to this flaw is to draw all knots tightly with an uniform, steady pulling force, avoiding any snapping or jerking motion. Hurriedly cinching up a knot too quickly can generate damaging heat that can weaken a knot significantly. It can also create a twist in the line directly in front of the knot, which results when the internal wraps slip under a pulling force. As a result, the twisted line generally will lose its elasticity that is critical to shock absorption.

Guidelines to Tying Strong & Dependable Knots

The general guidelines and fundamental techniques described below should be used when tying knots in nylon or fluorocarbon monofilament lines:

Follow the step-by-step instructions for tying a knot correctly. It is very important to be cognizant to the number of turns made around the standing part of the line. Many knots use a specific number of turns for a given range of line diameters, which were determined to prevent slippage. One less turn may cause the knot to slip internally, weakening it significantly. Conversely, one turn too many can make the knot more difficult to close and tighten properly.

When joining two nylon or fluorocarbon monofilament lines together of different diameters, use lines of the same apparent limpness whenever possible. This axiom applies primarily to building tapered leader sections. A knot, such as the blood knot, will close easier and more smoothly if the two sections of nylon or fluorocarbon monofilament line being joined together have similar limpness. It is more difficult to properly close two lines together when one line is medium-stiff and the other line is semi-limp.

Thoroughly lubricate the knot area before tightening the knot. Moistening a knot prior to tightening it has no effect on its ultimate breaking strength, but it does provide a less frictional surface for a smoother, easier draw and a tighter cinching of the knot. Equally important, wetting the knot area prior to tightening it reduces damaging heat buildup generated from the friction of the turns rubbing against themselves. Various substances of a low viscosity can be used as a lubricating agent including water, vegetable oil, fly line cleaner, dry-fly paste and even WD-40. Although the most commonly used lubricating agent is saliva, it is not the best lubricant and the saliva of some individuals can contain substances that can actually weaken a knot in nylon monofilament line.

Close the coils and wraps within a knot correctly. Another important factor in the construction of a strong, dependable knot is how smoothly and evenly the coils and wraps within a knot are closed. Coils must come together within the knot without crossing over one another. An improperly overlapped coil or wrap can result in line breakage under a severe load. When tying an Albright Special or nail knot, for example, if the wraps lie evenly next to each other, the knot will remain strong, but if one coil crosses over another during closure, the knot could fail under the stress of a violent strike or a powerful surge from a fleeing fish. The photo below shows a properly closed Albright Special knot using 8 turns of 16-pound line that is connected to 80-pound line. Note the tight and uniform wraps of the 16-pound line over the folded 80-pound line, assuring maximum knot strength. The tapering wraps also indicate the knot was cinched tight with a smooth and steady pulling force. The photo was taken with a digital microscope at a magnification of 30 times the normal size of the knot.

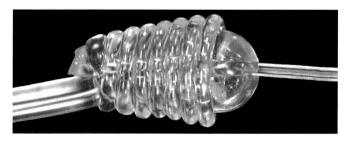

Check the knot area before pulling it completely tight. Preparing a knot just prior to closure is another prominent factor affecting the strength and reliability of a knot. Any slack in the wraps and spirals around the standing line should be removed. The prescribed method is to gently draw the tag end until it lies flush against the wrapped or spiraled portion of the knot.

Draw the knot with a slow, steady pull until it is taut. The most fundamental principle of a strong, reliable knot is it will not weaken or break until the line begins to slip internally. In fact, an improperly tied knot that has been closed tightly is less likely to fail as quickly as a properly tied knot that has not been closed firmly.

To insure proper closure of a knot tied in a nylon monofilament or fluorocarbon line stronger than 12 pounds, use gloves, pliers, vise grips, forceps or some other clamping device. Trying to properly cinch a knot tightly in a nylon or fluorocarbon monofilament line stronger than 12 pounds can result in severe cuts of unprotected hands and fingers. The use of gloves or some clamping device is usually required to develop sufficient cinching force to tighten a knot securely. Even trying to cinch a knot in 8- to 12-pound line can easily cut wet hands and fingers.

The photos below show the difference in using the proper amount of tightening force to satisfactorily close a knot. The photos depict 12 pound-test lines cinched to size 6 hooks using 6-turn improved clinch knots. The loosely formed knot in the top photo below was closed with 2 pounds of force, while the properly cinched knot below was closed with 6 pounds of force. As a result, the knot in the lower photo is more than 25% stronger, because it will not slip during extreme stress when setting the hook or fighting a powerful fish. The photos were taken with a digital microscope at a magnification of 30 times the normal size of the knots.

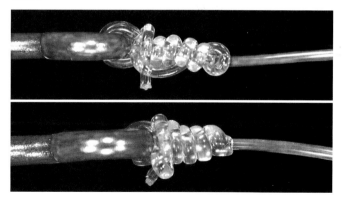

Dry the knot area of any residual lubrication and apply a partial drop of glue, such as Krazy glue, super glue or UV Knot Sense directly to the knot wraps only. The purpose of the glue is to prevent the wraps and coils within a knot from slipping under extreme strain. As a result, only a portion of the knot needs to be treated sparingly as shown in Step 9 of coating a Chermanski Loop knot on page 25. There are some special glues available that are specially designed to be used on nylon or fluorocarbon monofilament line to enhance knot strength, but most of the cyanoacrylate (CA) super glues are acceptable. It is not necessary the glue is waterproof. The key attribute of a glue for this purpose is to set and cure as quickly as possible. When tying knots at home, I typically use Krazy glue to secure all knots. When traveling or on the water, I will use UV Knot Sense.

UV Knot Sense is a liquid polyurethane knot dressing that cures in seconds when exposed to ultraviolet (UV) radiation either from direct sunlight or a UV light source. The glutinous consistency of the glue strengthens and smoothes a knot in about 30 seconds. A UV light will be required indoors or whenever direct sunlight is not available. UV Knot Sense requires a specific wave length of UV light to cure the chemicals, which is about 560 nanometer (nm) frequency. A LED bulb of the correct wavelength can be purchased at an electronics store and used as an acceptable light source. It is, however, cheaper and easier to purchase a mini-lamp from the manufacturer of UV Knot Sense.

Precaution should be taken when using a UV light source, because looking directly at the UV light beam can cause damage to the eyes. The reflected light can also create a problem, so wearing sunglasses even indoors is recommended when applying the UV light to the dressing. UV Knot Sense and the mini-lamp are extremely useful products in the field and they have become standard accessories in my tackle bag.

After the knot is tied and glued, trim any excess and test it one final time. If the turns, wraps or coils of a knot are not glued to prevent slippage, trim the tag end to within an 1/8-inch of the knot. If they are secured with glue, trim the tag end flush with the knot. After a knot is trimmed, examine it closely and test it thoroughly. If it does not look right or shows signs of slippage, cut it off and retie it. Obviously, it is better to have a knot break or slip in your hands than in an actual fishing situation.

The following table is a guide to the essential knots and connections I use in all of my fly fishing adventures. The step-by-step instructions to tying these knots are illustrated in Chapter 2.

Knot or Connection	Uses of Knot or Connection	Pages
PVC Fly Line Loop	Part of the interlocking loop system for connecting a leader system to a fly line.	**60**
Braided Nylon Mono Loop (1/4-inch long)	Part of the interlocking loop system for fastening the major components of a shooting taper (ST) system together.	**19**
Braided Nylon Mono Loop (6 to 8 inches long)	Part of the interlocking loop system for attaching a fly line to the braided Dacron or gel-spun polyethylene (GSP) backing.	**20**
Nail Knot	1) Binding the loop created at the end of a fly line. 2) Restraining the loop formed with braided nylon monofilament line from opening. 3) Cinching a braided nylon monofilament loop to a fly line.	**22-23**
Chermanski Loop Knot	1) Tying a fly to a tippet or shock trace to provide full freedom of movement. 2) The loop formed for connecting a leader to a fly line, a tippet to a leader and a shock trace to a tippet. 3) Attaching gel-spun polyethylene (GSP) backing to a fly line.	**24-25**
Blood Knot	1) Joining two lines of similar diameters together in a leader system. 2) Splicing braided Dacron and/or gel-spun polyethylene (GSP) lines together.	**25-26**
Improved Clinch Knot	1) Fastening a fly to a tippet. 2) An optional method to affixing a fly line backing to the spool arbor of a reel.	**26-27**
Bimini Twist	Creating a double line and a loop in the tippet section or the fly line backing.	**27-29**
Haywire Twist	Joining a fly to a solid wire shock trace to allow full freedom of movement.	**29-30**
Albright Special Knot (optional)	1) Attaching two lines of significantly different diameters together, such as a shock trace directly to a tippet, in a leader system. 2) Splicing gel-spun polyethylene (GSP) line to braided Dacron line.	**32-33**

Interlocking Loop System

Dyed-in-the-wool traditionalists consider the venerable nail knot the best method to attaching a leader and backing to a fly line. There are some fly line coatings, however, in which a nail knot may slip off a fly line under stress. In addition, I prefer to use an interlocking loop system for many reasons, although the nail knot is an important and essential knot utilized in this system. A permanent leader butt section may be acceptable with a floating fly line in many freshwater fishing situations, but its universal versatility and reliability is limited in most other fishing applications. Sinking fly lines, in general, and most saltwater fishing situations can render a considerable amount of wear and abrasive damage to a fly line and leader system, particularly the leader butt section. An interlocking loop system permits a fast and dependable replacement of any component of a leader system at the first sign of a problem, especially the more vulnerable elements such as the leader butt, tippet and shock trace sections.

An interlocking loop system, for example, allows for quick changes and adjustments of flies, fly lines and leader systems whenever it becomes necessary. This inherent versatility can be a major advantage in all fishing situations, particularly where ever-changing weather and water conditions, or a radical change in fly types or sizes dictate an adjustment in fly line type or density as well as a modification in leader design. In addition, this loop-to-loop connection system provides fast and reliable fly changes without the need to tying a knot, which is especially advantageous in low lighting conditions. This feature can also be particularly crucial in fishing situations where a hastily tied knot in a rushed circumstance can be tested within seconds by a powerful game fish. As illustrated in the photo on the right, I utilize an interlocking loop system in every facet of my fly-fishing arsenal.

The speed, convenience and reliability of using flies pretied to tippet or shock trace sections as part of an interlocking loop system is invaluable. The system inherently avails itself to minimum contact with a pre-rigged fly and, occasionally, a newly exchanged fly is not inspected closely enough for anomalies affecting its fish-catching qualities. For example, I recall the time the Reverend John Meyer and I were fishing a slough in Lake Okeechobee where the bluegills were bedding. It was the height of their spawning season and the big "copperheads" were actively feeding. Although they were aggressive, they were somewhat selective, because they did not strike our small foam poppers with abandonment until John switched to an orange sponge spider. His first ten casts yielded ten seemingly solid strikes although he failed to hook any of the 12- to 20-ounce giants.

Not having an orange sponge spider of my own, John graciously offered to share his arsenal of homemade concoctions, only to discover he was using the only orange sponge spider between us. A few minutes past when I saw and heard an explosive surface strike about 30 feet directly in front of John. At the time, he was in the act of casting perpendicular to the shoreline, so he tried to quickly redirect the cast 90 degrees to the spot where the surface activity occurred. In his haste and excitement, however, he created too much slack line in the back cast, wrapping most of the leader around my neck. Miraculously, the hook did not penetrate my skin or snare my clothing, and we were back fishing within a couple of minutes. After another 20 minutes of repeated strikes without a hookup, John was starting to get frustrated.

"These big copperheads must be grabbing the (rubber) legs (of the sponge spider)", John said in an uncharacteristic tone of disappointment, "I can't seem to get them to eat the thing like that bumble bee pattern you're using".

"You better check to see if the spider has any legs left", I replied.

Less than a minute after checking the fly and exchanging it for a bumble bee pattern, John swiveled his chair at the bow and glared at me for about 30 seconds before saying, "You knew the bend of the hook was missing when you untangled my leader, didn't you?", John murmured in a serious stare.

"You know, John, that is a serious accusation", I said trying to restrain my laughter, "you were having so much fun with those fish blasting the only orange sponge spider in the boat, I didn't want to ruin it for you. Besides, you were about 10 fish ahead of me before you changed to that orange fly."

Without a reply, John swiveled his chair back into position and resumed fishing. Within a cast or two, he was firmly hooked to a big bluegill and, as his 4-weight outfit bent in a deep arc, his spirited enthusiasm once again emerged. At the end of the day, John checked his fly box and found the bend of the hook to the orange sponge spider still embedded in the foam liner. The bronze metal had rusted from a previous fishing trip. The lesson learned: even though a fly is pre-rigged and ready for battle, it is prudent to take a few extra seconds to inspect it closely for any flaws.

In addition to the quick changes and adjustments to the major components of a fly outfit, an interlocking system can be utilized to affect the density of a leader system and the retrieval path of a fly. If the fishing situation dictates it, a mini or instant sinking section can be looped between the fly line and the leader butt section. The ability to interconnect mini or instant sinking sections of different densities and lengths to obtain various sink rates, while using only a floating fly line, can prove to be a real asset in many fishing situations. Conversely, when using a sinking fly line, a fly can be suspended over a rocky or obstructive bottom by looping a 3- to 4-foot section of floating fly line between the leader butt and tippet sections.

Alternative methods to this interlocking loop system are not nearly so quick and dependable; nor do they resist wear as effectively, or pass as easily through the rod guides with minimal bulk when casting and landing a fish. The basis of the interchangeable loop-to-loop system is in how the components ultimately connect. My system utilizes interlocking loops formed from single strand, double strand and braided nylon monofilament lines. The interconnecting loop between a shooting head (SH) and shooting line (SL) system, for example, must be durable and able to withstand repeated flexure, loading and abrasion. The loop material must also possess sufficient mass and stiffness, so that when sections are joined and cast, the kinetic energy of the casting loop transfers from one section to another efficiently with minimal interruption.

All fly line loop connections inherently form a bending stress at the end of the loop area, and this pressure can eventually create a failure as the line coating cracks. The strength of the fly line, however, comes from the strength of its core. Any cracks can be repaired with a flexible sealant such as Softex or Aquaseal. Sinking fly lines tend to fail more readily because of a thinner plastic coating over the line core, and the need to replace the loops can be expected periodically. When a loop becomes unusable, simply cut the damaged line off and form a new loop at the end of the fly line or replace it with a braided nylon monofilament loop. To protect mini or instant sinking line sections from rapid wear, which are looped between a fly line and the leader butt section, encase them in 20- or 25-pound braided nylon monofilament. The method for making mini or instant sinking line sections is discussed on pages 64-65.

There are several ways to make loops. For attaching leaders and mini or instant sinking line sections to a fly line, tie back-to-back nail knots on a short, doubled section of the fly line end. For 2- to 6-weight fly lines, a single nail knot can be used. The step-by-step instructions for forming a permanent loop at the end of a fly line are discussed and illustrated on page 60. For tying a loop in single and double strands of a nylon or fluorocarbon monofilament line for leader sections including the tippet and optional shock trace sections, I use the Chermanski Loop knot, which is illustrated on pages 24-25.

As demonstrated in the photos on the above right, there is a right and wrong way for connecting loops together. Never interlock loops in a girth hitch configuration, because this profile will weaken the connection and form a protuberance that can jam on the rod guides. The proper method for interlocking loops is in a square knot configuration. The technique involves passing the loop of one

section over the standing loop of the second section, then threading the opposite end of the first section through the standing loop of the second section and pulling the loops together snugly.

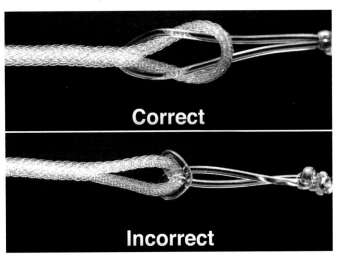

Building Braided Nylon Monofilament Loops

A braided nylon monofilament loop is used primarily to connect a fly line to the backing and to join the shooting head (SH) to the shooting line (SL) of a shooting taper (ST) fly line system. The step-by-step instructions for securing braided nylon monofilament loops to fly lines for these two purposes are illustrated on the next two pages. A braided loop can also be used at both ends of a mini or instant sinking leader section. The directions for fastening braided nylon monofilament loops to mini or instant sinking leader sections are related on pages 19-20 and 64-65. In addition, a braided nylon monofilament loop can be used as an alternative method to connect a leader to a fly line. The prescribed method, however, is using back-to-back nail knots on the end of a fly line that is doubled to form a loop. This recommended rigging technique is described on page 60.

Although commercial braided loops are available, I prefer to make my own loops from 20-, 25-, 30-, 35- and 50-pound braided nylon monofilament line. The size of the braided line is contingent upon the size of the fly line for the purpose of minimizing bulk without compromising toughness. For 2- to 5-weight fly lines, for example, I use 20-pound braided nylon monofilament line. I prefer 25- and 30-pound braided lines for 6- to 8-weight and 9- to 10-weight fly lines respectively. For 12-weight or heavier fly lines, I use 35- or 50-pound braided line. Cortland Line Company and Gudebrod manufacture quality braided monofilament lines, but I prefer the Gudebrod Butt Leader Material, because the braid is slightly tighter.

The best method to create a braided loop is with a splicing needle. Commercial splicing needles are available from Cortland Line Company and other sources or one can be made using a piece of #3 to #5 stainless steel trolling wire. Simply bend the wire about 3 inches from one end, forming a tight needle point at the apex of the bend. Shape the wires below the needle point to form an elongated opening similar to a bobbin threader used in fly tying. This opening is needed for passing part of the tag end of the braided nylon monofilament through it. At the opposite end of the homemade wire splicing needle, use the Haywire Twist, which is illustrated on pages 29-30, to attach a large nut or metal washer to serve as a grip for pushing and pulling the wire needle through the hollow core of the braided nylon monofilament line. Examples of a commercial and a homemade splicing needle are shown in the photo below.

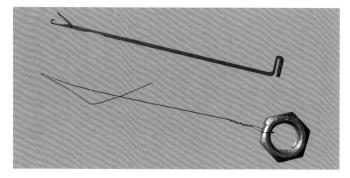

Forming a braided nylon monofilament loop is a quick and easy process. The following steps pertain to forming two loops of different sizes, which are used as part of the interlocking loop system for fly lines, leaders and backing. The smaller loop, about a 1/4-inch long, is secured at the back end of a shooting head (SH), the front end of a shooting line (SL) and at both ends of a mini or instant sinking leader section. The smaller the loop size, the better the transfer of the kinetic energy between the interlocking loops during a cast. The larger loop, about 6 to 8 inches long, is fastened at the back end of a fly line and a shooting line (SL), which is interconnected with the loop of similar size formed in the fly line backing.

Forming a Small Braided Nylon Monofilament Loop

The following steps will form a small loop in a braided nylon monofilament line, which can be used at the end of full-length and shooting head (SH) fly lines or built into a braided monofilament shooting line (SL):

Step 1: Insert the splicing needle approximately 3 to 4 inches from the end of the braided line. Carefully thread it through the hollow center about 3/4 to 1 inch toward the end of the braided line, and then force it partially out a side of the braided wall.

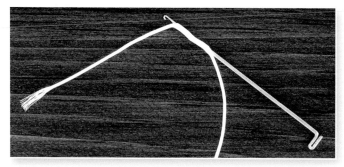

Step 2: Grasp the tag end about a 1/4-inch from the end in the splicing needle and slowly pull it through the center of the hollow core until the splicing or wire needle is withdrawn completely. Be careful not to embed the line forming the loop into the hollow core by pulling the splicing needle too forcibly.

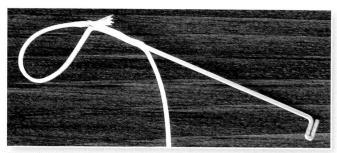

Step 3: After the splicing needle is removed, draw the tag end through its core to form a very small loop about 3/16-inch long. Trim the excess tag end flush to the standing part of the braided line.

Step 4: Lengthen the loop slightly to about 1/4-inch by pulling the loop slowly until the end of the tag end is embedded in the hollow core.

Step 5: To secure the loop in position, tie a 6- to 8-turn nail knot using 8-to 12-pound semi-limp nylon monofilament line about midway along the doubled standing part of the braided nylon monofilament. The step-by-step instructions for tying a nail knot are illustrated on pages 22-23. Partially coat only the wraps of the nail knot (photo inset below) with cyanoacrylate (CA) glue, such as Krazy glue or UV Knot Sense. Use the CA glue sparingly to prevent a capillary action, which will cause the cement to flow into and along the braid. After the glue has cured, cut the standing part of the braided line to a length of about 3 to 4 inches, which will be slipped over a fly line or a mini sinking leader section as described on pages 58-59.

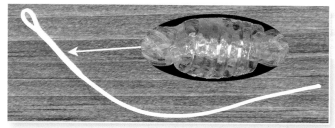

With 3 to 4 inches of the standing part of the braided nylon monofilament loop slipped over the end of a full-length fly line, shooting head (SH), shooting line (SL) or mini sinking leader section, it is almost self-adhering and similar to the "Chinese finger lock" principle. In theory, the tauter the loop is pulled, the tighter the braided line grasps the plastic fly line coating. The use of nail knots, however, assures maximum strength and durability to a braided nylon monofilament loop. I have caught literally tens of thousands of fishes using braided monofilament loops and I never had one fail primarily due to my vigilance to inspecting them at every opportunity. If a commercial braided monofilament loop is used, I recommend tying a 6- to 8-turn nail knot using 8- to 12-pound semi-limp nylon monofilament line at the cut ends of the braided line, instead of using the plastic tubing supplied with the loop. The thickness of the plastic tubing frequently interrupts the energy and flow of the entire system in motion as it travels through the rod guides and tiptop. For added security, an optional second nail knot is recommended to be tied midway between the first nail knot and the doubled standing part of the commercial braided nylon monofilament. The step-by-step instructions for tying a nail knot are shown on pages 22-23.

Forming a Large Braided Nylon Monofilament Loop

The following steps will form a large loop in braided nylon monofilament line, which can be used on the end of full-length fly lines and built into a braided monofilament shooting line (SL):

Step 1: Insert the splicing needle approximately 16 to 18 inches from the end of the braided line. Carefully thread it through the hollow center about 3/4 to 1 inch toward the end of the braided line, and then force it partially out a side of the braided wall.

Step 2: Grasp the tag end about a 1/4-inch from the end in the splicing needle and slowly pull it through the center of the hollow core until the splicing or wire needle is withdrawn completely. Be careful not to embed the line forming the loop into the hollow core by pulling the splicing needle too forcibly.

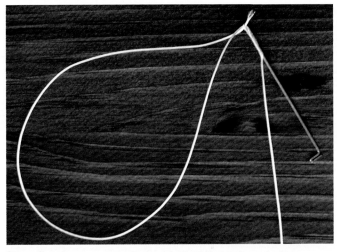

Step 3: After the splicing needle is removed, draw the line through its core to form a loop about 6 to 8 inches long. Trim the excess tag end flush to the standing part of the braided line. Lengthen the loop slightly by pulling the loop slowly until the end of the tag end is embedded in the hollow core.

Step 4: To secure the loop in position, tie a 6- to 8-turn nail knot using 8- to 12-pound semi-limp nylon monofilament line about midway along the doubled standing part of the braided nylon monofilament. The step-by-step instructions for tying a nail knot are illustrated on pages 22-23. Partially coat only the wraps of the nail knot (photo inset below) with cyanoacrylate (CA) glue, such as Krazy glue or UV Knot Sense. Use the CA glue sparingly to prevent a capillary action, which will cause the cement to flow into and along the braid. After the glue has cured, cut the standing part of the braided line to a length of 3 to 4 inches, which will be slipped over the back end of a fly line as described in pages 58-59.

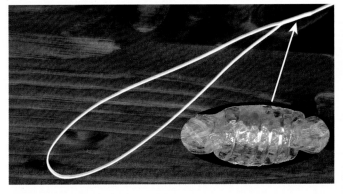

Chapter 2
Tying the Essential Knots

Since the late 1970s, the system I use for all my freshwater and marine fishing adventures consists of only six essential knots, which are: the nail knot, the Chermanski Loop, the blood knot, the improved clinch knot, the Bimini Twist, and the Haywire Twist. There is only one other knot, the Albright Special, which can be used to slightly modify my interlocking loop system configuration. Fishing exclusively for trout or panfish, for example, will require a maximum of five knots to learn. Furthermore, to fish for bass and other warmer water species, learning to tie an additional knot may be needed. To pursue every species in fly fishing, from brook trout in mountain freestone streams to giant tarpon on the saltwater flats, then all of the knots illustrated in this book will be necessary to learn and master.

Knot Tying Fundamentals

It is important not only to select the right knot for a certain task, but to tie it properly. Tying any knot requires some degree of practice, because the most difficult part is not learning how the knot is formed, but training the fingers with sufficient dexterity to handle the task. The secret to tying knots well is to practice them at home or in a controlled environment. Tying a knot repeatedly at home or in a controlled environment develops faster speed of operation, which translates to making a faster and more secure connection on the water when it becomes necessary. Some fundamental principles to ensure proper and efficient knot tying practices are:

- Check the hook eye for any rough spots that could fray the line.

- Use ample amount of working line, especially the tag end, when practicing to tie a knot until an improved level of proficiency permits minimizing excess quantities of line.

- Keep the wraps and turns of a knot lubricated to minimize buildup of damaging frictional heat and to allow the knot to cinch up smoothly and tightly.

- Tighten the knot with a steady, even and continuous pulling force.

- When trimming the tag end flush to the knot, use nail clippers carefully to avoid nicking or damaging the knot *after* part of the wraps or turns have been coated with UV Knot Sense or cyanoacrylate (CA) glue, such as Krazy glue. Allow at least a 1/16-inch tag end if the wraps or turns are not glued.

- Test the knot for slippage with moderate force before using it.

The following table is a guide to the tools and accessories for tying the essential knots and rigging the connections described in this book.

Tool or Accessory	Function & Usage	Page
The Third Hand (Knot Assistant)	Forceps tethered to a lanyard for holding the tag end of a line during the closing of a knot. A specially designed commercial version is available on the web at www.chermanski.com.	22-23, 25-27, 32-33
Hackle Pliers	Hackle pliers with rubber pads for holding the tag ends of two lines in tying the blood knot.	26
Splicing Needle	A device used for forming a loop in braided monofilament.	18-20
Monofilament Loop (20-pound)	The monofilament loop of 3 to 5 inches long is used to pull the tag end through the overwraps of a knot, such as the nail knot.	23
Hypodermic Needle (blunt point)	The needle is used as an alternative tool to the mono loop for threading the tag end through the overwraps of a knot, such as the nail knot.	23
Cyanoacrylate (CA) Glue	Fast-drying glue, such as Krazy glue, used for bonding wraps and turns of knots, and other connections.	15, 19-20, 23, 25-27, 29, 33, 59-60
UV Knot Sense	A glue activated by ultraviolet (UV) radiation and used for bonding wraps and turns of knots, and other connections in direct sunlight.	16, 19-20, 23, 25-27, 29, 33, 59
Lubricant Applicator	The applicator is used for lubricating a knot before it is tightened and it is typically a plastic squeeze bottle filled with water or vegetable oil.	25-27, 29, 33, 78
Line Straightener	A simple device used for removing twists and coils from monofilament line by pulling the line across two rubber pads being pressed against it.	80
Haywire Loop Twister	A homemade device for forming a small loop in a shock trace of solid wire for connecting to the loop at the end of a tippet section.	31
Needlenose or **Vise Grip Pliers**	The pliers can be used for holding a hook securely when considerable force is applied in cinching a connecting knot tightly. The pliers can also be used for holding solid wire in the formation of a Haywire Twist and a Haywire Loop, or twisting and burning plastic-coated cable wire.	30-32, 69
Bimini Twist Knotmaker	Forms a perfect Bimini Twist with 100% knot strength. The device is available on the web at www.chermanski.com.	28
Leader Stretcher	A homemade device used for stretching coils from the butt section and midsection of a leader system.	79-80

Many times having the right tool for a task will make performing it quicker and with less effort. The tools and accessories described in the previous table make it easier and more efficient to accomplish a specific task consistently. Some of these items you may already have available as a fly fisherman and fly tier, such as an applicator bottle, hackle pliers, leader stretcher, forceps and nail clippers. The remaining items are readily available for purchase with the exception of the Haywire Loop Twister and Third Hand, which you will have to assemble yourself.

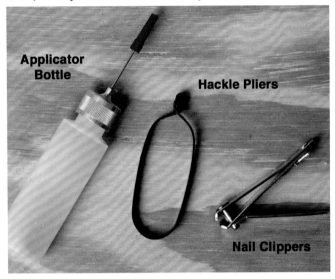

Applicator Bottle

Hackle Pliers

Nail Clippers

The Third Hand

When an additional hand is needed in closing a knot, many anglers rely on the gripping power of their front teeth to hold the tag end of a line securely. The long-term, potential damage to the front teeth when using this method is obvious. To preclude getting my front teeth repaired annually from chips and cracks, I developed a technique of using a pair of forceps tethered to a lanyard as a means of holding the tag end of a line when closing a knot. I call the contrivance the Third Hand and, for the past 25 years, it has actually worked better in closing a knot than my fingers or front teeth. The Third Hand has a more powerful grip on a line, which permits more pulling force to be applied without line slippage. It has been a real asset to tying strong, dependable knots quickly, safely and easily.

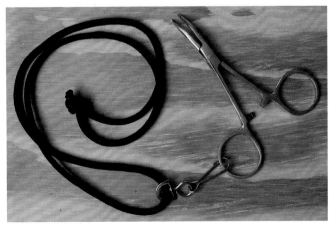

The most useful configuration of the Third Hand is having a pair of straight or curved forceps tethered to a lanyard and worn around the neck, as demonstrated in the photo below. This simple setup allows total mobility of both hands in the construction of a knot, while maintaining control of the tag end. In addition, varied or equal amounts of force can be applied independently in three different directions for smooth and consistent closure of wraps. The length of the lanyard should be large enough to fit over the head and manage the forceps at a comfortable working distance from the body. A variety of soft and limp materials can be used such as a braided shoelace or a lanyard from a coach's whistle.

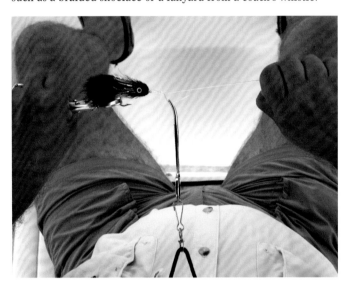

There is a specially designed commercial version to the Third Hand, marketed as the Knot Assistant, and it is available on the web at www.chermanski.com. The Knot Assistant features an adjustable lanyard and stainless steel pliers with a locking handle for aiding in the construction of any knot. The straight jaws and serrated teeth will safely and securely hold any line including 7X (.004") tippet material.

Tying the Nail Knot

As the name implies, a tapered nail was originally used to tie this knot when it was developed by the famed Florida Keys guide Jimmy Albright, but the nail knot can be tied in multiple ways using various tools. The differences stem primarily from the tool used to tie the knot, which can include a tube, a needle, a toothpick or a monofilament loop. The variation of the knot I tie most often uses a loop of 20- or 25-pound nylon monofilament for securing a PVC fly line loop and reinforcing a braided nylon monofilament loop, which are described on pages 60 and 19-20 respectively.

If it becomes necessary to tie a nail knot with stiff to medium-stiff nylon or fluorocarbon monofilament line of 20-pound or heavier, however, use the smallest diameter tube possible as a substitute for the monofilament loop. As depicted in the photo on page 23, I recommend using a hypodermic needle of 12- to 18-gauge with a blunt point. The cleaned out barrel of a ball-point pen shortened to about 1.5 inches long can also be used or even a toothpick. Any of these tools will make it easier than the monofilament loop to pass the tag end of stiffer and heavier line, such as leader butt material, through the wraps prior to cinching them tight.

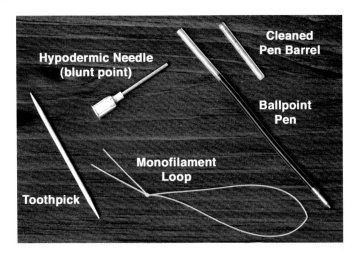

Hypodermic Needle
(blunt point)

Cleaned
Pen Barrel

Ballpoint
Pen

Monofilament
Loop

Toothpick

The following instructions apply to a right-handed person performing the steps in tying a nail knot to form a PVC fly line loop or a braided nylon monofilament loop.

Step 1: If the recommended nylon monofilament loop is to be used as shown in the photo above, double a piece of 20- or 25-pound nylon monofilament line and tie an overhand knot at the tag ends, forming a loop of 3 to 5 inches long.

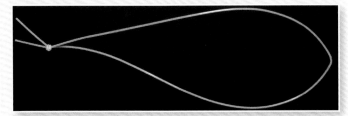

Step 2: With the thumb and index finger of the left hand, grasp the object being secured (the PVC fly line loop or braided nylon monofilament loop for example) where the nail knot is to be tied. Use a section of 8- to 12-pound semi-limp nylon monofilament to serve as the binding line. Lay it parallel and in the opposite direction to the object being secured. Securely grasp the line with the thumb and index finger of the left hand, allowing about 6 inches of the tag end to extend past the grip area.

Binding Line

Step 3: Place the monofilament loop, hypodermic tube or pen barrel parallel the binding line and the object being secured. With the thumb and index finger of the left hand, grasp the monofilament loop, hypodermic tube or pen barrel about midway along its length where the nail knot is to be tied.

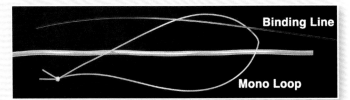

Binding Line

Mono Loop

Step 4: With the right hand, make a series of 6 to 8 wraps of the 8- to 12-pound binding line around the object being secured as well as the monofilament loop, hypodermic tube or pen barrel and the start of the binding line. Grasp each wrap with the thumb and index finger of the left as the binding line is being advanced (from left to right) to the tag end of the object being secured. Be careful to wrap the binding line firmly to avoid any overlap. The closer the wraps are made to each other, the easier it will be to tighten them evenly.

Mono Loop

Tag End
(Binding Line)

Step 5: Thread the tag end of the 8- to 12-pound binding line through the monofilament loop, pen barrel or hypodermic tube. Slowly pull the standing part of the 8- to 12-pound binding line to remove any slack. Carefully pull the monofilament loop or withdraw the hypodermic tube or pen barrel from the grasp of the thumb and index finger of the left hand.

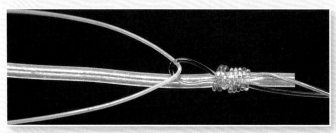

Step 6: Once the tag end of the 8- to 12-pound binding line is closed securely, grasp the standing part with the right hand and slowly pull them both in opposite directions with moderate force. The wraps should be tight, but not cinched to the object being secured. Hold the tag end of the 8 to 12 pound-test binding line with the Third Hand and slowly pull the tag end to close the wraps. Remove the grasp of the thumb and index finger of the left hand and inspect the knot. If there are no overlaps of the wrap, pull both ends of the binding line until the knot is tight as possible.

Pull Standing Part

Pull Tag End

Step 7: Trim the tag end and standing part of the 8- to 12-pound binding line as close as possible and coat the wraps with cyanoacrylate (CA) glue, such as Krazy glue, or UV Knot Sense. For added strength, abrasion protection and enhanced passage through the rod guides, the wraps can be coated with Pliobond, Goop, Aquaseal, Softex, marine silicone or similar products.

Tying the Chermanski Loop Knot

I developed the knot in 1970 from the frustration of trying to form a reliable and permanent loop in stiff nylon monofilament shock traces of a 100 pounds or heavier. At the time, the Home Rhode Loop was the standard knot to use, but it was difficult to tie securely in stiff and thick monofilament line. The knot was easier to tie and cinch tightly with lighter monofilament, but its low breaking strength of 70% or less limited its use to 20-pound or heavier nylon monofilament line. For the first ten years, I called this hybrid variation the Improved Homer Rhode Loop Knot whenever I demonstrated it. After more than twenty-five years of people referring to the knot as the Chermanski Loop, I officially renamed it in 1996. I also did not have to explain who Homer Rhode was anymore, although I greatly admire his pioneering achievements in saltwater fly fishing.

The maximum size of a nylon or fluorocarbon monofilament line that I ever used to tie a Chermanski Loop is 150 pounds. Since 1990, I do not use a nylon or fluorocarbon monofilament shock trace heavier than a 100 pounds. I also use the knot with pliable shock traces of stranded or braided wire. Whenever I am attaching a 4- to 8-pound tippet directly to a fly, I pass the tag end through the overhand knot in front of the figure-8 twists twice as shown in Step 6. I also use this variation with 4X and 5X tippets, and notably on dropper-fly rigs. It is interesting how much added movement is given a fly drifting freely with the current, especially in the main chutes of freestone streams and rivers.

I use the Chermanski Loop knot to attach all my freshwater and saltwater flies to a tippet or shock trace, except when I am fishing with 6X, 7X and 8X tippets for trout. I do not use the knot for securing a fly to these tippet sizes, because the lines are too fine to see the openings in the figure-8 twists. As a caveat to this exception, however, I do tie the Chermanski Loop in double lines of 6X, 7X and 8X tippet material, which are formed using the Bimini Twist. The loop tied in the double line is interlocked with the loop at the end of the semipermanent leader section. The use of this special rigging for these ultralight tippet sizes is utilized in the Type B leader system design illustrated in Chapter 9 and the Type K leader system design shown in Chapter 10.

The following instructions are based on a right-handed person performing the steps to tie the Chermanski Loop knot.

Step 1: Hold the standing part of the line with the index finger and thumb of the left hand about 5 to 6 inches from the end and the tag end in the right hand. Fold the tag end back and in front of the standing part, forming a small loop about a 1/4-inch in diameter above the intersection.

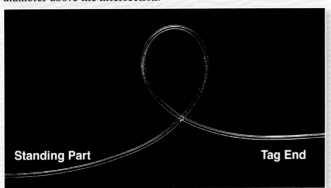

Step 2: Holding the base of the loop in position with the thumb and index finger of the left hand, pass the tag end through the loop then pass it around and through the loop a second time.

Step 3: Slowly pull the tag end away from the loop, causing the loop to collapse, twist and form a figure-8.

Step 4: Pass the tag end through the eye of the hook from below and, with the figure-8 positioned above the standing part, pass the tag end through the first part of the figure-8, over and across the internal line twists, and through the second part of the figure-8.

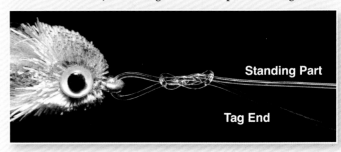

Step 5: Holding the figure-8 twists with the index finger and thumb of the left hand and the tag end with the right hand, slowly slide the figure-8 twists against the eye of the hook.

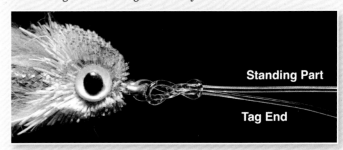

Step 6: Position the figure-8 above the internal line twists and hold the figure-8 twists with the left hand. Wind the tag end over and around the standing part, passing the tag end through the formed loop. When using 4- to 8-pound line, it is important to pass the tag end through the formed loop a second time, creating a figure-8 twist.

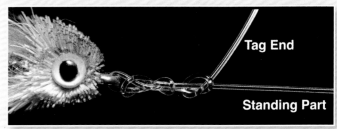

Step 7: Slowly pull the tag end to close the loop snugly directly in front of the figure-8 twists. The loop should not be cinched too tightly to the standing part since the figure-8 twists must slide towards the loop in the next step.

Step 8: Lubricate the figure-8 twists and the front overhand or figure-8 knot before forming the loop knot. Holding the hook with the left hand and grasp the tag end with the Third Hand, slowly pull the standing part with the right hand to cinch the figure-8 twists tightly against the overhand or figure-8 knot, forming about a 1/4-inch loop in front of the eye of the hook.

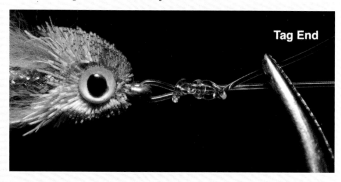

Step 9: Trim any excess tag end line close to the knot. It is highly recommended to moisten the overhand part of the knot sparingly with a fast-drying cyanoacrylate (CA) glue, such as Krazy glue, or UV Knot Sense.

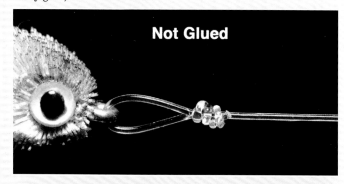

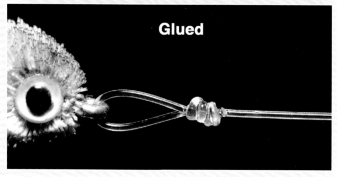

Tying the Blood Knot

The blood knot, or barrel knot as it also commonly called, is used for joining two sections together of similar diameter in the construction of a leader system. I also use this knot to create a tandem or dropper rig for attaching a second or third fly to a leader system. Other knots used for these purposes can cause a substantial loss of strength as well as other disadvantages. The blood knot, however, is more difficult to tie properly than these other knots. The principle impediment to tying this knot properly is the dexterity required, which can be remedied with practice. The knot is the easiest to cinch tight and the most reliable when the difference in the diameters of the lines to be joined is approximately .005 inches or smaller. It is also important the conjoining lines are similar in suppleness. In terms of line strength, for example, joining a 12-pound line to a 6-, 8-, 10-, 16- or 20-pound line will provide optimum knot strength. Coupling a line smaller or larger in diameter outside of this range can reduce the strength of a blood knot significantly and a knot, such as the Albright Special, is usually a better choice.

The following instructions apply to a right-handed person performing the steps to tie the blood knot.

Step 1: Overlap the two lines to be joined and grasp them at their intersection with the thumb and index finger of the left hand, forming an "X". Allow about 3 inches of their tag ends to extend beyond the intersection. If a tandem or dropper rig is being made, lengthen the tag end of the heavier line to about 12 inches.

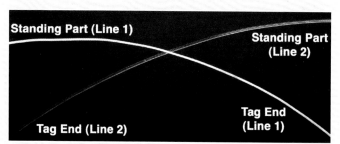

Step 2: With the right hand, wrap the right tag end of Line 1 about 4 or 5 times clockwise around the standing part of the Line 2 and thread the tag end between the two lines at the start of the wraps. Hold the tag end in position and switch the grip of the intersection with the thumb and index finger of the right hand.

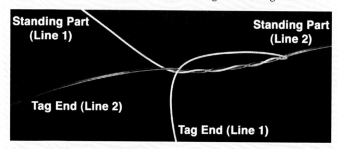

Step 3: Wrap the left tag end about 4 or 5 times in the counterclockwise direction around the standing part of the first line and thread the tag end in the opposite direction between the two lines at the start of the wraps. The tag ends should be protruding in opposite directions from the same opening between the lines.

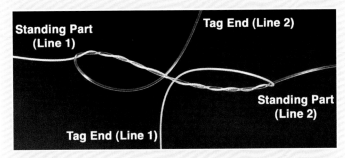

Step 4: Transfer the grip of the tag ends at their intersection back to the thumb and index finger of the left hand. Fold the lower tag end next to the upper tag end and pull each line separately to minimize the size of the formed loops. Grasp the tag ends with the Third Hand or hackle pliers as close as possible to the standing parts of both lines at their intersection.

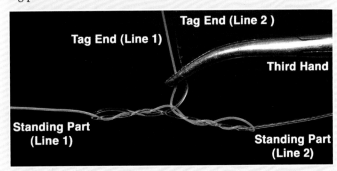

Step 5: Lubricate the wraps and slowly pull the standing parts of the two lines in opposite directions with a steady force to close the wraps evenly. It is critically important the tag ends do not slip from the grip of the forceps or hackle pliers during this process.

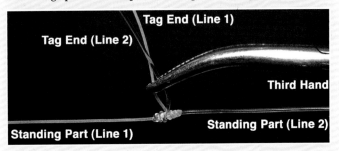

Step 7: Once the wraps are compressed, tighten the knot with a steady, even and continuous pulling force. Remove the forceps or hackle pliers and trim the tag ends as close to the knot as possible. If a tandem or dropper rig is being made, remove only the shorter tag end. Coat the wraps with cyanoacrylate (CA) glue, such as Krazy glue, or UV Knot Sense.

Tying the Improved Clinch Knot

The improved clinch knot is a quick and easy knot to tie when connecting a fly to a tippet. It is an alternate knot to the Chermanski Loop knot in fishing situations where a knot cinched tightly to the eye of the hook is desired. The improved clinch knot is a strong and reliable knot to tie with any size of nylon or fluorocarbon monofilament line less than .023 inches in diameter or 25 pounds. The use of this knot is recommended primarily for ultra-light tippets, 4 pounds or lighter, that are attached directly to a fly. Since it is a knot typically tied on the water, it is important to practice tying this knot so it can be tied quickly, easily and reliably under any fishing condition.

The following instructions apply to a right-handed person performing the steps to tie an Improved Clinch knot.

Step 1: Holding a fly in the left hand, thread the tag end of the tippet material through the hook eye and grasp the tag end and standing part of the tippet material in front of the hook eye with the thumb and index finger of the left hand. Allow about 2 to 3 inches of the tag end to protrude beyond the grip area.

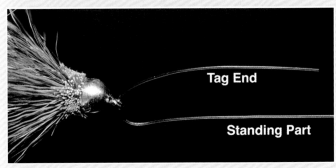

Step 2: Wrap the tag end 4 to 5 times around the standing part of the tippet material away from the hook eye using the right hand. For tippet strengths of 16 pounds or stronger, wrapping the tag end 3 to 4 times around the standing part is sufficient.

Step 3: Thread the tag end back through the loop between the hook eye and the first wrap being held with the left hand, creating a large loop over the wraps.

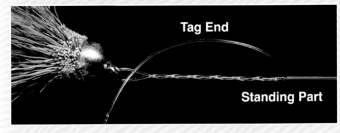

Step 4: Thread the tag end through the large loop and pull the tag end with a slow, steady force to close the wraps loosely. Do not cinch the wraps tight against the standing part of the tippet material.

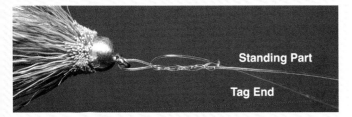

Step 5: Lubricate the knot area and slide the wraps against the hook eye using the thumb and index finger of the right hand.

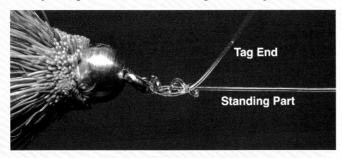

Step 6: Grasp the tag end with the Third Hand and tighten the knot with a steady, even and continuous pulling force away from the hook eye. It is important to keep the wraps tight against the hook eye when cinching the knot closed. Remove the forceps and trim the tag end as close to the knot as possible. Allow at least a 1/16-inch tag end if the knot will not been glued.

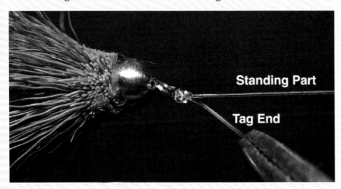

Step 7: Coat the knot with cyanoacrylate (CA) glue, such as Krazy glue, or UV Knot Sense.

Tying the Bimini Twist

The Bimini Twist and the Chermanski Loop are the two most important knots in my arsenal. They are both unique in their purposes, but retain the same qualities in knot strength, durability, reliability and functionality in a leader system. The Bimini Twist is a simple technique to producing a loop, or two strands, of a nylon or fluorocarbon monofilament line that proves stronger than the original single strand of the unknotted line. Originally, it was developed for offshore big-game sportfishing and it was known as the "20 times" knot, because of the number of twists applied to tie it.

When properly tied, the Bimini Twist is a knot with 100% breaking strength. It retains the original strength of the line being used. As a result, when the two strands of the formed loop are used to tie the next knot in a leader system, the knots used for this task, such as the Chermanski Loop and Albright Special, will be stronger than the standing part of the original line. If the line such as the tippet section should break, for example, the failure will not occur in the knot itself, but at the weakest area in the original single strand.

The most unique feature of the Bimini Twist is its shock-absorbing qualities. The elasticity of the twists forming the knot, and the double strands resulting from the knot, provide built-in shock absorption or impact resistance from sudden, jolting strikes or powerful runs from certain fish species. During a battle with a powerful fish, the tippet section will be subjected to the forces of stress and strain. When nylon or fluorocarbon monofilament line is initially pulled, all the force or stress is used to stretch the line. The total elongation of a nylon monofilament line, for example, ranges from 20% to 30%.

In fighting a fish, the early elongation of nylon monofilament serves as a safety cushion in setting the hook. For this reason, it is essential that the hook is honed to razor-sharp edges. Once the initial stretch has been achieved, there is an immediate transfer of stress to the line. The more force exerted on it, the more it continues to strain. When the tension is relaxed, the line recovers and the stress is zero. These are the elastic limits of the line and, while these limits are not exceeded in battling a fish, there will be no irrevocable damage to the line. If the elastic limits are exceeded, however, permanent deformation will occur and the line can be fatally weakened. Exceeding the elastic limits with a steady pull is one way to break a line, but impact is another, occurring more frequently than most anglers realize.

Under actual fishing conditions, the strain rate can be tremendous and the impact force can be considerable. A little tunny, for example, can swim at a burst speed of at least 14 miles per hour or 1,232 feet per minute. If a little tunny was hooked on a 9-foot leader with a 24-inch tippet and it swam directly away from the angler, the strain rate would be slightly more than 600%, including the strain rate for the fly line and its backing. With a fish moving that fast for even a short distance, it only takes about a half-second for it to stretch the line to its limit and break it.

Consider another example when a 4-pound largemouth bass strikes a popping bug or fly violently and immediately surges for cover away from the angler. The fish may be moving at a speed in excess of 1,000 feet per minute while the flyrod is sharply swinging from the horizontal to the vertical position trying to set the hook. The strain rate on a 9-foot leader with a 24-inch tippet can be an astonishing 500% and the impact force definitely becomes a concern to the reliability of the tippet to withstand these forces.

In addition to its shock-absorption qualities, the untrimmed tag end of a Bimini Twist can be used to create a tandem or dropper rig for attaching a second fly to a tippet section. This tandem design is actually a stronger and more reliable rig than using a blood knot for this purpose. The shock absorption qualities of this configuration can be significantly beneficial in many fishing situations, particularly in saltwater. It provides an added buffer to withstand the opposing forces of two powerful fish on the same tippet section.

Most books and magazine articles typically illustrate tying the Bimini Twist with one end of the loop being held under a foot and the other end on a knee. Although this method may be acceptable to most sport fishermen in general, I fail to understand why a fly fisherman would want to produce a 2- to 3-foot section of double line when the maximum length they would need to tie the next knot is about 6 to 8 inches long. In addition to the technical and physical difficulties associated with this procedure, it is a gross waste of expensive tippet material, because I use the Bimini Twist in virtually all of my freshwater and saltwater leader systems with few exceptions.

There are many common objects that can hold the loop firmly during the tying process. From a standing position, for example, a door knob, a drawer handle or a boat cleat can serve this purpose effectively. Conversely, from a seated position, a bent knee, the arm of a chair or the shaft of a tying vise can provide the necessary constraint for holding the line loop in position during the tying process. For many years, I tied the Bimini Twist with the loop held firmly on a bent knee or over a foot until I developed a tool called the Bimini Twist Knotmaker. The patent-pending device creates a perfect Bimini Twist knot in any line size as small as 7X (.004") tippet material. Although there are no restrictions to the length of the double line being produced by the tool, it

will render a short double line 8 to 10 inches long more suitable to the fly fisherman and the applications detailed in this book. In addition, when it is needed in the field, this device can be secured to a flat surface or other stationary tubular object, such as a steering wheel or boat railing. The Bimini Twist Knotmaker is available at local fly shops and other retail fishing tackle stores, or it can be purchased on the web at www.chermanski.com.

The following instructions apply to a right-handed person performing the steps to tie the Bimini Twist.

Step 1: Grip the line about 6 to 8 inches from its end with the thumb and index finger of the left hand. Double the line to form a single strand loop about 10 to 12 inches long, securing it with the tag end in the left hand. To tie a Bimini Twist as a tandem or dropper rig, grip the tag end 10 to 12 inches from its end.

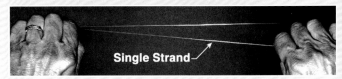

Step 1A: (Forming a double strand loop) Due to its ultra-thin and super slick nature, it is suggested a double strand loop is formed when using gel-spun polyethylene (GSP) line. This recommendation also applies to the most fragile tippets, particularly the ones used in saltwater. Grip the GSP line about 6 to 8 inches from its end with the thumb and index finger of the left hand. Double the line to form a loop about 24 to 28 inches long. Fold the loop back onto itself, forming a double strand loop about 10 to 12 inches long and securing it with the tag end with the thumb and index finger of the left hand.

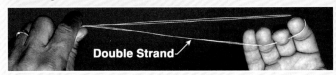

Step 2: Insert the three middle fingers of the right hand inside the closed end of the loop and rotate the right hand clockwise 16 to 24 times to create twists in the loop. For nylon and fluorocarbon monofilament lines, I make 16 to 18 twists for 16- and 20-pound line, 18 to 22 twists for 8- and 12-pound line, and 20 to 24 twists for 2-, 4- and 6-pound lines. For a single strand loop of braided Dacron and a double strand loop of GSP lines, I twist the loop at least 15 times.

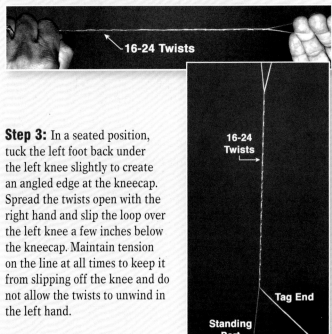

Step 3: In a seated position, tuck the left foot back under the left knee slightly to create an angled edge at the kneecap. Spread the twists open with the right hand and slip the loop over the left knee a few inches below the kneecap. Maintain tension on the line at all times to keep it from slipping off the knee and do not allow the twists to unwind in the left hand.

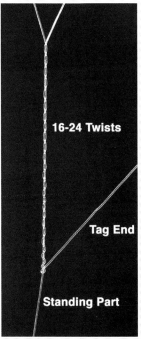

Step 4: Grasp the tag end securely with the thumb and index finger of the right hand and hold the standing line firmly in the left hand. Lubricate the twists and slowly separate the hands apart evenly, forming a large "V" in the tag end and standing part. This action will cause the twists to compress tighter together, reducing the size of the loop. Do not allow the twists to wrap over each other. Pull the tag end at about a 45-degree angle towards the knee until the twists are compressed as tightly as possible.

Step 5: With the twists tightly packed together, lift the tag end slightly so that it will jump or skip loosely over the first wrap. Maintain tension on the tag end while repositioning the standing part

in the left hand to insert the index finger in the loop. Hold the standing part firmly and slowly move the index finger towards the twists, simultaneously releasing some tension on the tag end. This action will cause the tag end to wind towards the index finger, further compressing the twists and wraps. The wraps should coil tightly against each other. Hold them in place with the thumb and index finger of the left hand. Some practice may be necessary to feed the tag end

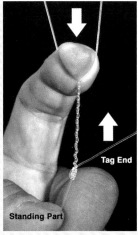

until it completely wraps over all twists.

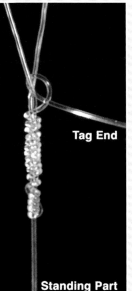

Step 6: If necessary, lubricate the area again and make a half hitch with the tag end on the right leg of the loop. Carefully cinch the half hitch tight against the wraps to lock the knot and to prevent the wraps from unraveling.

Step 7: Make one or two half hitches

on both strands of the loop to prevent the wraps from unraveling.

Step 8: To finalize the locking of the knot and to prevent the wraps and the previous half hitches from unraveling, tie a 3- to 4-turn half hitch on both strands of the loop. Cinch it tight against the previous half hitches, being careful to prevent the wraps from overlapping each other.

Step 9: Coat only the half hitches with cyanoacrylate (CA) glue, such as Krazy glue, or UV Knot Sense before trimming the tag end as close as possible unless it is intended to be used as a tandem or dropper rig. If the half hitches are not coated, allow at least a 1/16-inch of the tag end to remain.

Making the Haywire Twist

When confronted with the problem of trying to catch certain fish possessing exceptionally sharp teeth, such as wahoo and king mackerel, I use about 9 inches of solid, stainless steel wire as a shock trace. These species, as well as a few others with razor-sharp teeth, can easily shred the plastic coating on a braided wire shock trace and sever the individual strands, fatally weakening it. In addition, the smaller diameter of the solid wire fits more easily between the teeth of certain fish species, such as sharks, making it more difficult for the wire to be scored or cut.

The Haywire Twist is the strongest connection for securing single strand wire to a fly. The Haywire Twist gains its strength through a series of tightly formed twists that fortify the section where the wire joins the hook eye of a fly. As a result, this otherwise major stress point is stronger and less prone to kinking under increased pressure and torque. The barrel wraps are important, because they prevent the twists from unraveling.

It is advisable to practice forming the Haywire Twist before trying to test its formation on the water under actual fishing conditions. I would recommend starting with #7 or #8 wire, because lighter wire is more difficult to handle. The larger size wires are easier to see how the wires are twisting together and easier to twist off at their ends. The extra tag of wire must be twisted off correctly to ensure a smooth finish at the point of separation. Solid wire can penetrate the skin as easily as a needle and the slightest burr can cut hands and fingers severely.

The following instructions apply to a right-handed person performing the steps to form the Haywire Twist. Whenever possible, I prefer to form the Haywire Twist with the fly secured in a tying vise.

Step 1: Since solid wire is commonly packaged in a large coil, loop the wire through the hook eye so that the bow of the coil is orientated downward with the sinking alignment of the fly. Carefully fold back about 3 to 4 inches of the wire, making certain there is not a kink at the bend.

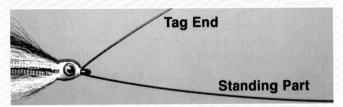

Step 2: Lay the tag end under or behind the standing part, crossing the wires so that a small loop is formed. It is important the tag end and standing part are spread equally apart to form a small loop. The size of the loop is defined by shortening or expanding the point where the wires intersect. Firmly hold the crossing point of the wires between the thumb and index finger of the left hand or with a pair of needlenose or vise grip pliers.

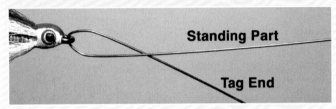

Step 3: Holding the tag end and standing part evenly apart at a 45-degree angle with the thumb and index finger of the right hand, twist the wires in a clockwise direction, forming an "X". Continue twisting the wires 3 to 4 more times. With each progressive twist, it is helpful to move the grip with the left hand and continue the pressure closer to the twists. A tight grip close to each wrap makes it easier to twist the wire, helps to keep it straight and prevents kinking.

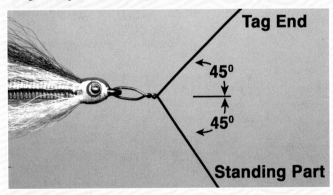

Step 4: At the conclusion of the last twist, change the orientation of the tag end to be perpendicular to the standing part. Make 4 to 5 barrel wraps with the tag end around the standing part. It is important these wraps be spiraled closely together, because they lock the twists in position.

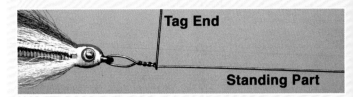

Step 5: After making 4 to 5 barrel wraps, use a pair of needlenose or vise grip pliers to bend the tag end to a 90-degree angle that is also perpendicular to the standing part.

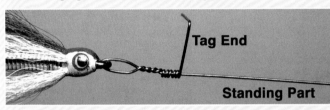

Step 6: Hold the barrel wraps securely with the thumb and index finger of the left hand and grasp the 90-degree section of the tag end with the pair of needlenose or vise grip pliers. Using the bent tag end as a lever, rotate the tag end back and forth, parallel to the standing part. It is very important the focal point of this action be directed at the termination of the barrel wraps. After a series of rotations, the tag end will break free cleanly at the base of the barrel wrap, leaving a smooth finish.

Step 7: A completed Haywire Twist.

Making the Haywire Twist Loop

The strongest and most dependable configuration for attaching a solid wire shock trace to a tippet is with interlocking loops. There are at least two ways of accomplishing this task. The method I use to create a quick-change rig involves a simple wire-forming tool fashioned from an open eye screw and a wooden dowel. The home-made tool, which I call the Haywire Loop Twister, forms a Haywire Twist loop in the wire and the thickness of the eye screw determines the width of the loop. The wooden handle aids in forming a Haywire Twist loop by providing leverage and a secure hold.

To build a Haywire Loop Twister, start by using an open eye screw with about a 5/8-inch outside diameter and a 1/8-inch thickness. Bond the open eye screw to a pre-drilled wood dowel, about 1/2 to 3/4 inches in diameter and 3 to 4 inches long, using an expandable wood glue. After the glue cures, cut a slot about a 1/16-inch deep at the apex of the eye screw using a hacksaw blade. The slot holds the wire loop from moving during the formation of the Haywire Twist loop. The tool will produce a small, compact loop about a 5/16-inch long and 3/16-inch wide, which is connected to the loop at the end of a tippet section.

The following instructions apply to a right-handed person performing the steps to form the Haywire Twist Loop. Although the Haywire Loop Twister can be used to form a complete set of 4 to 5 "X" twists in the wire, I prefer to use a pair of needlenose or vise grip pliers to firmly grip the wire after the first complete "X" twist. The pliers provide better control in completing the twists and wraps as well as preventing the wire from becoming bent or distorted.

Step 1: To form a loop, pass the wire through the center of the eye screw, seat it in the slot and bend it across the radius.

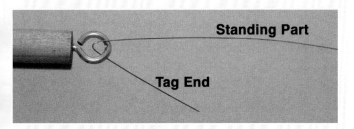

Step 2: Lay the tag end under or behind the standing part, crossing the wires so that a small loop is formed. Firmly hold the crossing point of the wires between the thumb and index finger of the right hand. It is important the tag end and standing part are spread equally apart to form a small loop.

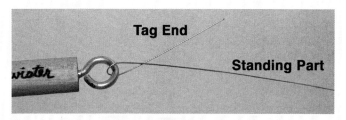

Step 3: Holding the tag end and standing part evenly apart at a 45-degree angle with the thumb and index finger of the right hand; rotate the Haywire Loop Twister one or two revolutions in a clockwise direction, forming an "X" with each complete turn.

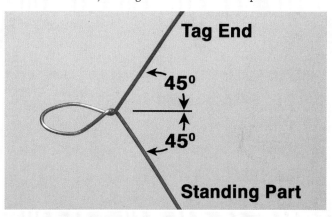

Step 4: Remove the wire from the Haywire Loop Twister and grip the crossed wires at the twist with a pair of needlenose or vise grip pliers. Continue twisting the wires 3 to 4 more times. With each progressive twist, it is helpful to move the grip with the left hand and continue the pressure closer to the twists. A tight grip close to each wrap makes it easier to twist the wire, helps to keep it straight and prevents kinking.

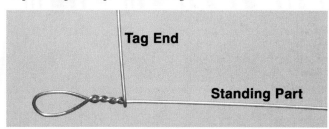

Step 5: At the conclusion of the last twist, change the orientation of the tag end to be perpendicular to the standing part. Then make 4 to 5 barrel wraps with the tag end around the standing part. It is important these wraps be spiraled closely together, because they lock the twists in position.

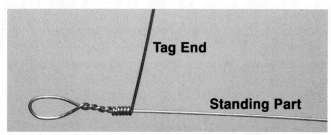

Step 6: After making 4 to 5 barrel wraps, use a pair of needle-nose or vise grip pliers to bend the tag end to a 90-degree angle that is also perpendicular to the standing part. Hold the barrel wraps securely with the thumb and index finger of the left hand and grasp the 90-degree section of the tag end with the pair of needlenose or vise grip pliers. Using the bent tag end as a lever, rotate the tag end back and forth, parallel to the standing part. It is very important the focal point of this action be directed at the termination of the barrel wraps. After a series of rotations, the tag end will break free cleanly at the base of the barrel wrap, leaving a smooth finish.

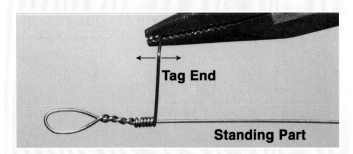

Step 7: A completed Haywire Twist Loop.

Tying the Albright Special Knot

Although famed Florida Keys guide Jimmy Albright has been credited with developing this knot, it was actually designed by J. Lee Cuddy of South Florida. The Albright Special is used primarily for joining two lines of significantly different diameters, most commonly a monofilament or wire shock trace to the tippet section of a leader system. The knot has increased strength when tied with a Bimini Twist to a wire or a much large diameter monofilament shock trace. I also apply the knot as an alternative option to splicing gel-spun polyethylene (GSP) backing to braided Dacron backing as well as when I want to attach a shock trace directly to a tippet section. In tying the Albright Special, it is important to note the knot should be closed in stages with only moderate force, so follow the instructions carefully.

The following instructions apply to a right-handed person performing the steps. For simplicity, these instructions are applied to a single strand of the smaller or binding line, such as a fly line backing material. If the lighter or binding line is a tippet material, however, it is suggested the line is doubled, using the Bimini Twist, before securing it to a shock trace with the Albright Special for example.

Step 1: Form a loop about 1 to 2 inches long in the tag end of the wire or larger line and hold it between the thumb and index finger of the left hand, allowing about half of the loop to protrude. Insert about 4 to 6 inches of the tag end of the smaller or binding line from the back of the loop and pinch both lines firmly between the thumb and index finger of the left hand.

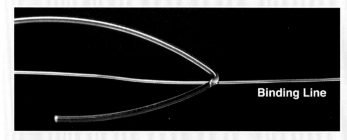

Step 2: Using the right hand, wrap the first turn of the smaller or binding line over itself and secure it in place by pinching it firmly between the thumb and index finger of the left hand. Continue wrapping the smaller or binding line towards the closed end of the loop for 5 to 7 more times around all three strands. The wraps should be moderately tight. After each wrap, pinch the coil between the thumb and index finger of the left hand.

Step 3: While holding the coils securely, thread the tag end of the smaller or binding line through the front side of the open loop. It is important the tag end exits the loop on the same side it initially entered. Grasp the tag end with the Third Hand and slowly pull on the standing part of the smaller or binding line with the right hand to moderately tighten the coils still firmly

held with the left hand. Do not cinch the coils too tightly, because they must be repositioned on the loop in the next step.

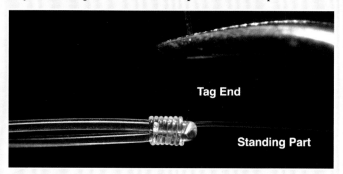

Step 4: With the thumb and index finger of the left hand, slide the coils of the smaller or binding line along the loop, stopping about a 1/16-inch from the end. If it is necessary to close the loop to a smaller size, slowly pull on the tag end of the larger line. Hold the tag end of the smaller or binding line perpendicular to the loop with the Third Hand to prevent the coils from slipping off the loop. Lubricate the coils and tighten them firmly by pulling the standing parts of both lines with a slow, even and continuous force. It is important the coils do not overlap each other. Trim both tag ends as close as possible and coat the coils with cyano-acrylate (CA) glue, such as Krazy glue, or UV Knot Sense.

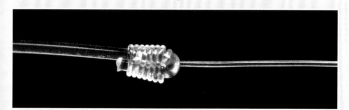

Step 5: (optional). This step and the next one are recommended only when tying this knot on the water or whenever it is not possible to secure it with glue. Make one to two half-hitches around the standing part of the smaller or binding line, cinching them tight against the base of the heavier line.

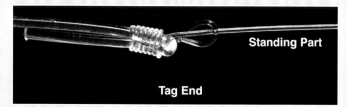

Step 6: (optional). Tie a 3- to 4-turn half hitch, pulling it tight to lock the half-hitches in position and to prevent the wraps over the heavier line from unraveling.

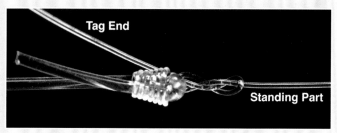

Step 7: Completed Albright Special knots with and without a "lock".

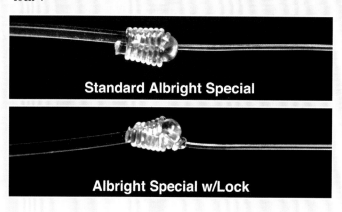

Chapter 3
Fly Lines

Introduction to Fly Lines

Despite the seemingly endless volumes of information written about fly fishing, the subject of fly lines has been mentioned in somewhat of a cursory commentary except to identify them as to their taper and densities. I find this ambivalent attitude somewhat surprising, because the fly line is the only means to present a fly to a fish. In this sense, it appears to me the fly line is a most critical component relative to the fly rod and fly reel in many fishing situations. Consider how the fly line assimilates into what I offer here as an abstract definition of "normal" fly fishing: An artificial fly, made of any natural or synthetic material, is cast by means of a long, cylindrical weight called a fly line, which extends beyond the tip of a double-fulcrum lever called a fly rod that is used to propel this line and fly to the fishing area.

It should be apparent from that definition, therefore, the fly line has always been a critical part of the fly fishing outfit. This importance has been true ever since the days when fly lines were made of braided horsehair. The purpose and function of the fly line becomes the most significant when trying to reach fish that are feeding much deeper in the water column. To illustrate the importance of the fly line in all types of fly fishing, I will briefly describe two experiences in which the difference between catching fish and not catching them was the fly line and not the fly, the fly rod or the fly reel. You should also note in these instances the degree to which I was willing and able to customize my fly lines, because there are times when it is necessary to "think outside of the box" to be successful.

In 1968, I was fishing for large rainbow trout in a relatively shallow lake in eastern Pennsylvania, which had grasses emerging from the bottom as high as four feet. The problem was to get the fly down to the feeding level of the trout, maintain it at that level during a retrieve and still keep it from getting snarled in the bottom vegetation. To solve this problem, I added a six-foot section of level floating fly line between the sinking fly line and the leader using an interlocking loop system. As a result, I proceeded to catch rainbows instead of the bottom, because I was able to work an unweighted fly safely above the vegetation, but still within the feeding zone of the fish.

In 1971, my good friend and longtime fishing companion, the Reverend John Meyer, and I looked down from the lighted catwalk under the Sebastian Inlet bridge in Florida through turbulent water to observe large snook stacked like cordwood near the bottom. The tidal turbulence, in excess of 5 knots, was of such magnitude that our normal lead-core shooting taper (ST) systems and weighted flies just would not penetrate deep enough for the

fish to respond. Later that day, in preparation for another planned late-night fishing trip, I made a special extra-fast-sinking "fly line" using five-amp lead fuse wire I strung through about 30 feet of squidding line. The process took nearly two hours to complete, the lead stuck out at frequent intervals and the finished "fly line" looked ragged and awful, but it had weight. Despite its appearance, the makeshift fly line cast surprisingly well, but more importantly, it proved to be heavy enough to penetrate the turbulence, keeping the fly near the bottom at the feeding level of the snook.

For two consecutive nights, before the fish moved offshore to a nearby reef, I enjoyed terrific snook fishing while John struggled in discontent to entice an occasional strike. His patience was virtuous, his determination was unyielding and his dedication was unwavering as he tried to lure snook with his Meyer Mullet fly higher in the water column.

The same

John Meyer

fly was not used, in these two examples, of course, but the vital factor in each case was the fly line and not the fly or the fly rod and the reel. The fly line may not be the most ostentatious item of fly fishing equipment, but it is frequently the only way to effectively get a fly to a fish. Consequently, no fly will be effective unless it is presented to the fish at the level at which the fish will accept it. That means you may need to evaluate the line you are using in accordance to the situation and conditions. It does not seem logical or very productive to fish on or near the surface when the fish will only take on or near the bottom, or vice versa.

Because a detailed discussion of fly lines have generally treated so trivially as a topic unto themselves, there are some anglers who arrogantly disparage the idea that fishing with anything but a floating fly line is not really fly fishing. To claim that only one type of fly line constitutes fly fishing is to foolishly ignore the reality and purpose of a fly line and its historical evolution.

In Western Europe during the 1400s, and probably earlier, horsehair was the basic material used in the construction of a fly line. Most anglers made their own, preferably of hairs from the tail of a white stallion, which were believed to be the strongest as well as the most easily dyed. Equal lengths of the hairs were either twisted or braided. In the former case, the hairs were twisted in one direction to form strands to be subsequently joined, and then the strands were twisted in the opposite direction for such joining. The strands were then knotted together with what was called a "water knot". Tapers were achieved by reducing the number of strands from butt to tip.

These lines were generally as long as, or slightly longer than, the length of the rods that prevailed at the time, which were typically 16 feet long. Little, if any, casting was done in the conventional sense as it is done today. The line and attached fly were tossed with the wind, since the horsehair line lacked sufficient weight to be cast into the wind. This situation prevailed at least until the advent of silk lines in the middle of the 1800s, when lines were heavy enough to allow the development of actual casting.

Various other products were used to make fly lines before the advent of silk, notably gut from the intestines of sheep and Indian grass called jute. But because of the difficulties inherent in the physical characteristics of the materials involved, they did not function very well. A combination of silk and hair was used during the days of Walton in the mid-1600s, but the technological problems of marrying the two materials into a single fly line went largely unsolved, and horsehair alone remained the dominant material.

In the latter part of the 1800s, due primarily to technological advancements in the manufacturing of braided lines and wire, fly lines were designed and built to cast more efficiently and effectively. In the 1880's, for example, tapered fly lines with either a copper wire or steel wire core were used. In 1952, Sunset Line made a braided nylon and fine metal wire tapered line, which Jim Green, an international fly casting champion who also designed rods for the Fenwick Company, used to cast in the dry-fly accuracy event at a national tournament.

The invention of nylon and its use in the production of fly lines created a stronger tapered core that was coated with a molten polyvinyl-chloride (PVC). By 1954, the PVC coating on a level nylon core could be varied to create a taper. In the early 1960s, micro balloons were injected between the nylon core and PVC coating to allow a fly line to float without the need for an external silicone application. The 1990s marked a significant leap in fly line technology, which has taken the use and function of a fly line to its fullest potential; that is, to present a fly at the level at which a fish will take it. Consequently, whatever the material used to make a fly line and regardless of its density, if it can be cast in the normally accepted manner, then it conforms to my definition of a fly line.

Fly Line Selection

With literally hundreds of styles and types available, it can be a daunting task to select the optimum fly line, especially for someone new to the sport of fly fishing. Using the wrong type of fly line for a specific fishing situation can be a very frustrating and unproductive experience. The process can be simplified, however, when the selection is based on certain parameters such as the perceived fishing situations desired and the probable species targeted in these fishing situations. The first step in the selection process is understanding the basic characteristics and attributes of a fly line design and how these elements affect performance.

The fly line is a very important component in the delivery system that propels a fly to the intended target. The weight of a fly line extended beyond the rod tip during a cast loads a rod, causing it to bend and recoil, and advances the developed kinetic energy to the target. For example, a fly line too light for a fly rod will present potentially difficult casting challenges in which the fly rod will never be fully loaded to develop sufficient line speed during the cast. Likewise, a fly line inordinately heavy will cause a fly rod to bend excessively during the cast, making line control and line speed an uncertain proposition at best. A fly line can also play a pivotal role in determining whether a fish will actually strike a fly and whether a hooked fish will be captured or lost.

Most fly lines are made with a braided nylon or monofilament core, which is coated with polyvinyl-chloride (PVC) although there is one manufacturer who uses polyurethane instead of the traditional PVC in the production of its fly lines. The main characteristics of a fly line are its weight, its taper and its density. The weight of a fly line extending beyond the tip of the fly rod provides the necessary mass for loading the rod for a cast. The taper of a fly line is suited to the casting preference and the presentation of the fly. The density of a fly line determines its floating or sinking qualities.

Key Elements to Fly Line Performance

Many fly lines, particularly specialty models, are designed with a preconceived system of fishing in mind and deliver a specific type of performance. The key elements determining the performance of a fly line are: the core, the coating, the taper design and the line weight. Every fly line is composed of two major components: the inner core and the outer jacket coating. It is the modification of these two components that affect the specific performance characteristics of a fly line, such as castability, shootability, durability and density.

Fly Line Cores

The core of a fly line, as shown in the following drawing, determines its tensile strength and the amount of stretch or elasticity it produces under stress. The type of core material used also affects the stiffness of a line. The breaking strength of a fly line is generally contingent upon its size. A 2-weight fly line, for example, has a breaking strength of about 20 pounds while the core of a 13-weight fly line can test more than 40 pounds. Most fly lines will stretch 25-30% before they break. If the fly line coating does not stretch as much as the core material, stretching could damage the coating. The most common problem is the coating will eventually crack and ultimately separate from itself, exposing the core to the elements. A PVC fly line coating, however, stretches more than a nylon line core so moderate stretching of a fly lines causes no damage.

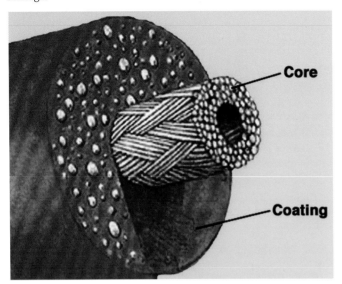

The amount of stretch in the core material of a fly line is a very important factor in casting performance and fish-fighting tactics. A core material with little or no stretch can cause a fly line to develop memory problems, which can severely affect shooting a fly line to a distant target. The only way to effectively straighten a line in the field is to stretch the coating. If the fly line is made of a core material, such as Kevlar, that prevents or minimizes stretching, memory cannot be removed and the line will retain its troublesome coils. In addition, the lack of stretch can cause light tippets to break suddenly during the setting of the hook if an angler is not careful.

Conversely, too much stretch in the core material and a fly line can become difficult to control during a cast as well as on the water. In most fishing situations, minimizing slack in the fly line during a retrieve is important, because the less slack in the fly line, the quicker the response to a strike. A core material that stretches more than 30% will make it difficult to drive a hook into the flesh of a fish, especially if the strike occurs more than 30 feet from the angler.

The type of core material used also plays an important part in the stiffness of a fly line. Fly lines intended for use in tropical climates are designed to withstand high heat extremes and maintain their inherent stiffness. Conversely, fly lines developed for use in more temperate climates are made with a less stiff core material, reducing the problem of line memory that occurs when a stiff line is subjected to cool weather or cold water conditions.

Fly lines are comprised of a core material and an outer coating. The type of core material has an effect on the performance of a fly line, because it affects the stiffness, strength and elasticity of a line. Core materials are either braided or single strand. The stiffness of the core material is an important consideration to the weather and water conditions you will be fishing most of the time. Supple core materials for colder weather and water conditions and stiffer braids for warmer fishing situations ensure loose loops, or tight coils between the rod guides, will not impede the cast.

A braided multifilament core satisfies colder weather and water conditions more adequately by providing lower memory and greater suppleness. Conversely, for tropical temperatures,

a braided monofilament core performs better in the heat and provides better shootability for longer casts. Braided fly line cores can consist of braided nylon monofilament or braided multifilament nylon, braided Dacron or braided polyester. A braided nylon monofilament core is constructed from a number of nylon strands braided together and, when the outer coating or jacket is added, the end result is a relatively stiff line.

Conversely, a braided multifilament nylon core is constructed from multifilament strands braided together, which results in a more supple fly line when the outer coating is added. A braided nylon core is used for most freshwater fishing situations, because it provides a strong limp line with an acceptable amount of memory. Fly lines with a braided multifilament Dacron or polyester core is not as popular as a normal fishing line, although it is used by many tournament fly casters.

Single strand nylon can be manufactured as a high- or low-memory core as required and it is often used for saltwater fly lines. One manufacturer uses gel-spun polyethylene (GSP) line for the core of its fly lines, which has very little stretch combined with high breaking strength. Low stretch cores have the benefit of allowing a quicker, more solid response in setting the hook to a strike, but they lack the shock-absorbing qualities that help protect fragile tippets when fighting large, powerful fish.

Stretching a Fly Line

Stretching a fly line to remove its memory coils can be accomplished in various ways. When wading a stream, I will wrap the maximum length of fly line I intend to use around the trunk of a tree. With the rod parallel the ground, I will grasp the fly line at the cork grip with one hand and hold the leader above the tippet section with the other hand and step backwards to slowly pull the line and leader taut. In wading situations where a tree or other fixture is not available, I will cast and shoot the amount of fly line I intend to use without the fly attached. As I retrieve the line, I will stretch it by slowly pulling 3- to 4-foot sections apart in my hands. On land or in a boat, I can stretch longer sections by stepping on the line and slowly pulling it above my head as illustrated in the photos below.

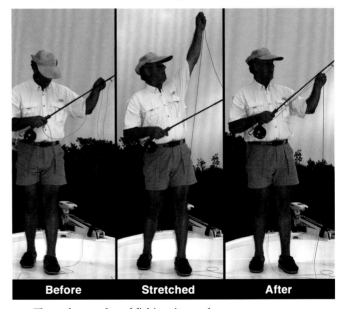

Before | Stretched | After

Throughout a day of fishing, it may become necessary to stretch a fly line more than once. Bulky, air-resistant flies and poppers are notorious for spinning during a cast, causing the fly line to twist and eventually coil. Whenever twists and coils develop, I simply remove the fly, shoot all the fly line I had been using and retrieve it quickly. In situations of moving water, I will remove the fly, cast the entire length of fly line I was using and retrieve it against the current. When fishing from a boat, I will remove the fly and let the entire length of fly line I was using trail behind the boat as I slowly move to another location. After retrieving the line, I reattach the fly and I am ready for the next fishing location.

Fly Line Coatings

How a fly line coating is formulated, and how it is applied to the core of a line, determines the remaining performance characteristics of a fly line. One of the most basic and important functions of the line coating is to provide the casting weight needed to load the fly rod, causing it to bend and recoil. Precise weight standards for a fly line are set by the fishing tackle industry, which are listed on page 42, and the proper amount of coating must be applied to a line in order to meet this standard.

Other purposes of the coating are to reduce friction when casting, to encourage floating lines to float high on the water, and sinking lines to descend below the surface. The lubrication in the coating helps reduce friction, minimizes wear and diminishes the risk of cracking. The coating also helps to resist the collection of dirt and other debris, which increases friction and thus reduces casting distance. A coating that allows a fly line to shoot through the rod guides with minimal resistance will aid in distance casting.

Some manufacturers offer fly line coatings for either coldwater or warm water applications that have different internal core configurations to suit the prevailing weather and water conditions under which they are designed to be used. Since their functions frequently overlap, it is easy to select fly lines that will perform best at the prevailing air and water fishing temperatures. For example, fly lines used in the tropics have monofilament cores and hard coatings to prevent them from becoming too limp in high temperatures. This same fly line design can also be used effectively in moderately warm air and water temperatures. A fly line suited for warm weather trout fishing, for example, can be used for cool weather saltwater fishing. The line should be exchanged for a model featuring a stiffer coating and monofilament core, however, when the water and especially the air temperatures rise.

All manufacturers have their own specialized coating formulations, which include axially orienting polymer, specific plasticizers and super slick lubricants. There are three main base materials used for fly line coatings: PVC, polyurethane and polyethylene. PVC is the most popular but one manufacturer uses polyurethane and another company is the sole user of polyethylene as fly line coatings. Combining polymers with plasticizers produces a stable coating that prevents premature brittleness. The addition of ultraviolet (UV) light inhibitors will also help to protect a fly line from the damaging effects of sunlight. Fly line coatings also contain the color pigments, which determine the visibility of the fly line to both the angler and the fish.

It is primarily the density of the coating material that determines whether a fly line will float or sink. Fly lines lighter than water, of course, will float. To aid in their floatation, most floating lines have special micro balloons mixed into their coating to provide their essential buoyancy and to allow for accurate control

of line density. A polyethylene coating, however, does not require any floatation additives because this substance has a specific gravity less than water so it floats naturally. In addition, most floating fly lines are treated with hydrophobic agents to make their coating water resistant. These lines actually repel water, making them float higher than other lines of the same density.

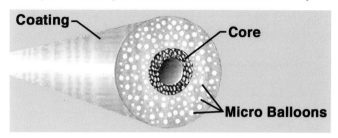

Conversely, sinking lines incorporate a high-density material into their coatings to make them heavier than water and therefore sink at a prescribed rate. Most sinking fly lines are designed to sink with the addition of tungsten particles to the coating as shown in the drawing below. Tungsten is nontoxic and it is 170% denser heavier than lead. By precisely controlling the formulation of how much metal powder is added to the fly line coating, a specific range of sink rates can be achieved. Most sinking fly lines have a descent rate ranging from as little as 1.25 inches per second (ips) to as much as 10 inches per second (ips). The standard sink rates for sinking fly lines are discussed on pages 44-46.

Fly Line Taper Designs

Many years ago, fly line tapers consisted only of very basic double taper and weight-forward designs. Since the 1980s, however, the popularity of fly fishing has broadened its base to well beyond trout, bass, salmon, steelhead, panfish and a few marine species. In addition, technical improvements in rods, leaders and flies has spawned a vast array of general and specialty taper designs for use in both freshwater and saltwater.

The taper design is perhaps the most important component of a fly line because it affects the castability and presentation of the fly. The flexibility of a fly line is also important in forming narrow loops during a cast of either long distances or precision accuracy in restrictive places. This attribute is also essential in resisting memory sets in a fly line after being stored on a reel for any length of time. A fly line can lose its flexibility, however, when subjected to lengthy exposure from infrared (IR) and ultraviolet (UV) radiation that is emitted by sunlight.

Fly line tapers have evolved to complement the faster, lighter and more efficient fly rods. Their multifilament braided nylon and monofilament core materials are also stronger and more uniform. The plastic coatings are more durable, slicker and float higher or sink faster. The most commonly used tapers are double taper (DT), weight-forward (WF) taper and shooting taper (ST) as shown in the drawing on the next page. For all my fishing requirements, which range from bluegill to billfish, I use some variation of either a weight-forward (WF) or shooting taper (ST) line almost exclusively, because these taper designs deliver a fly to the target effectively and efficiently. I do, however, customize a double taper (DT) line into a shooting taper (ST) system for specific fishing situations, which is discussed in detail on pages 61-62.

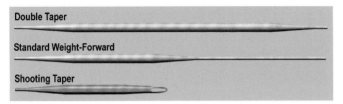

The shape or taper design of a fly line determines its performance. In essence, the taper design designates how energy is transmitted and dissipated during a cast. By varying the lengths and diameters to the major parts of a fly line design, manufacturers are able to produce fly lines with accentuated performance characteristics for specific types of fishing situations and fish species. For example, special tapers, such as bass and saltwater tapers, have shorter and heavier front tapers, which are designed for casting large, wind-resistant flies with a minimum of false casting for quick and accurate delivery of the fly. There are also specialty tapers for specific fish such as pike, salmon, steelhead, bonefish, redfish, tarpon, billfish and other popular species. There is even a specialty freshwater nymph taper for anglers who fish with heavy, weighted nymphs or add weight to their leaders for sinking their flies deeper in the water column.

To better comprehend the dynamics and characteristics of fly line tapers, it is helpful to have a basic understanding of the fly line nomenclature and the six major parts of a fly line. Since the most popular taper used by most fly fishermen is some variation of a weight-forward fly line, I will use that taper design as the primary example as illustrated in the drawing below. The front section of a weight-forward fly line is referred to as the head, which includes the tip, forward and rear tapers, and the body. The remaining portion behind the head, which comprises at least 60% of the total length of a fly line, is a small-diameter level line referred to as the running line. By varying the lengths and diameters of the tip, front taper, body and rear taper, fly line manufacturers can design heads with unique and specialized casting characteristics.

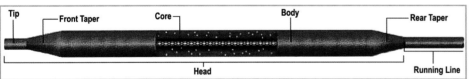

Tip: The leader connects to the tip, which is a thin, level and short section usually six to twelve inches long. Its length allows a permanent leader to be cut off and reattached several times without significantly affecting the shape and performance of the front taper. The diameter of the tip affects the way the fly line turns over during a cast. A thinner tip section provides a more delicate presentation, while fly lines with thick tip sections create a more powerful delivery.

Front Taper: This section of a fly line taper design determines how delicately or powerfully the fly is delivered onto the

water. Its length typically ranges from 4 to 8 feet as it decreases in diameter from the body to the tip section. This graduation of mass (weight) along the length of the front taper affects the transfer of casting energy to the fly. The length of the front taper, combined with the diameter of the tip, ultimately determines how delicately or powerfully a fly will land in the target area. The combination of these parameters also affects how the casting energy dissipates as it moves forward from the body of the fly line to the leader and eventually to the fly. Fly lines with long front tapers disperse the energy slower than those with short front tapers.

Extended front tapers that graduate to small-diameter tip sections, however, sometimes collapse when matched to heavy leaders and bulky, wind-resistant or heavily weighted flies. Windy conditions can also produce a collapse in the delivery of the fly line and leader because this configuration cannot sustain sufficient energy to turn them over on the final forward cast. Conversely, a comparatively short front taper has a more powerful turnover, but it may not cast as smoothly. When matched to a large-diameter tip section, the powerful turnover of a short front taper makes casting large or weighted flies easier even in windy conditions. These more blunt tapers, however, have a tendency to produce a "hook" or "kick" at the completion of the cast, especially when mismatched with short leaders and very light tippets. In addition, fly lines with larger diameter front tapers and tip sections may land with too much impact for skittish fish in calm, shallow water.

Body: This section of a fly line is located between the front and rear tapers. It is the longest section of the head with the largest diameter where most of the weight of a fly line is concentrated and, consequently, where the casting energy is carried. When the rod is stopped at the end of both the forward and back casts, the energy stored in the rod is transferred to the line at the rod tip. Because the body is the thickest part of the head, it holds most of the energy in a cast, which is then dissipated through the forward taper and leader. It is easier to control a fly line with a long body and thus increase accuracy on long casts than a short body. It is also easier to achieve distance with a long-bodied line because of the delayed turnover, but these specialized, longer versions may require more false casting for the average caster.

Head: This term describes the combination of the front taper, the body and the rear taper of a fly line. The length and weight of the head alone is not sufficient to turn over a big or heavily weighted fly. Fly size and weight are the primary determinants in selecting the ideal fly line weight and matching fly rod, but perceived wind speed is also a factor to consider as well. For example, a heavier weight fly line may be needed to comfortably cast less bulky flies in open water where a constant breeze is almost a certainty.

The heavier and more wind-resistant a fly, the more mass, or the heavier the line, is needed for turnover at the conclusion of a cast. Fly line sizes are determined by their weight. The weight of a fly line is expressed in the form of a numerical scale starting with 1, the lightest weight. According to the standards developed by the American Fishing Tackle Manufacturing Association (AFTMA), fly line weight designations are based on the weight in grains of the first 30 feet of a fly line excluding the level tip section. For example, all 8-weight lines weigh an average of 210 grains (+/- 8 grains) in the first 30 feet of the body regardless to the length, shape or density of the head. The weight standards for a given fly line weight are listed on page 42.

There are several factors to consider when looking for the best head configuration to match a given typical fishing situation, including the expected average casting distance, the delivery speed of the fly to the target, and the casting ability of the angler. The overall length of the head can significantly affect the casting distance and the number of false casts needed to make a presentation. Longer heads generally require more false casting and they are usually harder for the average caster to keep airborne.

Additional false casting required to extend a longer head beyond the rod tip can present a problem to the average caster, for example, when a cruising fish suddenly materializes and there are only a few precious seconds available for the fly to be delivered accurately. Conversely, a shorter head offers a distinct advantage in this situation, because it is designed for executing quick, relatively short casts. A longer head, however, may be a better choice when longer casts are required and there is ample time to deliver the fly to the target.

Regardless of the taper or head design of a fly line, every caster will get slightly different results from the same fly line configuration, even under identical circumstances. An experienced, skilled caster can reach extreme distances with the same number of false casts regardless of the length of the head. The average caster, however, may be more effective using a short length head for moderate casting distances, because there is less line to manage when false casting.

Rear Taper: This section is the transitional area between the thin-diameter running line and the thicker body. The length of the rear taper affects the degree of control in managing the head section and, therefore, provides smooth casts beyond 35 feet. An average caster can control a cast more easily and throw a smoother line more efficiently by keeping the end of the rear taper just inside or slightly outside the rod tip on the final forward cast. Compared to the thin diameter of the running line, the relatively larger diameter of the rear taper transmits the kinetic energy from the rod tip to the head section of the fly line more efficiently. Although a long rear taper provides the best line control and casting smoothness, a short rear taper is better suited for quick casts at moderate distances.

Running Line: This section consists of a small diameter level line and it is an integral part of a weight-forward (WF) fly line, which is described on page 40. The primary purpose of the running line is to make distance casting easier. Since a reversible double taper (DT) line, is essentially a long body with front tapers at both ends, there is no running line section by definition. This large diameter body does not shoot through the rod guides as easily as a running line and, therefore, it is not a line for distance casting. The smaller diameter running line creates less friction. Once the head of a weight-forward (WF) line is extended beyond the rod tip, its weight loads the rod and the momentum generated at the final forward cast can pull the trailing running line for relatively long distances. For this reason, the running line comprises at least 60% of the length of a standard weight-forward (WF) fly line.

Types of Fly Line Tapers

There are four basic types of fly line tapers and two general types of hybrid tapers. The principal fly line tapers include level (L), double taper (DT), weight-forward (WF) and shooting taper (ST) while the basic hybrids include the specialty weight-forward (WF) and the extreme sinking shooting taper (ST). The myriad of specialty tapers available are variations of weight-forward (WF) and double taper (DT) fly lines. The weight-forward configuration is the most popular for a variety of reasons and it also has the most taper variations. The following topics are a synopsis to the performance characteristics and general uses of each basic taper design.

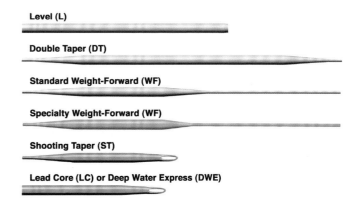

Level (L) Fly Line

The level (L) line designation simply means this floating fly line has the same diameter throughout its total length with no front or rear tapers and no running line. It is the oldest form of the modern, plastic-coated fly line. A level (L) line has poor casting characteristics in general fishing situations and it is not recommended in circumstances requiring either long casts or delicate presentations. It transfers energy variably, it is hard to control while casting and it has limited shootability beyond the length of line outside the rod tip. The only advantage to a level (L) line is its economic value. About the only use a level (L) floating line has sustained in recent years is casting surface poppers, foam spiders, wet flies, small streamers and weighted nymphs short distances to panfish, where a delicate presentation is not normally required.

Double Taper (DT) Fly Line

A double taper (DT) line is essentially a longer level fly line with front tapers of equal length and design on each end, although it does have improved casting characteristics. It is the second oldest form of the modern, plastic-coated fly line and it is used exclusively in freshwater situations where floating line applications prevail. A double taper (DT) fly line is aptly named, because it can be reversed when one end of the line becomes worn or damaged, which is a definite economical advantage.

This style of line is designed for short- to medium-range casts, where achieving maximum casting distance is not required in normal freshwater fishing situations. A double taper (DT) fly line provides excellent line control since the entire body of the line is a large, uniform diameter. It is designed for delicate and accurate presentations and it is easy to mend and roll cast, which makes it most useful on moving water.

Weight-Forward (WF) Taper Fly Line

There are two basic types of weight-forward (WF) tapers as illustrated in the drawings below. A standard weight-forward (WF) taper, with its longer front taper, allows more fly line to be extended beyond the rod tip during a cast. This results in better casting control for increased accuracy, a softer landing on the water and improved line management once it is on the water. Conversely, a more specialized weight-forward (WF) taper, such as fly line designated for saltwater or for casting heavily weighted flies, has its own unique advantages. This taper features a shorter head and front taper, which can be extended beyond the rod tip with one or two false casts for quick presentations to mid-range targets that may be constantly moving. In addition, the shorter front taper delivers unwieldy flies better than a standard weight-forward (WF) fly line.

A standard weight-forward (WF) fly line is comprised of a head, which includes a tip, a front taper, a body and a rear taper, and a level running line of a smaller diameter. The weight or mass of a weight-forward (WF) fly line is concentrated at its head. When extended beyond the rod tip during a cast, the momentum achieved by the head is used to carry the running line behind it. Momentum is a quantity of motion and, in fly casting terms, it is the product of the weight of the fly line head extended beyond the rod tip during a cast and the velocity it is traveling at the completion of the power stroke.

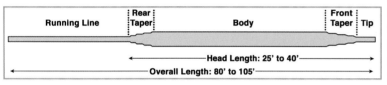

Weight-forward (WF) lines are the most versatile of the fly line tapers and perform well over a wide range of fishing conditions. The mass or weight of this taper design is concentrated in the head as shown in the drawing above. The line then tapers to a small diameter running line, which is less resistant and, therefore, travels through the rod guides more smoothly and easily. As a result, this taper design allows for longer casting distances of 60 feet or more with minimum false casting and more delicate presentations at short to medium range then either a double taper (DT) or a level (L) fly line. In essence, any fly line, regardless of its density, consisting of a head and running line section that are seamlessly joined together can be technically termed a weight-forward (WF) fly line.

Although it does not execute an extended roll cast as efficiently as a double taper (DT) line, a weight-forward (WF) taper will cast further and deliver a fly to a target into a head wind more effectively. Due to its versatility, its performance characteristics and its availability in a variety of densities, the weight-forward (WF) taper has replaced the double taper (DT) design as the standard line for most fly fishermen. It is also the best choice for anyone learning to fly cast, because the head serves as a controlled length so that the same amount of line is outside the rod tip during repetitive casting practices. As a result, the beginner can apply a more consistent amount of load to a rod and, therefore, become better acquainted with the dynamics and "feel" of a casting cycle more easily and quicker.

Weight-forward (WF) lines are obtainable in both floating and various sinking densities. The taper design is available in

many head configurations to comply with specialized fishing situations or perceived presentational improvements. They are marketed under a myriad of names and variations, such as rocket taper, bass bug taper, saltwater taper, steelhead taper, triangle taper, bonefish taper, tarpon taper, just to name a few. The bass bug taper (BBT) and the saltwater taper (SWT), for example, are variations of the standard weight-forward (WF) line with a shorter and more concentrated head configuration for handling bulkier flies and quicker casts.

The triangle taper (TT) is somewhat different from other weight-forward taper designs. It features a continuous front taper in the head that varies in length from 27 to 40 feet depending upon the line size or weight, and a very short rear taper to the running line. This unique concept, developed by the legendary Lee Wulff, provides an efficient transfer of casting energy as it unrolls, because the heavier line is constantly turning over the lighter line. When casting 30 feet beyond the rod tip, for example, the line will perform as a 5-weight, but if the full 40-foot head is extended, it will perform as a 6-weight. With excellent turn over properties for short to medium casts and softer, more delicate presentations from the continuous front taper design, the line is a particularly good choice for dry-fly fishing.

Specialty Weight-Forward (WF) Fly Lines

If choosing a fly line from all the standard optional designs available is not confusing enough, there are also dozens of different specialty weight-forward (WF) fly lines to consider. These lines mostly target specific fish species and types of flies, but there are also other specialty lines designed for specific environments and fishing situations. The two most common environments for which a specialty line may be needed are marine and cold water. Some fly lines get stiff and unmanageable in very cold water, while other lines become too soft and limber in very hot weather. Fly lines constructed of a polyethylene copolymer coating, for example, will remain supple in the coldest of temperatures.

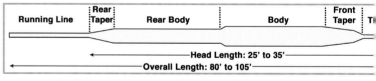

The largest assortment of these specialty lines have been developed for use in the tropics and in temperatures above 65 degrees F. Many of these fly lines feature a high performance coating and a stiff monofilament core to help create tight loops and positive turnover of long leaders, while minimizing line tangles. Some of these lines also emphasize a slightly shortened front taper, which allows for quick accurate casts and the turnover of the biggest flies.

Another popular group of specialty lines promote a no-stretch gel-spun polyethylene (GSP) core for quick hook setting response, increased strike sensitivity and more positive hookups. One manufacturer claims the no-stretch power of their GSP core will hook a fish from 100 feet, which I find doubtful for various reasons. Nevertheless, these fly lines are primarily designed for use on a wide variety of marine species including redfish, bonefish, permit, tarpon, striped bass, tuna, sharks, billfish, bluefish and false albacore.

Still another type of specialty fly line is the clear coating with a monofilament core, which is used primarily in clear, shallow marine environments. Some of these lines are clear their entire length, while other lines include a clear tip section. The MONIC Tropical Clear fly line, for example, is the first clear floating line and it has the potential to be an effective tool when pursuing tarpon, permit, and bonefish in saltwater, because it is designed for use in warmer water and weather conditions. In theory, a cast can be made closer to a quarry and a shorter leader can be used, which can provide an advantage in better line control for a more accurate presentation. Nevertheless, the impact of the line hitting the water close to a skittish quarry can negate both apparent advantages. A translucent line or tip section, however, does present some interesting possibilities for a skilled caster capable of making accurate presentations.

There is also a myriad of specialty fly lines for the trout, salmon and steelhead enthusiasts. One of these lines was designed to cope with the added weight of fishing a strike indicator with a split shot. This line is intended to pick up and deliver the extra weight needed to fish strike indicator systems effectively at any depth. There is also a similar fly line design, with its unique reverse compound taper and a bullet front taper, built to turn over heavy flies with less effort being cast into the wind and smoothly transfers energy to prevent the characteristic "kick" with heavily weighted flies.

There is also a weight-forward (WF) floating design made specifically for the casting demands of steelhead and Atlantic salmon fishing. The line was developed with a long body and long back taper for long controlled mends, roll casting, and single-handed Spey casting. A shortened front taper turns over large flies more easily and it works well with a greased line or the waking fly technique. On the opposite end of the spectrum is a fly line designed for casts of 60 feet or less. This special sinking line has 20 feet of a sinking tip and 40 feet of floating line. It is extremely easy to cast and control for close-range fishing situations.

Double Taper (DT) vs. Weight-Forward (WF)

Over the many years since the development of the weight-forward taper, there has been an ongoing argument primarily among trout fishermen which is the better taper, double taper (DT) or weight-forward (WF). The answer is neither taper is inherently better, because the best performance and use of either taper is contingent upon many factors, including the specific fishing situation. Double taper (DT) lines, for example, are proclaimed to deliver a more delicate presentation and roll cast better. In many fishing situations, these performance features are true, but not always.

The delicate delivery of a presentation is determined by the mass or weight of the front taper of a fly line, which is defined by line diameter and taper length. The diameter of the line is directly related to its mass. A fly line with a small diameter tip and a long taper has much less forward mass than a line with a large tip and short taper, which results in a more delicate delivery. A fly line with a long front taper and a large tip diameter will deliver a fly with less delicacy.

A double taper (DT) and a weight-forward (WF) fly line of the same taper and tip diameter will deliver a fly with the same impact on the water. For many years, most double taper (DT) and a weight-forward (WF) lines were constructed with the same tip diameter and front taper length so there was no discernible dif-

ferences in their deliveries. More recently modern double taper (DT) lines, however, are actually designed with longer tapers and smaller tips specifically for soft and delicate presentations.

Whenever a fly line is designed for a specific application, there will be compromises in some of its other performance characterics. For example, fly lines designed to deliver a delicate presentation will have minimal mass in the front taper and tip section to efficiently cast larger or heavier flies. Also, the line will not handle as well in windy conditions. Conversely, a weight-forward (WF) line will be more accurate, because of the smaller diameter running line passing through the guides more easily, augmenting increased line speed. Also, a double taper (DT) does not necessarily deliver a fly more accurately to the target than a weight-forward (WF) line. Nevertheless, a skilled and experienced caster can generally manage these situations and conditions satisfactorily regardless of the line taper used.

A double taper (DT) fly line is usually easier to control, mend on the water and roll cast at distances beyond 50 feet than a weight-forward (WF) line. At casting distances less than 50 feet, though, there is really no difference in performance and simply a matter of preference. There are not many typical fishing situations in freshwater that require longer casts. As a result, a double taper (DT) and a weight-forward (WF) fly line will perform comparably at the distances most often fished in freshwater. For wide rivers, which may require longer roll casts and line mends, a double taper (DT) or a specialty weight-forward (WF) line with a long head would be more beneficial. A longer fly rod would also be an important asset in this situation.

Roll casting, and to a lesser degree line mending, is best accomplished when the body of the line is inside the rod tip. If only the small diameter running line of a weight-forward line (WF) is inside the rod tip, for example, there will not be sufficient energy transmitted from the running line to the head for a proper execution. It is similar to trying to throw a ping-pong ball as far as a baseball. Realistically, the continuous body of a double taper (DT) line makes roll casting and line mending easier beyond 40 feet. As a result, for most anglers in common freshwater fishing situations requiring casts of 50 feet or less, it probably does not make much difference which taper they choose.

Shooting Taper (ST) Fly Line

A shooting taper (ST) is a special type of fly line. Also called a shooting head (SH) system, a shooting taper (ST) consists of two separate lines which are joined together with an interlocking loop-to-loop system. The head or front section is basically the same configuration as the body and front taper of a standard weight-forward (WF) fly line. The remaining section consists of a very small diameter running line, which is called the shooting line (SL). Its purpose is to significantly reduce friction as it travels through the rod guides and in the water. Various materials can be used as a shooting line (SL), including nylon monofilament, which are discussed in detail on page 48.

A shooting taper (ST) system will allow an angler to achieve extreme casting distances, 100 feet or more, when required. Since they are available in a wide range of densities, the shooting taper or head can be interchanged with the shooting line (SL) quickly and without having to restring a rod, change the reel or reel spool. The various densities available for a shooting taper (ST) system are discussed on pages 45-47 or you can make your own customized system, which is discussed on pages 61-63.

Choosing a Fly Line Taper

If you are uncertain to the taper on the fly lines you currently own or are considering purchasing a fly line, there are several ways to ascertain the taper design in determining the best type of fly line for any given fishing situation. Relying on the name of a fly line alone, which was contrived by a manufacturer, can be misleading and often erroneous to your intended use of the line. There is a large assortment of tapers designed specifically for bass, tarpon and bonefish, for example, and each version has its own distinctly formulated head and tapers. Since these fly line designs are not standardized by name, the best method of determining the most suitable choice for your needs is to examine the head and taper dimensions carefully and consider their effects on the performance you desire.

Conversely, there are some fly lines with different names that have the same taper design. For instance, some saltwater tapers and bass tapers are identical. Similarly, there are saltwater and bonefish fly lines with identical tapers. The only perceivable difference between the two lines is the type of core material used. The bonefish taper, for example, generally has a braided monofilament core that performs at its best in hot weather and a tropical environment. The typical saltwater taper, however, has a braided multifilament core, because it performs better in cooler weather and water conditions.

When trying to choose a fly line with an appropriate head configuration and taper design for an intended fishing situation, I would suggest considering the following variables that are perceived to be encountered most of the time:

- fly size and weight
- expected casting distance
- delicacy of presentation
- accuracy at distant targets
- delivery speed of a presentation
- line management on the water
- nominal wind speed
- casting ability

By incorporating these variables in the selection process, the final decision will include most, if not all, of these considerations that closely match your perceived fishing requirements. There will certainly be compromises made, but they should not affect the overall performance of your choice. Conversely, unless your fishing requirements specifically dictate the use of a specialty taper, I would suggest contemplating the use of a standard weight-forward (WF) fly line to meet your general-purpose demands. The line can deliver a proficient, all-around performance under a variety of fishing situations and conditions. In summary, my advice when buying a fly line is to buy the best line you can afford for your most common and frequent fishing situations. With most products, including fly lines, you generally get what you pay for. Any fly line can help catch fish, but a more suited, quality line will be more productive and efficient, which hopefully will make the whole experience more pleasurable.

Fly Line Weight

Fly line standards were developed by the former American Fishing Tackle Manufacturers Association (AFTMA), now the American Sportfishing Association (ASA), to help fly fishing tackle manufacturers create a system that would match the weight of a fly line to fly rod performance. In theory this initiative would standardize fly line manufacturing throughout the industry and enable anglers to select and balance their equipment for optimum performance.

The ASA system uses the weight in grains of the first 30 feet of a fly line as a standard, excluding any tapers and regardless of line density. Thus, if a fly line has a taper, the measurement begins on the first level 30 feet of a fly line after the taper. The weight of a fly line is represented on a numerical scale ranging from 1 to 15 with the lowest number representing the lightest fly line weight. A 5-weight fly line, for example, is lighter than a 9-weight fly line. The table below shows the line size designation and its associated average weight measured in grains (437.5 grains = 1 ounce) for a given fly line. The table also displays the tolerance level or range of weight that is acceptable for each line size.

Line Size	Weight (grains)	Weight Range (grains)	Line Size	Weight (grains)	Weight Range (grains)
1	60	54-66	9	240	230-250
2	80	74-86	10	280	270-290
3	100	94-106	11	330	318-342
4	120	114-126	12	380	368-392
5	140	134-146	13	450	435-465
6	160	152-168	14	500	485-515
7	185	177-193	15	550	535-565
8	210	202-218			

Fly Line Color

The choice of fly line color is a very subjective topic among anglers. I, of course, have my own opinion and it is simply unless a fly line is translucent clear, its color does not matter for two reasons. When two floating fly lines are sitting on the water side-by-side, for example, one fluorescent orange color and the other buckskin color, the orange line is clearly more visible to an angler. From an underwater perspective, however, both lines cast similar silhouettes. Given the turbidity of water and fish not having the visual acuity of humans, I do not think the issue is whether the line is visible in the water or not. I think the issue is how the visibility appears in a context to a fish. Both colored lines cast a silhouette of equal magnitude, but more importantly, they both reflect light polarized light. Similarly, sinking lines also reflect polarized light to a depth where sunlight is still present, regardless of their color.

Polarized light reflection from fly lines, leaders, tippets and shock traces have been spooking fish since the beginning of their use, unbeknownst to most anglers. It is definitely a factor in our angling productivity, which is rarely taken into consideration or fully understood. The polarized light theory as a means of prey enhancement should work favorably and not adversely for the angler. As a result, a fly should reflect polarized light since it is designed to emulate a prey, not the fly line or leader and especially not the tippet, which is attached directly to the fly in most cases.

Scientific studies have proven fish can see polarized light, which is a particular characteristic of ultraviolet (UV) light that humans cannot see. In fact, it is a major factor in their prey detection and recognition process. The amount of polarized light refracted into the water is greatest when the sun is about 30 degrees above the horizon. When polarized light is reflected by a fly line, leader, tippet or shock trace, it causes them to become luminous and more easily seen by the fish. Interestingly, a natural quirk in the structure of the human eye gives us, by accident, the ability to tell apart different states of polarization. Thanks to this small aberration or defect of the eye we are not completely blind to polarization; nevertheless, we cannot see polarized light as fish do and there lies the significance.

In summary, I would recommend choosing a floating fly line that is easy to see in the most frequently fished waters and lighting conditions, because the fish will see its silhouette regardless of its color. As a result, the ability to track a fly line is crucial to fishing success, particularly in low-light conditions and when working a fly below the surface. Most sinking lines are dark color, however, so the choices of line color are limited. These lines still reflect polarized light higher in the water column, but it is in a different perspective to a fish and seemingly less intrusive.

Fly Line Densities

The density of a fly line refers to its buoyancy or ability to either float or sink. There are three general categories of fly line buoyancy: floating (F), sinking (S) and floating/sinking or dual-density (F/S). Sinking lines are further grouped into categories or classes of a predictable sink rate, which are discussed on pages 44-46 and 63. The following guide is a synopsis of different fly line densities and their general fishing applications:

Floating Fly Lines

A floating fly line does just what the name suggests; that is, it floats on the surface of the water along its entire length. A floating fly line is the most popular and commonly used density for various reasons, but I believe being the easiest to fish and the most enjoyable to cast are probably the two most important ones. The visibility of the line during a cast and floating on the surface of the water is another reason for its popularity.

In addition to the inherent floatability designed in its coating, most floating fly lines are treated with some type of hydrophobic agent to make their coating water resistant. These floating lines actually repel water, making them float higher than other lines of the same density. The higher a line floats on the water, the easier it will be to pick up and cast. For this reason, it is important for a floating fly line to be clean and free of dirt or other debris particles.

A floating fly line is best suited to working flies on or just beneath the surface of the water in relatively shallow-water fishing situations. The fishing range of a floating line can also be extended further down the water column with the use of weighted flies or a small split-shot attached to the leader. In either case, the subsurface effectiveness of a floating fly line can be increased to a depth of three or four feet in most fishing situations and conditions.

A standard, floating weight-forward (WF) taper design provides an all-around performance to longer casts, accuracy to the target, sufficient line control and the easiest to lift off the water for a recast or correction. The shorter heads and tapers of specialty floating weight-forward (WF) fly lines allow for a quick cast to moving targets and positive leader turnover of bulkier or weighted flies, but casting accuracy and delicacy of presentation may be slightly compromised. These specialty lines are available in various taper designs for more customized applications. Some versions feature a stiffer core and harder coating to resist becoming limp in hot weather or warm water conditions as previously mentioned.

Dual-Density Fly Lines

A dual-density fly line features a sinking front section typically of 6 to 15 feet that transitions to a full-length floating fly line. This type of line density is commonly called a sink tip (F/S). The benefit of a dual-density line is the ability to present a fly deeper in the water column and still being able to watch the floating portion of the line on the surface of the water. A dual-density line retains the advantages of a floating fly line in which less fly line is needed to be retrieved before being lifted from the water for another cast in comparison to a full-length sinking line. In addition, visibility of the floating line on the water provides improved strike detection. The floating section of the line can also be mended on the water to reposition it during a drift or a retrieve.

Prior to the late 1980s, floating fly lines were the standard unless you wanted to battle the pioneering sink-tip fly lines for added depth in the water column. The aerodynamic imbalance of the weighted front taper of a dual-density fly line creates the risk of casting a tailing loop, which can cause knots in a leader or a chance of getting hit by the fly. Contemporary sink-tip lines, however, cast better than their predecessors, but they still produce a hinge effect to a lesser degree during a cast. The hinge effect is manifested by the differences in the mass or weight of the floating section of the line and the heavily weighted sinking section. During a casting cycle, the hinge is created by the increased momentum of the sinking section in comparison to the floating section of a dual-density fly line. A solution to lessen this effect is to create a wider, unrolling loop in the forward and back casts, and to minimize the amount of fly line head extended beyond the rod tip during a cast.

Although it is a more challenging line to cast, a sink-tip fly line broadens the fishing zone in a variety of situations and conditions. They are used frequently when extra depth is needed in shallower water for working flies on or near the bottom. In shallow water, however, these lines should be used cautiously, because their somewhat emphatic entry on the water can startle a wary quarry. Sink-tip lines are also commonly used in fast or deep water such as along shoreline drop-offs, around docks, pilings, jetties, gaps of deeper water surrounded by shallow water, deep holes, channels and saltwater flats. In addition, a dual-density line with an intermediate sink-tip has become a practical substitute for a full-length floating fly line, particularly in saltwater on the flats and over grass beds.

Dual-density fly lines are available in mini and standard sink-tip configurations as well as in different sink rates although most sink-tip lines tend to sink quickly. The maximum sink rate is attained only in still water, or when the line is moving at the same speed of the current. Once the retrieval of line starts, however, the line will cause the fly to rise slightly higher in the water column, depending upon various factors including the weight of the fly, retrieval rate and current speed. As a result, the best sink rate of a sink-tip line for use in moving water will be determined by the speed of the water, the intended fishing depth and the rate of retrieve.

A modern hybrid to the dual-density fly line is the multi-tip fly line system. This interchangeable tip configuration typically features four, 15-foot tip sections of different densities, which are looped to a floating, tapered belly section. The loops are generally fused to provide a stiff, non-hinging connection between the belly and tip sections. The densities of the tip sections are commonly floating, intermediate, fast sinking and extra-fast sinking to accommodate a wide range of fishing situations. The best assets of interchangeable tip sections are portability and compactness, especially when traveling to more remote fishing locations.

The variations within each sink rate type or class are due to the different line sizes themselves. For example, the tip section of a Type 2, 6-weight line will sink faster than a Type 2, 4-weight line. To further complicate the equation, manufacturers vary on their definitions and scope of a sink rate type or class. As a result, a fly line should be selected by its sink rate rather than by its type or class. It should also be noted that sink rates are measured under controlled conditions and may not always be duplicated in actual fishing conditions. The table below relates the sink rates for each type or class of sink-tip lines.

Type or Class	Sink Characteristic	Sink Rate (inch per second)
1 or I	intermediate (slow)	1.25 to 1.75 ips
2 or II	medium	1.5 to 2.0 ips
3 or III	fast	2.5 to 4.25 ips
4 or IV	faster	3.5 to 5.25 ips
5 or V	fastest	5.5 to 6.5 ips

The lighter weight sink-tip lines, which are normally used with smaller flies in short to moderate fishing distances, generally feature a shorter sinking tip section and head. Conversely, heavier weight lines, used for larger flies and longer casting distances, have longer sinking tip sections and heads. The scope and diversity of using sink-tip lines provides unparalleled control to the movement of a fly through the water.

A more customized version known as the mini or instant sink-tip typically features a 4- to 6-foot section of sinking line in various sink rates, which is attached to the front end of any floating fly line using an interlocking loop-to-loop system. The other end of the mini sink-tip section also has a braided monofilament loop for interchanging leaders. This mini sink-tip system, which is usually covered with braided nylon monofilament, provides a quick and easy method for getting a fly slightly deeper in the water column. The details to making mini or instant sink-tip sections are discussed on page 64.

Full-Length Sinking Fly Lines

There are times when a floating or dual-density fly line is just not the right tool for the fishing situation, especially when the fish are holding in deeper water. The solution may be using another type of sinking fly line. There are three major forms of sinking fly lines: dual-density, full length and shooting taper. Full-length sinking fly lines constitute the core of fishing in deepwater situations to realistic depths of about 30 feet. They are designed to dredge flies on or near the bottom in the deep, slow-moving pools in big rivers, in lakes and reservoirs as well as in many saltwater situations.

Most sinking fly lines are composed of a braided nylon monofilament core that are coated with a molten polyvinyl-chloride (PVC) material. Some sinking lines feature low-stretch, monofilament cores with urethane polymer coatings. This latter coating provides a faster sink rate, because it is about 30% smaller in diameter than a PVC-coated line and, therefore, produces less resistance during its descent. In addition, the low-stretch core material improves strike detection, which can be challenging when working flies deep in the water column. Tungsten is added to the coatings to make the line sink. By varying the amount of powdered tungsten, manufacturers can produce fly lines that sink at precise and predictable rates.

Full-length sinking fly lines will cast bulky flies farther and easier because of their less air-resistant, smaller diameter than their floating line counterparts. A standard weight-forward (WF) fly line, for example, is about 35% larger in diameter and surface area when compared to a sinking fly line of the same line weight. The efficiency of casting a full-length sinking line also applies when confronting a wind, which can be an expected daily occurrence in most situations where a sinking line is typically used. The most common uses where a smaller diameter sinking line can deliver moderate to long casts, even in breezy conditions, are on lakes and reservoirs, on large rivers and in saltwater.

The early sinking lines had a major problem of sinking in a bowed profile in which the body would sink faster and deeper than the front taper and tip sections. The angle at which a fly was retrieved made strike detection difficult. To resolve this problem, density compensation was developed to produce a fly line whose front taper and tip sections will sink at the same rate as the body of the line. As a result, a density-compensated sinking fly line greatly improves the linear retrieval path of the fly, enhances depth control, magnifies strike detection and increases hook-setting capability.

Sinking fly lines are rated by the speed at which they sink, which is measured in inches per second (ips). The actual sink rate of a sinking fly line will vary considerably and its rate will be listed on the packaging along with the weight and taper. A sinking fly line can sink from approximately 1 to 10 inches per second (ips), although the typical range for full-length sinking lines is from 1 to 7 ips. Knowing the sink rate and the predetermined depth for the retrieval process, an angler can use a countdown method to attain the proper level. And once the acceptable depth is reached, a full-length sinking fly line will maintain that depth throughout most of the retrieve.

In addition to numerical sink rates, sinking lines are generally classified as intermediate, slow, moderate, fast and extra-fast, but each manufacturer has its own nomenclature. The choice of sink rate is contingent upon the fishing situation and conditions. For fast moving water, deep pools or dredging the bottom in deep water, for example, a fast sink rate may become necessary to sink and maintain a fly at the desired depth. Otherwise, a slower sink rate generally works well in most fishing situations, especially with a weighted fly.

Eventually all sinking lines reach the same depth. However, the speed in which the line reaches the various depths is often the deciding factor in fishing success. The table below relates the sink rates for each type or class of full-length sinking lines. The variations within each sink rate are due to the different line sizes themselves. For example, a Type 3, 8-weight full-length sinking line will sink faster than a Type 3, 5-weight line. To further complicate the equation, manufacturers vary on their definitions and scope of a sink rate type or class. As a result, a fly line should be selected by its sink rate rather than by its type or class. It should also be noted that sink rates are measured under controlled conditions and may not always be duplicated in actual fishing conditions.

Type or Class	Sink Characteristic	Sink Rate (inch per second)
1 or I	intermediate (slow)	1.25 to 1.75 ips
2 or II	moderate	2.5 to 3.0 ips
3 or III	fast	3.5 to 4.0 ips
4 or IV	faster	4.25 to 5.0 ips
5 or V	extra fast	5.25 to 6.0 ips
6 or VI	super fast	6.25 to 7.0 ips

A full-length, slow-sinking, intermediate fly line has become a practical substitute for a full-length floating fly line in many fishing situations. This line density has become a popular choice in saltwater where a shadow cast by a high floating line will often spook a fish in shallow water even in discolored water conditions. In addition, a full-length intermediate fly line will generally cast farther and easier than a floating line, because of its slightly smaller diameter. Whenever the need arises, the line can be dressed with a silicone-based gel or paste to further reduce its slow sink rate sufficiently to use poppers, sliders and other surface flies effectively.

An intermediate fly line has numerous advantages in certain fishing situations and conditions. For example, they are generally immune to wave action at the surface and the collection of vegetation and other debris in the water that typically afflict floating fly lines. On lakes and saltwater flats with emerging grasses and other bottom vegetation, an intermediate line can work a fly just above these obstacles. And because it sinks, the line tracks linearly at a more natural angle especially when the surface is disturbed, enhancing strike detection and hook setting response.

Sinking Shooting Taper (ST) Fly Lines

A shooting taper (ST) line is simply the head of a weight-forward (WF) fly line without the rear taper and running line sections. It is comprised of two major components: a shooting head (SH) and a small diameter shooting line (SL). The term "head" relates approximately to the front 30-foot section of a typical full-length fly line, whose weight determines its line size. Early shooting taper (ST) systems, previous to the 1980s, were just the body and

front taper cut from weight-forward (WF) or double taper (DT) fly lines and they were reattached to a 25- to 40-pound nylon monofilament shooting line (SL). Since that time, manufacturers and anglers have developed shooting head (SH) and shooting line (SL) systems of various materials, lengths and densities to achieve different purposes. Similar to a weight-forward (WF) line, the shooting head (SH) is the part of a shooting taper (ST) system that provides the mass required to make a cast. The difference is a shooting head (SH) will pull the much smaller diameter shooting line (SL) to considerably farther distances than any other type of fly line. The longer head of a standard full-length weight-forward (WF) line, for example, creates approximately 50% more resistance through the air and water.

A shooting head (SH) can be made any length and density. The low-friction shooting line (SL), ranging from 75 to 150 feet in length, is composed of either nylon monofilament, braided nylon monofilament or a small diameter, commercial shooting line (SL). The latter type is typically 100 feet long, PVC-coated and available in various densities. I connect the shooting head (SH) to a shooting line (SL) using an interlocking loop system. The leader is looped to the shooting head (SH) and the shooting line (SL) is looped to the backing on the fly reel. The system is completely adaptable to interchanging the shooting head (SH) and/or the shooting line (SL) quickly and easily to accommodate any fishing situation. Detailed information on how to rig a shooting taper (ST) system is discussed on pages 61-63.

A shooting taper (ST) system offers several other advantages in addition to achieving long casts. The capability to interchange a shooting head (SH) of a different density quickly and easily to accommodate changes in fishing conditions or situations is a paramount feature of the system. This versatility is especially important when the situation changes from surface and near-surface fishing techniques in shallow water to dredging a fly on or near the bottom in deeper water. I typically find this system extremely effective when the situation requires a slightly slower or faster sinking shooting head (SH) than the one I am using at the time. The change to a different density is generally very quick and the results are usually immediate. Also, the interchangeability of the system eliminates the need for additional fly reels or spare spools.

Sinking lines are designed to present a fly at depths unattainable with a floating line. In my opinion, a conventional sinking shooting taper (ST) system is the most versatile, practical and effective method of attaining this goal as well as achieving extreme casting distances. In fact, I use these systems more often in both freshwater and marine fishing situations than all of the other types of fly lines combined. In saltwater, for example, I use a full-length floating fly line almost exclusively for topwater flies and poppers, and only in certain applications. My primary line in most of these fishing situations is an intermediate shooting taper (ST) connected to a floating shooting line (SL). I do use full-length floating fly lines more often in most freshwater environments, though, but a sinking shooting taper (ST) system is my first choice on lakes and reservoirs.

I view the versatility of a shooting taper (ST) system, with its assortment of densities, analogous to golf clubs, particularly the irons. Instead of carrying multiple fly outfits rigged with different fly line tapers and densities, I can exchange a shooting head (SH) of a different density within two minutes without changing spools or reels to accommodate the specific fishing situation or condition at the time. I have homemade wallets with labeled, ziplock bags for each specific line weight. Each line density is rolled in 4-inch coils and stored in these bags for easy and quick access, which is discussed in more detail on page 65.

In many freshwater and marine fishing situations, I generally carry at least two fly outfits sometimes of the same line weight and, at other times, of different line sizes. For example, for general inshore saltwater fishing, I typically use a 7-weight outfit rigged with an intermediate or sinking shooting taper (ST) system and a 9-weight outfit setup with full-length weight-forward (WF) floating line. The different line weights are matched to the size, bulk and weight of the flies intended to be used. For river smallmouth bass, as another example, I will use two 7-weight outfits rigged with a full-length weight-forward (WF) floating line and a sinking shooting head (SH) attached to a floating shooting line (SL).

Sometimes I carry two fly outfits of the same line weight that are rigged with shooting heads and shooting lines of different densities. The first outfit is setup with a floating shooting line (SL) line and the other outfit is equipped with a braided nylon monofilament shooting line (SL) line. The former configuration is usually employed with a floating or intermediate shooting head (SH), while a faster sinking shooting head (SH) is used with the braided nylon monofilament shooting line (SL) line.

For ocean and bluewater fishing, all my fly outfits are rigged with shooting head (SH) lines. Regardless how many fly outfits I take on a fishing trip, at least one of them will be rigged with a shooting taper (ST) system. The only exceptions to this rule is when I am fishing exclusively with topwater flies and poppers, and a fly line density other than floating is not a viable option, which is rarely the case. In many fishing situations where I will have only one outfit, it is usually rigged as a shooting taper (ST) system with a floating shooting line (SL). If the need suddenly arises for working topwater flies and poppers, I either change to a floating shooting head (SH) or loop a 6-foot section of floating fly line into the front of an intermediate or slow sinking shooting head (SH).

If you decide to use a floating or intermediate shooting taper (ST) system rather than a full-length weight-forward (WF) floating or intermediate line, I would recommend making your own floating shooting head (SH) from a floating double taper (DT) fly line. It is easy to do and the length of the shooting head (SH) can be literally customized to your casting ability. The complete steps for making and rigging a shooting taper (ST) system are covered on pages 61-64 with specific instructions on building a floating or intermediate shooting head (SH) line on pages 61-62.

The versatility of making your own custom shooting head (SH) extends beyond traditional applications. For example, I thoroughly enjoy casting poppers and flies on 4- and 5-weight outfits to fish, particularly snook and bass, in closely restrictive areas. These tightly confined, secluded spots prohibit standard equipment from being used effectively and efficiently. In these situations, I use an 8-foot, 5-weight outfit rigged with an 18.5-foot, 9-weight floating shooting head (SH) looped to a floating shooting line (SL). The length and weight of the shooting head (SH) is comparable to the weight of a full-length 5-weight floating fly line, but it delivers quick and accurate casts to close-range targets.

If purchasing a commercial shooting taper (ST) line for general fishing applications, I would recommend using a shooting head (SH) one size larger than the fly line rating for the fly rod being used. When making a longer cast with a full-length weight-forward (WF) fly line, usually more than 30 feet of fly line is extended beyond the rod tip before shooting it to the target on the final forward cast. Using a 30-foot shooting head (SH) one size larger will compensate for this weight differential and create more line speed, propelling it longer distances before it straightens and falls to the water. In addition, the smaller diameter 30-foot shooting head (SH) line is more aerodynamic.

The variations of the sink rates within a given type or class are due to the different line sizes themselves. For example, a Type 3, 9-weight shooting taper (ST) will sink faster than a Type 2, 9-weight line. To further complicate the equation, manufacturers vary on their definitions and scope of a sink rate type or class. As a result, a fly line should be selected by its sink rate rather than by its type or class. It should also be noted that sink rates are measured under controlled conditions and may not always be duplicated in actual fishing conditions. To determine the exact sink rate for any sinking fly line, consult the catalog or Internet web site of the manufacturer to ascertain the range of line weights associated with a specific sink type or class. The sink rates for each type or class of sinking shooting taper (ST) are shown in the table below.

Type or Class	Sink Characteristic	Sink Rate (inch per second)
1 or I	intermediate (slow)	1.5 to 1.75 ips
2 or II	moderate	2.25 to 3.0 ips
3 or III	fast	2.8 to 3.5 ips
4 or IV	faster	3.75 to 6.5 ips
5 or V	extra fast	6.25 to 6.75 ips
6 or VI	super fast	6.5 to 7.0 ips

Advantages & Disadvantages of Shooting Taper (ST) Systems

With a shooting taper (ST) system, a considerable amount of water can be explored more effectively, because it will cast a fly farther and sink it faster and deeper than any other type of fly line. Shooting tapers offer the convenience of enabling an angler to switch from a floating head to various sinking densities without changing reels or reel spools. The compactness and portability of carrying a selection of shooting heads in labeled, ziplock bags is a real advantage for the traveler or anyone who wants to minimize the quantity of tackle taken on a fishing trip.

There are, however, some disadvantages to a shooting taper (ST) system. The major disadvantage is the entire length of the shooting head (SH) outside of the rod tip cannot be lifted from the water. Some of the shooting head (SH), usually about 8 to 10 feet, should remain inside the rod tip before a pick up is attempted. I typically retrieve the shooting head (SH) to where the interlocking loop connection with the shooting line (SL) touches the stripping (middle) finger of my casting hand before I start a roll-cast pickup of the shooting head (SH). Nevertheless, the next cast can be delivered quickly and accurately to the target with no or only one false cast.

Sinking fly lines, in general, tend to crack more readily because of their thinner plastic coating over the line core. The strength of a fly line, however, is derived from its core, and any cracks in the coating can be repaired with a flexible adhesive such as Softex or diluted Aquaseal. The outer coating of a sinking shooting taper (ST) system has the propensity of cracking in the immediate vicinity of the interlocking loop connection of the shooting head (SH) and shooting line (SL). All loop connections inherently form a bending stress where the loop zone ends, and this area eventually can create a stress-zone failure as the line coating cracks. The problem occurs with wear from prolonged use and it can be remedied quickly and effectively when it develops by replacing the connection loop on the affected line section.

The latest innovation of a shooting taper (ST) system features the shooting head (SH) permanently fused to the shooting line (SL). This configuration eliminates the worry of knots or integral loop connections from affecting the optimum performance of a cast. Depending on the density of the shooting head (SH), this system presents flies from a few feet to very deep in the water column. The only disadvantage is a different density shooting head (SH) can not be interchanged with the same shooting line (SL). As a result, an entire system of different densities must be stored on separate reels or spare spools.

Ultra Fast-Sinking Shooting Taper (ST) Systems

From a fly fishing perspective, nothing sinks faster or deeper than a shooting head (SH) line with a lead core or lead impregnated such as the Kerboom or Deep Water Express (DWE) fly lines. For anyone who takes the time to master the explicit casting discipline and fishing techniques associated with these ultra sinking lines, an expanding panoply of exciting and unequaled opportunities can present themselves to an otherwise bevy of unattainable species. These specialized lines are very heavy and super-fast sinking for getting and maintaining a fly very deep in the water column. In certain fishing conditions, this system can sink a fly to depths of 100 feet if necessary.

The original concept of the lead-core line was utilized by lake and ocean sport fishermen to provide a manageable method for deep trolling without resorting to the use of solid wire that was an unacceptable alternative. In the 1960s, this supple line was initially adapted for use by fly fishermen in pursuit of salmon and steelhead in deep, swift rivers. This unique shooting head (SH) system, made up of 30-foot sections of different weight lead-core lines, quickly evolved for use in deep lakes and later in saltwater.

Traditionally, a lead-core shooting head (SH) was cut from the commercially available lead-core trolling lines. The outer sheath of these lines determines their breaking strength (pound-test) and their weight, or sink rate, is predicated on the diameter of the lead core, which in most cases, weigh between 10 and 15 grains per foot. At 13 grains per foot, for example, a standard 30-foot length for a lead-core shooting head (SH) will weigh 390 grains. Conversely, the head, or first 30 feet, of a 9-weight fly line ranges in weight between 230 and 250 grains.

The lead-core shooting head (SH) differs from the conventional shooting taper (ST) and full-length sinking fly lines in casting and handling. There are more modern alternative products by fly line manufacturers, such as the Deep Water Express (DWE) and Kerboom that are considerably more durable than a conventional lead-core line. These alternative products are available in 30-foot lengths and they range in weight from 400 to 850 grains with the lead or tungsten impregnated in the PVC jacket rather than containing a lead core. Due to their extreme weight, however, lead-core lines and their commercial alternatives usually require some customizing of their length to achieve increased overall manageability. The steps to rigging these specialized shooting head (SH) and shooting line (SL) systems are discussed on pages 62-64.

Casting a Shooting Taper (ST) System

Casting a shooting taper (ST) system does have a slightly different feel compared to casting a full-length fly line, but the same basic casting principles apply for a cast to be executed properly and efficiently. The high weight-to-diameter ratio, coupled with their relative stiffness, of a conventional lead-core line and the modern alternatives, with the lead or tungsten impregnated in the PVC jacket, present an unique casting discipline that can be mastered with some practice. These ultra fast-sinking lines fall and move through the casting cycle at faster speeds than standard shooting taper (ST) and full-length fly lines. The abbreviated casting stroke is often non-synchronous and the casting loop is generally unrecognizable with the speedy delivery and turn over of these specialized lines.

Understanding the basic principles to the casting mechanics for any type of fly line is paramount and it is worth reiterating with respect to a shooting taper system. At the conclusion of the final back cast, the rod is accelerated forward and stopped. The shooting head (SH) portion of the system travels forward; parallel to itself, forming a loop or candy cane on its side as it unrolls in the direction the rod tip is pointed. It is important to realize the unrolling loop begins at the rod tip. The amount of shooting line (SL) extended beyond the rod tip during a false cast or at the completion of the final back cast is called the overhang. Too much overhand will cause the unrolling shooting head (SH) to quickly decay, because the small diameter shooting line (SL) does not have sufficient mass and rigidity to transfer the proper amount of kinetic energy to sustain the velocity of the shooting head (SH) in its forward travel to the target.

When too much overhang extends beyond the rod tip during a cast, a phenomenon known as the "hinge effect" will occur. This circumstance manifests itself either as a total collapse of a cast or an erratic, almost uncontrollable movement of the line during the casting cycle. The hinge effect is caused by the vast differences in the mass and stiffness of the shooting head (SH) and shooting line (SL). As a result, the kinetic energy of the shooting line (SL) does not transfer sufficient energy to the shooting head (SH) during a casting cycle. The loop material, which interconnects the shooting head (SH) and shooting line (SL) sections together, must also possess sufficient stiffness for the energy transfer to be sufficient.

The extent of the overhang allowed during the cast of a shooting taper (ST) system is critical. Determining an acceptable amount of overhang is a simple process. Start with some of the shooting head (SH) just inside the tip of the rod. Perform a false cast and gradually extend the shooting head (SH) beyond the rod tip until shock waves develop or the unrolling loop begins to collapse on itself. These symptoms indicate too much overhang has occurred.

With an ultra fast-sinking lead-core shooting head (SH) and its modern alternatives, the normal casting rhythm is somewhat exaggerated. The back and forward casting strokes are slower and more deliberate to control the momentum of the heavily weighted shooting head (SH). The tendency for these specialized lines to quickly fall on the back cast should be offset by a slow, and wide open loop that is gradually accelerated in the forward cast in a controlled, pushing stroke. In addition, the final forward cast does not respond to the usual wrist snap of the power stroke. Once the casting stroke is mastered, however, the line will propel through the air like D'Artagnan's rapier.

When casting a shooting taper (ST) system, I will retrieve the line until the connection between the shooting head (SH) and shooting line (SL) is inside the rod tip and at least halfway down the rod. I will roll cast the shooting head (SH) out, letting a few feet of shooting line (SL) slip through my line hand in the process. I then immediately lift the line using the water haul pickup to help load the rod, and, after one back cast, I will make a final forward cast. No false casting is usually necessary and almost the entire shooting line (SL) line will be pulled by the shooting head (SH) to the target.

With some practice, the water haul pickup is a simple and easy casting technique to learn. To execute the water haul pickup, instead of roll casting the shooting head (SH) into the air and making a back cast, roll cast it forward so that all of the sinking head is lifted from the water and rolls out straight and back on the water. When the front end of the head unrolls and contacts the water, start the back cast.

Shooting Lines

The smaller diameter shooting line (SL), looped to a shooting head (SH), passes through the rod guides more easily than the running line of a traditional, full-length weight-forward (WF) fly line. As a result, a shooting taper (ST) system can cast a fly to extremely long distances when it becomes necessary, which is a definite advantage the deeper a fly must be worked in the water column. If a fly must be fished at the 20-foot level in the water column, for example, only about 11 feet of a 60-foot cast will maintain the fly at that level before it starts ascending. A 90-foot cast, however, will maintain the fly at the 20-foot level for about 41 feet or 79% longer and farther in the water column, which is a significant difference. In most cases, the longer a fly can be retrieved at the feeding level of a fish or school of fish, the better chance for success.

There are numerous materials that can be used as a shooting line (SL), ranging from stiff nylon monofilament to various commercial PVC-coated lines designed specifically for this purpose. The most commonly used stiff nylon monofilament is 25-pound Amnesia and Cobra lines that provide the maximum casting distance and achieve the greatest depth. Stiff nylon monofilament, however, is more difficult and often frustrating to use than other shooting line (SL) materials. It has a tendency to coil and tangle, and its small, slick diameter is more difficult to handle during a retrieve and when setting a hook. In addition, the retrieved line lying on the deck of a boat is easily affected by the wind and highly susceptible to getting entangled on the nearest obstacle.

The more popular and widely used commercial shooting lines consist of a low-friction, plastic-coated nylon monofilament core, which is either single strand or braided. A shooting line (SL) with a braided nylon monofilament core is stiffer and more manageable in tropical conditions. These commercial lines range in length from 100 to 120 feet, from 25- to 40-pound, and from

.029" to .042" in diameter. They are available in three densities: floating, slow-sinking intermediate and faster sinking. Their small diameter and specially formulated coating provide minimal resistance through the rod guides for optimum casting performance over long distances.

Braided nylon monofilament leader material is another option for use as a shooting line (SL) and it is available in 15-, 20-, 25-, 30-, 35- and 50-pound on spools of 50 and 100 yards. In fact, Braided Butt Leader, a product made by Gudebrod is my favorite line, which I use with a floating or sinking shooting head (SH) for most freshwater and marine applications. It is the easiest to handle and it provides the best resistance to memory sets and tangling as well as to wear and abrasion. I also use this braided nylon monofilament leader material for building connection loops, which is discussed on pages 18-19.

In addition to braided nylon monofilament leader material, I use three other materials as a shooting line (SL), but in more specialized applications. In freshwater and marine fishing situations requiring a fly to be worked just below or within three feet of the surface, I use a commercial floating shooting line (SL). Depending upon the circumstance, I will attach either a Type I (intermediate) or II (slow sinking) shooting head (SH) to it. When a fly must be worked deeper in the water column to about 10 feet, I will attach a faster sinking shooting head (SH).

I use a .029" Monocore shooting line (SL) as a substitute to the braided nylon monofilament line whenever I need to sink a fly quickly in deep water or maintain its retrieve level in strong currents. Braided nylon monofilament does not sink as quickly and it has a tendency to hydroplane upward in the water column during a long retrieve. In the most specialized situation, I will use stiff nylon monofilament for extreme depths of 50 to 90 feet, which is attached to an ultra fast sinking shooting head (SH). The methods I use for rigging a shooting line (SL) to a shooting head (SH) as well as to the fly line backing are discussed on pages 61-62 and 58-59 respectively.

Fly Line Identification Codes

Any angler who has purchased a fly line undoubtedly knows there are a lot of abbreviations and codes associated with the identification of a fly line. The following chart is an explanation of these codes, which is used primarily when purchasing a fly line. In addition to the codes for a taper design and a line density, there are codes for the sink rates of lines as shown on pages 44-46 and 63.

Taper Design	Line Density
L = Level	**F** = Floating
DT = Double Taper	**I** = Intermediate
ST = Shooting Taper	**F/S** = Floating with a Sinking Tip
WF = Weight-Forward Taper	**S** = Sinking
TT = Triangle Taper	

Below are some examples of the descriptive nomenclature of these codes and their meaning in the purchase of a fly line.

L4F: This code signifies a level (L) taper fly line, with a weight of 4 for a matched 4-weight fly rod, and it floats (F).

DT5F: This code denotes a double taper (DT) fly line, with a weight of 5 for a matched 5-weight fly rod, and it floats (F).

WF6F: This code indicates a weight-forward taper (WF) fly line, with a weight of 6 for a matched 6-weight fly rod, and it floats (F).

WF7S: This code implies a weight-forward taper (WF) fly line, with a weight of 7 for a matched 7-weight fly rod, and it sinks (S) with the sink rate of the line, specified as inches per second, listed on the box.

WF8F/S: This code suggests a weight-forward taper (WF) fly line, with a weight of 8 for a matched 8-weight fly rod, and part of the line sinks while the remainder floats (F/S). The sink rate of the line, specified as inches per second, will be listed on the box and the length of line that actually sinks.

ST9F: This code signifies a shooting taper (ST) fly line, with a weight of 9 for a matched 9-weight fly rod, and it floats (F).

DWE 550: This code refers to a 550-grain Deep Water Express (DWE) fly line that sinks. The sink rate of the line, specified in inches per second (ips), will be listed on the box and information pertaining to the weight of the line per foot will be enclosed.

LC-13: This code denotes a lead core (LC) line weighing 13 grains per foot. The diameter of the line and its breaking strength will be listed on the box.

Fly Line Identification System

Maintaining a variety of fly lines, in different sizes and densities, organized and identifiable is a necessary and important custodial task. There are many ways of accomplishing this menial function and, in an effort to minimize time and effort, I have developed a system to keep the task as simple as possible. I have been using this system ever since the necessity arouse after I had acquired more than one fly line size and density in the late 1960s. Since that time, the number of fly line sizes has expanded significantly to more than ten different line weights. Add to this number two or more densities per line weight, and the amount of fly lines to identify and maintain permutates to more than 40. To further complicate the situation, my wife also has a comparable assortment of fly lines to manage.

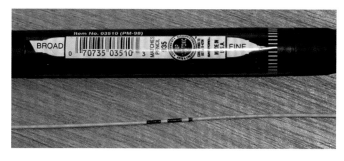

To annotate a fly line for identification by its weight, I use a permanent, waterproof Prismacolor or Sharpie marking pen to make a series of narrow and wide slashes. A narrow slash denotes a "1" and a wide slash signifies a "4". A Sharpie marking pen is more widely available at craft, office supply and other retail stores. A Prismacolor marking pen, as shown in the previous photo, is used principally for coloring various types of fly tying materials. The drawing below shows the complete code for fly line weights ranging from 1 to 15.

Fly Line ID System

1	|	6	██|	11	██|||
2	||	7	█|||	12	███
3	|||	8	██	13	███|
4	&#9608;	9	██|	14	███||
5	█|	10	███|	15	███|||

The photo below shows how a specific code or arrangement of narrow and wide slashes indicates the weight of a fly line, regardless of its length or taper. The example identifies a floating fly line as a 9-weight with one narrow slash and two wide slashes. The series of narrow and wide slashes can be marked on the fly line in any order although it is more easily identifiable to keep the same width of slashes in a set. I will mark a fly line about a foot or two from each end. By marking both ends, I am able to quickly identify a fly line whether it is spooled on a reel or hanging in coils from a storage rack.

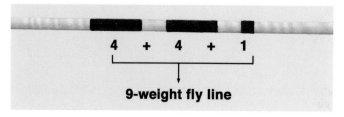

9-weight fly line

I also use this marking code to identify the sink rate of a full-length or shooting head (SH) sinking fly line with the number of narrow slashes corresponding to the sink rate. A single, narrow slash indicates a Type I (slow sinking intermediate) sink rate. I mark the light-colored fly lines with the appropriate number of narrow slashes a few inches to a foot from the front end of the lines. For dark-colored, full-length lines, for example, I mark the slashes on the standing part of the braided monofilament loop connecting the fly line to the backing. I identify the sink rates of the dark-colored shooting head (SH) lines by marking them with the appropriate number of slashes on the standing part of the braided nylon monofilament loop connecting the shooting head (SH) to the shooting line (SL). If you choose to use a braided nylon monofilament loop for connecting the shooting head (SH) to the leader butt section, you can also mark its standing part with the suitable number of slashes. As the example shown in the photo on the follwing page, a 13-weight fly line is also identified as having a Type 4 or IV sink rate. The markings were made on the standing part of the braided monofilament loop connecting the shooting head (SH) to its shooting line (SL).

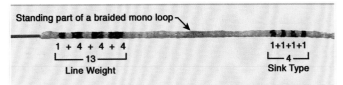

The series of Deep Water Express (DWE) lines, and other super-fast-sinking, are often described solely in terms of grains, because they are too heavy for the parameters established by the American Sportfishing Association (ASA). To identify the weight of these lines, therefore, I use a single, wide slash of a different color on the braided nylon monofilament loop connecting the shooting head (SH) to the shooting line (SL). I use a green marker for the 550-grain, a blue marker for the 700-grain and a red marker for the 850-grain DWE line. These markings relate grains per foot as well as the sink rate. I do not specify the actual weight of these lines with a marking code, because they are stored in wallets designated to a specific fly rod weight. The photo below is an example of the markings on a DWE shooting head (SH). The weight code of the line is a wide red slash indicating 850 grains and it has been constructed for a 17-weight outfit, specified by the one narrow and the four wide slashes.

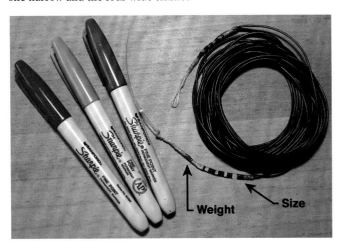

General Uses of Specific Fly Line Weights

The versatility, efficiency and effectiveness of any line weight can be utilized for many applications beyond its standard and accepted usage. For example, I will typically use a 4-weight outfit, rigged with a customized floating fly line, for working foam-bodied poppers and sliders on the surface of windless days for many inshore marine species such as spotted seatrout, redfish, snapper, ladyfish, small snook and baby tarpon. At other times I will use a custom 7-foot fly rod, rigged with a specialized 9-weight shooting taper fly line, for casting large, bulky flies to a variety of freshwater and marine species in very restrictive fishing areas such as beneath overhanging trees and vegetation as well as under low bridges, docks and piers.

The following information is intended to be used as a basic primer regarding the general usage of a fly line weight. This information does not cover the entire scope and diversity of a specific fly line weight. The use of a specific line weight in situations other than those mentioned is dependent upon many factors, including casting skill, angling ability and the innovative nature of the angler. We are limited only by our desire, imagination and

perseverance. I would encourage any serious angler to experiment and "think outside of the box" when it applies to tackle selection, fly designs and fishing techniques. An innovative approach in the face of conventional wisdom can sometimes pay large dividends in angling success and fishing pleasure.

2- to 4-weight: These fly lines are generally used in fishing situations requiring small flies, softer presentations and relatively short casts of 40 feet or less. Fly tackle matched to this line weight is best suited for small trout, panfish and smallmouth bass in small streams and ponds.

5- & 6-weight: These fly lines are typically the most versatile of the line weights for many freshwater fish species and fishing situations. The momentum generated by these line weights can deliver a wide range of fly types and sizes to a variety of fish species in freshwater streams, rivers, ponds, lakes, reservoirs and inshore saltwater ecosystems. The fly rods associated with these line weights are usually capable of efficiently handling fish ranging from small to medium size.

7- & 8-weight: These fly lines are designed for longer casts of medium to large flies in wide rivers, lakes and reservoirs as well in saltwater for an extensive variety of fish species including large trout, smallmouth bass, largemouth bass, Northern pike, muskellunge, carp, steelhead, light salmon, bonefish, spotted seatrout, redfish, small striped bass, baby tarpon and snook, just to name a few species.

9- & 10-weight: These fly lines are used mainly for general saltwater fishing and a seemingly endless list of marine species as well as sizable freshwater species including large trout, smallmouth bass, largemouth bass, Northern pike, muskellunge, striped bass, steelhead and salmon, just to name a few species.

11- to 13-weight: These fly lines are matched with stout fly rods and large flies for subduing tarpon, large salmon and steelhead as well as large pelagic species such as sharks, billfish, tuna, mackerel and dolphin, just to name a few species.

15- to 17-weight: These fly lines are used to hurl the biggest and bulkiest flies to the largest pelagic species, such as large sharks, giant tarpon, yellowfin, dogtooth and bluefin tuna, billfish and wahoo.

Cleaning, Protecting & Storing Fly Lines

Fly line performance is contingent upon many factors and one of the most important of these aspects is the condition of the outer coating or jacket. Obviously, a well-maintained fly line will last much longer and perform better than one that is subject to regular or even occasional abuse and neglect. Although fly lines are somewhat resilient and durable, they are susceptible to damage and deterioration from extreme cold, heat, ultraviolet (UV) radiation, mud, dirt, being stepped on, sunscreen, solvents and insect repellants. Insecticide sprays and liquids containing DEET, which is a brand of diethyltoluamide, a colorless and oily liquid with a mild odor, are particularly harmful to plastic fly lines.

In addition, fly lines have the propensity of collecting microscopic particles such as algae, which will attract and aggregate dirt, debris and other matter. Accumulation of these materials will eventually affect the buoyancy of a floating fly line and the shootability of all fly line densities. In general, the overall casting performance of a fly line can be affected, because dirt and most other matter absorbs water and the added weight can influence the castability of lightweight fly lines. Dirt and salt deposits, for example, can also accelerate the wear of the rod guides, particularly the tiptop guide. A worn guide, in turn, can scratch and chaff the fly line coating, causing it to crack and peel.

Faulty rod guides are a major cause of fly line and backing failures. It is prudent and good practice to check the condition of the rod guides periodically, especially the tiptop and the first stripper guide nearest the reel. The tiptop and the stripper are maximum stress and wear points. Because of their importance and delicate nature, I use a cotton-tipped swab or a piece of nylon stocking to detect signs of wear by running the swab or stocking through and around the guides. If cotton or nylon fibers become snagged, I automatically replace the damaged guide, because it can severely fray the plastic coating on a fly line as well as the backing material.

Cleaning a fly line is an easy task. After a day of fishing, I normally rinse my tackle in the shower or under a faucet, using lukewarm water. I clean floating fly lines by pulling them through a cleansing pad treated with a commercial line dressing. When cleaning sinking fly lines I pull them through a damp cloth moistened with a mild, detergent-free soap. With shooting taper (ST) systems, I also clean the shooting line (SL) in the same manner. This quick and simple procedure has helped to preserve and protect all of my fly lines, some of which I have been using for more than 20 years.

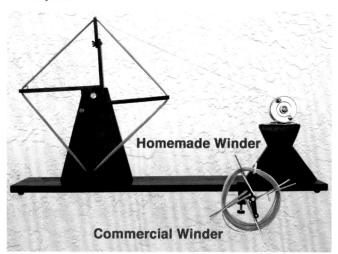

Homemade Winder

Commercial Winder

Unless I am traveling on an extended fishing trip or fishing on numerous consecutive days, I do not store my fly lines on their reels and spools for more than a few days. I use a line winder to remove a fly line from the reel spool as I am pulling it through a cleaning agent as previously mentioned. There are various types of commercial fly line winders available on the market or you can choose to make your own as shown in the photo above. Commercial fly line winders are generally portable, which can be an asset for cleaning fly lines during long periods of travel. The disadvantage to these devices, however, is the size of the coiled fly line is not much larger than the size produced by a large arbor fly reel.

From a storage standpoint, however, there is no real advantage to using one of these commercial fly line winders, except for the fact a fly line can be coiled external to the fly reel spool. Since

the coils are relatively small, memory sets can still remain a problem. As a result, I built my own fly line winder that forms 18-inch coils. The homemade winder is part of a two-component system I designed many years ago to store and protect fly lines and reels. The storage unit is secured to a wall where it stows fly line coils hung on pegs as well as reels and spare spools stored on shelves as illustrated in the photo below. In addition, the fly lines can still be connected to the backing and stored with their reels if desired. I use this unit to store all my fly lines, reels and spare spools in

this manner, because the system provides different storage options and variations, which allow me to quickly prepare an outfit for the next fishing adventure. Unfortunately, the storage wall unit was built many years ago and, since that time, I have accumulated more than twice as many reels, spare spools and fly lines, not to mention the arsenal of comparable equipment my wife has amassed.

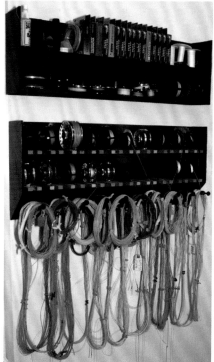

There are times when I need to stretch a braided nylon or stiff monofilament shooting line (SL) of a shooting taper (ST) system. To accomplish this task, I keep the shooting head (SH) and shooting line (SL) elements connected and I stretch them across the width of my garage at its opening, just below the tracks for the garage door. This method has worked well for more than 30 years and it allows the entire shooting taper (ST) system to be cleaned, dried and treated. Occasionally I will stretch a full-length fly line in the same manner whenever the running line portion develops obstinate memory coils. In either case, I typically stretch fly lines across my garage for a period of 24 to 48 hours. There are many innovative and creative ways to store, clean and stretch a fly line. Regardless of the storage method used, it is important to keep a fly line from the exposure to direct sunlight, chemicals, solvents, heat and extreme cold.

Chapter 4
Fly Line Backing

Purposes & Advantages of Fly Line Backing

Once the weight, taper and density of a fly line is selected, the next step in the process of rigging a fly outfit is choosing a small-diameter line to spool onto a reel and connect to a fly line. This thin line of various materials is known as backing. In essence, it "backs" up a fly line from being lost if it is stripped completely from the reel spool during a long-running battle with a powerful quarry. Fly line backing is the least talked and written about fly fishing topic, because it is the simplest and probably the least understood component of a fly outfit. Nevertheless, it is an important element to angling efficiency and success.

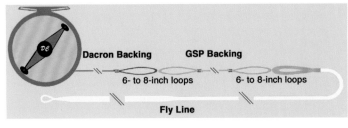

Fly line backing serves two essential purposes. It provides a higher retrieve rate for every revolution of the spool and it allows an angler to battle large, powerful fish that can run considerably farther than the length of any fly line. In most freshwater and many inshore saltwater situations, the latter purpose is generally a secondary concern. Obtaining the highest possible retrieve rate when reeling, however, is a major asset to fishing productivity, effectiveness and overall success. In addition, the increased size of the spool where the fly line is wound will prevent tangles, which can be caused by the line being wound into very small coils.

To satisfy the two essential purposes of fly line backing, it should be a material of low stretch or elasticity and have a relatively small diameter for its breaking strength. Nylon monofilament is not a recommended choice for use as backing under any circumstances, because it has too much elasticity when pulled taut. If the line is retrieved on the reel spool while stretched, it will constrict once the pressure is relaxed and start to bury itself into the other layers of monofilament already on the reel. This action of the monofilament over-wrapping itself can cause a potentially serious tangle. For example, when a fish pulls enough line to reach the stretched portion on the reel, which has now become thinner and has dug into the bed of line, it is likely to produce a sudden jerk in the line. The result may, and usually does, cause the tippet, which is the weakest component in a leader and fly line system, to fail.

Reel spools with thin-walled side plates can be warped, or even blown apart from the spool arbor in some extreme cases, due to the stretched nylon monofilament constricting back to its original form. The constriction of a hundred feet or more of nylon monofilament can apply considerable outward pressure against the spool walls. In addition, nylon monofilament deteriorates more quickly from the infrared (IR) and ultraviolet (UV) radiation of sunlight, and it has a lower breaking strength for its diameter than other fly line backing materials of comparable size and strength.

Braided Dacron Backing

The type of backing, the amount, sometimes the color and even the combination of backing materials used can all play an important role in successfully fighting and landing a fish. The most popular and widely available materials used as a backing material for fly lines are braided Dacron, manufactured by a number of companies, and Micron, a small diameter braided Dacron derivative made by the Cortland Line Company. Braided Dacron exhibits minimal stretch under stress and it lies flat on the spool, which maximizes its storage capacity. The bedding is generally firm on the spool when the line is retrieved under a slight pressure, which precludes the overlapping line from digging into itself.

Braided Dacron is similar in diameter to standard nylon monofilament. Twenty-pound backing is the most common size used for freshwater and most inshore saltwater fishing situations. Thirty-pound backing is used in saltwater applications pertaining primarily to 12-weight or heavier fly outfits. The only impediment to using braided Dacron is it can wear out or become easily frayed if subjected to an abraded rod guide or sharp obstruction, such as a coral reef or a barnacle-encrusted piling. As a result, abusive conditions and circumstances can degenerate even newly applied Dacron backing.

It is important to note that when the backing is the cause of a lost fish and a fly line, in most cases the loss was not caused by the type of backing material being used, but rather the improper installation or maintenance of it. This sudden and often mysterious breakage can occur with any type of backing material. The breach usually occurs near the connection to the full-length fly line or shooting line (SL) where wear and frictional stress are the most severe. It is, therefore, prudent to occasionally check all line connections, including the coupling between the backing and the full-length fly line or shooting line (SL).

Gel-Spun Polyethylene (GSP) Line

The latest innovation as a fly line backing is gel-spun polyethylene (GSP) line, which was originally marketed as Dyneema or Spectra. It is a synthetic fiber based on the ultra high molecular weight of polyethylene, which is 15 times stronger than steel and nearly 40% stronger than Kevlar. Dyneema or Spectra is usually used in bulletproof vests, bow strings, climbing equipment and fishing line. Dyneema was invented by DSM High Performance Fibres of Holland in 1979. It has been in commercial production since 1990 at a plant in Heerlen, the Netherlands. In the Far East, DSM has a cooperation agreement with Toyobo Company for commercial production in Japan. In the United States, DSM has a production facility in Greenville, North Carolina which is presently the largest production facility in the United States for UHMWPE fiber. Honeywell has developed a chemically identical product of its own. The Honeywell product is sold under the popular brand name Spectra.

In more recent years, numerous other companies now produce GSP line, which is a product of polyethylene gel, either as a braided strand or as a fused parallel strand. The lines are then treated with a lubricant such as silicone or Teflon to create a very slick finish. Each manufacturer incorporates different coatings or heat treatments with additional plastics during the finishing process. In essence, however, all gel-spun polyethylene (GSP) lines are similar.

Knowing the characteristics of gel-spun polyethylene (GSP) lines can help dictate how they can be best used to optimize a fishing experience. To begin with, GSP lines have a much smaller diameter in comparison to nylon monofilament and braided Dacron lines. Fifty-pound GSP line, for example, has a diameter of .013 inches, which is comparable to 12-pound Dacron or 15-pound nylon monofilament. As a result, GSP lines increase the capacity of a given reel to hold as much as 75% more backing than standard braided Dacron and, at the same time, more than doubling the strength of the backing material. The photo below demonstrates the diameter and strength of GSP line in comparison with the two sizes of braided Dacron.

20-pound Braided Dacron

30-pound Braided Dacron

50-pound Gel-Spun Polyethylene (GSP)

Because more and thinner backing material can be stored on a reel spool, a faster recovery rate on the retrieve can be maintained even if a considerable amount of line is taken off the reel by a fish. In other words, a larger arbor can be effectively maintained throughout a battle with a long-running fish. In addition, and equally important, the drag pressure will remain more consistent, because the effective spool diameter changes only slightly. This characteristic of a GSP line also means that a smaller, lighter and probably less expensive reel can be used to the same relative advantage as a larger arbor reel, assuming the drag system is comparable and adequate.

The reel arbor is the center area of the spool where the GSP or braided Dacron backing material is secured and then wound around. The fly line is attached to the backing and it is also wound around the arbor until all the line and backing are safely stored on the reel. The larger the spool arbor the more efficient the reel is in retrieving the backing and fly line, because the fly line is further from the axis of rotation (center of the spool). Note the differences of the two reels in the photos on the following page, which are designed to handle the same range of fly line sizes. The obvious advantages of a larger arbor reel are the fly line is stored in larger coils, which means less memory and a faster retrieval rate, because the fly line occupies 25% or less of the reel spool. In addition, there is a smaller increase in drag force and less revolutions of the reel spool from a fleeing fish.

In addition to its ultra-thin diameter for its strength, there are other important attributes of GSP lines to consider when ascertaining their most effective use as a fly line backing material. GSP backing retains 100% of its strength while wet, because it is waterproof, and it is impervious to UV rays, gas, oil, salt, and other damaging elements. Its smooth, exceptionally slick coating has a low coefficient of friction (COF) that minimizes wear on the rod guides. However, as a higher modulus material, which translates into brittleness and low stretch, its extremely high abrasion resistance can make it more susceptible to weakening if it does become frayed.

Due its small diameter and slickness, GSP line generates less drag or resistance through the water, which is especially important when battling extremely fast-swimming or long-running fish and often crucial in big game fly fishing. Line drag is caused by its resistance through the water and it is a product of diameter and weight. The drag of 20-pound nylon monofilament through the water, for example, is comparable to 20-pound braided Dacron, because the two lines are approximately the same diameter. To decrease drag, the diameter of the backing must be reduced, which is most significantly accomplished by using a GSP line as the backing material.

GSP line, however, is not the panacea for the angling ills associated with fly line backing. It does have some disadvantages and issues related to its high modulus, which translates to brittleness and low stretch. Its reduced drag through the water, coupled with its low stretch of less than 3%, for example, does not provide a shock-absorbing buffer for lighter tippets, particularly in situations dealing with fish making long, powerful runs. In most cases, however, a slight reduction in the drag setting on the reel will compensate for the minimal line stretch in the GSP backing.

The major issue besetting GSP lines hinges on the topic of knot strength. In general, due to its modulus and thinness, a given knot can be potentially weaker and fatigue faster with a GSP line in comparison to braided Dacron and even nylon monofilament. GSP line has a tendency to twist while tying and, because of its low stretch, some knots are more difficult to tie properly and most conventional knots usually provide poor or marginal performance. Because GSP backing is so thin and slick, all knots must be tied

carefully, tightened properly, and tested thoroughly before use. It is also more likely to cut through a fly line and a finger than braided Dacron. In addition, the brittleness and smallness of the braided fibers can fracture more easily from the impact of a knot hitting a rod guide or the tiptop guide as well as when the line is grazed against a sharp object.

The most important factor to obtaining the best performance of GSP backing is how the line is positioned on the spool. Due to its thin diameter, even 30-pound GSP line can dig into the bedding and cause a lost fish or fly line. To reduce compression on a reel spool and to avoid pressure on its ported side plates, the initial installation of GSP backing should be slightly cross wound under a modest amount of pressure. This procedure also helps to avoid layer slippage caused by the slickness of GSP backing. When installing new GSP line on a reel spool, use cotton gardening gloves to apply slight tension on the line as it is being reeled onto the spool.

Using Braided Dacron & GSP Lines Together

Due to some of the attributes and characteristics of GSP line previously mentioned, I would recommend using a minimum of 30-pound as a backing material. It provides improved manageability at a greater breaking strength and it significantly reduces the chances for problems associated with smaller diameter and lighter line tests. As a result, I use 30-pound GSP line for backing with 9-weight or lighter fly lines, 50-pound for backing with 10- to 13-weight fly lines and 65 pound-test for backing with 15-weight or heavier fly lines.

Except in rare situations, I do not fill an entire reel spool with GSP line. I typically setup most of my reel spools with a combination of GSP and braided Dacron lines when using 7-weight and heavier outfits as illustrated in the photo below. In addition to the economy, it is not necessary to have more than 200 to 500 yards of GSP backing on any reel, depending upon its capacity. My largest reels, for example, store about 800 yards of backing, but the GSP portion does not exceed 500 yards. If a fish runs more than 300 or 400 yards of backing from the reel, it is highly unlikely the outcome will be successful. Beyond these distances,

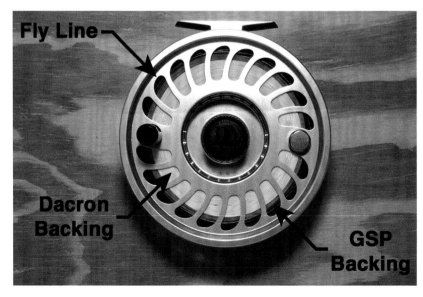

the ability to control and fight a fish is significantly ineffective. In general, the farther a hooked fish is from the angler, the greater amount of forces are exerted on the connections, knots, leader and particularly the tippet. As a result, the chance of landing a fish under these circumstances is reduced significantly.

The major advantage of using both backing materials is to maximize the rate of retrieve. Even 100 or 200 yards of ultra-thin GSP line, connected between the braided Dacron and a full-length fly line or shooting line (SL), does not occupy much space and only slightly changes the rate of retrieve. This dual combination of backing materials also reduces their chances to bury themselves in the bedding, especially in situations when many yards of backing are retrieved grievously relaxed. The most common occurrence of this condition typically is when a hooked fish runs directly towards the angler.

When rigging a reel with a combination of GSP and braided Dacron lines, I tie a Bimini Twist at the end of the braided Dacron line already stored on the reel and the spooled GSP line to form a 6- to 8-inch long loop. The loops are connected together and the system of different backing materials interlocked with a fly line remains modular for quick and easy interchangeability. The instructions for attaching the backing to a reel spool, splicing two different backing materials together and connecting the backing to a fly line are discussed and illustrated in Chapter 5.

Chapter 5
Rigging Fly Lines & Backing

To the uninitiated, the knots and connections compulsory to rigging a fly fishing outfit can seem like a daunting assignment that is reserved only to the skills of an expert. These tasks are not nearly as difficult or complicated as they seem. The process to accomplishing these tasks is actually quite simple and straightforward once the overall concept of the interlocking loop system is understood and the detailed rigging methods are practiced. The apparent complexity stems from the fact this book is describing in detail the rigging and interchangeability of fly lines and leader systems for every possible fishing situation. The table below serves as a guide to cross-referencing the various types of rigging and connection tasks associated with fly line backing, fly lines and leader systems.

Major Element	Component	Rigging & Connection Tasks	Page
Fly Line Backing	Backing	Preparing the backing for attachment to the spool arbor.	57-58
		Securing the backing to the spool arbor.	57-58
		Splicing Dacron and GSP lines together.	25-26 or 32-33
		Building the loop for interlocking with the PVC fly line loop.	28-29
		Connecting the backing & PVC fly line loops together.	59
Full-length Fly Line	Fly Line	Making a braided nylon mono loop for linking to the backing.	20
		Interlocking the fly line & backing loops together.	58-60
		Forming a PVC fly line loop for attachment to the leader butt.	60
		Fastening the fly line & leader butt loops together.	18
Shooting Taper (ST) System	Shooting Head (SH)	Rigging a braided nylon mono loop for coupling to the SL.	19-20
		Customizing a SH.	61-63
		Forming a PVC fly line loop for securing to the leader butt.	60
		Connecting the fly line & leader butt loops together.	18

Major Element	Component	Rigging & Connection Tasks	Page
Shooting Taper (ST) System	Commercial Shooting Line (SL)	Building a braided nylon mono loop for joining to the backing.	20
		Creating a braided nylon mono loop for linking to the SH.	19-20
		Attaching the SH to a commercial SL.	64
Shooting Taper (ST) System	Braided Mono Shooting Line (SL)	Forming a braided nylon mono loop for joining to the backing.	20
		Building a braided nylon mono loop for attaching to the SH.	19-20
		Attaching the SH to a braided mono SL.	63-64
Shooting Taper (ST) System	Nylon Mono Shooting Line (SL)	Tying a loop in the mono for linking to the backing.	28-29
		Preparing a braided nylon mono loop for joining to the SH.	64
		Attaching the SH to a nylon mono SL.	63-64
Leader System	Butt Section	Preparing the end loops.	24-25
Leader System	Midsection	Tying the end loops.	24-25
Leader System	Tippet	Doubling the line at one or both ends.	28-29
		Forming the end loops.	24-25
		Tying to the fly.	24-25 or 26-27
Leader System	Shock Trace (monofilament)	Connecting to the fly.	24-25
		Preparing the end loop.	24-25
		Securing directly to the tippet.	32-33
Leader System	Shock Trace (solid wire)	Fastening to the fly.	30
		Constructing the end loop.	31-32
		Optional method to create the end loop with an Albright Special.	32-33
Leader System	Shock Trace (braided wire)	Securing to the fly.	24-25/69
		Shaping the end loop.	24-25/69
		Optional method to create the end loop with an Albright Special.	32-33
Mini or Instant Sinking Sections	Sinking Fly Line Section	Constructing braided nylon mono end loops.	19-20 & 58

Major Element	Component	Rigging & Connection Tasks	Page
Mini or Instant Sinking Sections	Lead-core Section	Rigging a lead-core section & creating end loops for linking to the fly line & leader loops.	19-20 & 65

The seemingly endless tinkering of knots, riggings and connections is part of the fun and enjoyment of fly fishing. I enjoy experimenting with different fly line and leader configurations, for example, in an attempt to better my fishing proficiency and success. This chapter is organized to provide the detailed steps in assembling two major components of a fly outfit; namely, a fly line and fly line backing. The drawing below depicts the configuration for the assembly of the fly line backing and fly line as interchangeable elements. The logical order of tasks defined in this chapter is based on the assumption these components are newly purchased and have not been rigged or assembled previously.

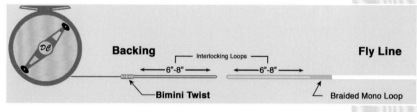

Rigging a Reel Spool with Backing

In nearly all books and magazine articles, the Arbor Jam knot is used to attach the fly line backing to the reel spool arbor. I never fully understood the reason for this specialty knot when there are other more commonly used knots that will perform the same task, such as the Bimini Twist and Improved Clinch. The Arbor Jam knot is considerably weaker than these knots. I just never saw the logic in learning to tie a knot that is weaker, not any less bulkier and I may only use a few times in a lifetime. I am a firm believer that it is not how many knots an angler knows how to tie, but rather how many knots an angler knows how to tie properly. The least number of knots an angler needs to know how to tie and the more times a knot is tied, the more efficient and reliable the knot-tying process will be. Consistency is the operative word in tying strong and dependable knots and the key to consistency is developing the manual dexterity derived from the repetition of tying the same knot.

Consequently, I prefer to use the Bimini Twist in rigging a reel spool with backing, because it is a knot I tie regularly as opposed to the specialized and weaker Arbor Jam knot that I may tie only a few times in a lifetime. In addition, a Bimini Twist on each end of the backing material allows the line to be reversed regularly, which prolongs its durability and usefulness. Except in extreme cases, dealing primarily with the heaviest line weights and the most powerful fish species, most of the backing on a reel is rarely used. The entire amount of backing is often discarded prematurely when signs of wear occur in the first hundred feet behind the fly line. In most fishing situations, extended use can be achieved by reversing the backing material on the spool without cutting it free and retying it.

The first step to setting up a reel spool with backing material is to determine how much backing is needed to fill the spool to its maximum capacity for accommodating both backing and fly line. The amount of backing a spool can hold is contingent upon the size, length and type of fly line to be stored on the spool. Once the backing and fly line are secured to the spool, the other end of the fly line will be rigged with a loop, which connects the leader system. The following steps apply to filling a reel spool with the maximum amount of backing material that will render the highest possible retrieve rate.

Step 1: Measure the depth of the reel spool (A) as shown in the photo below, which will fill the spool to its maximum capacity. Write down the inside dimension. Secure the end of the fly line to the spool arbor with a piece of masking tape and wind the entire fly line onto the spool in even layers under slight tension. If the backing is being setup for a shooting taper (ST) system and the shooting line (SL) or shooting head (SH) components are not already rigged with braided nylon monofilament loops and connected together, use a small piece of masking tape to temporarily secure each element to the spool. These components do not have to be joined together to determine the amount of space they occupy on the spool.

Step 2: With the fly line wound on the reel, measure the depth of the spool (B) as shown in the photo on the right and write down the new inside dimension. Subtract this dimension from the original depth of the empty spool to determine how much of the exposed spool will be left after filling it with the backing material.

Step 3: Tie a Bimini Twist at the end of the backing material to create a loop 6 to 8 inches long as illustrated in the photo on the left. The steps to tying the Bimini Twist are illustrated on pages 28-29. Coat only the half hitches with cyanoacrylate (CA) glue, such as Krazy glue, or UV Knot Sense, before trimming the tag end as close as possible.

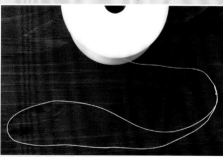

Step 4: Remove the fly line from the spool. Fasten the backing material to the arbor by wrapping the Bimini Twist loop around the reel spool from above the arbor and passing the spool of backing through the loop as shown in the photo below. Draw the loop tight and keep it cinched against the arbor when starting to wind the backing onto the reel spool. If both Dacron and gel-spun polyethylene (GSP) lines are intended to be used on the spool, perform optional Steps 5 and 6; otherwise, fill the spool with the backing material to the calculation (A - B = C) derived in Step 2 as shown in the second photo below, cut the Dacron line from its spool and skip to Step 7.

Step 5: (optional). If both Dacron and GSP lines are intended to be used, wind the Dacron evenly on the spool arbor with moderate tension and fill the spool to within an 1/8- to 1/4-inch of the calculation (A - B = C) derived in Step 2 and shown in the photo below. Either tie a Bimini Twist knot in the ends of the Dacron and GSP backing to form 6- to 8-inch loops, or cut the Dacron line from its spool and join it to the GSP line using a Blood knot. The steps for tying a Blood knot are illustrated on pages 25-26. Forming interlocking loops using a Bimini Twist, however, is the recommended method. Coat only the half hitches of the Bimini Twist or the wraps of the Blood knot with cyanoacrylate (CA) glue, such as Krazy glue, or UV Knot Sense before trimming the tag ends as close as possible.

Step 6: (optional). Interconnect the two backing materials together by slipping the GSP loop over the Dacron loop and passing the spool of GSP line through the Dacron loop from behind or below. Cinch the loops together tightly. Wind the GSP line evenly under moderate tension and fill the spool to the measurement (A - B = C) derived in Step 2. Cut the GSP line from its spool.

Step 7: With the proper amount of backing now on the reel spool, tie a Bimini Twist knot in the end of the Dacron or GSP backing, forming a 6- to 8-inch loop to accommodate coils of a full-length fly line or a hundred feet of a shooting line (SL) to pass through the loop. It is recommended a double strand loop

is formed in GSP line to enhance its connection with a braided nylon monofilament loop. Refer to Step 1A on page 28 to form a double strand loop. Coat only the half hitches of the Bimini Twist with cyanoacrylate (CA) glue, such as Krazy glue, or UV Knot Sense, before trimming the tag end as close as possible. The steps to interconnect the end of a fly line or a shooting line (SL) to the loop of the Dacron and GSP backing material are described on pages 59-60.

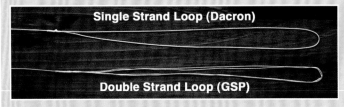

Single Strand Loop (Dacron)

Double Strand Loop (GSP)

Rigging a Fly Line for Connection to the Backing

The criterion for a proficient connection between the backing material and the fly line is its smooth passage through the rod and tiptop guides in both directions. Some knots and connections, however, pass easily through these guides when traveling in only one direction. The interlocking loop system provides the smoothest travel in both directions. In addition, the loops are quick and easy to disconnect when removing a fly line for storage or exchanging it for another.

To interconnect a fly line or a PVC-coated shooting line (SL) to the loop of the backing, build a braided nylon monofilament loop, as illustrated on page 20. The length of the loop at the end of a full-length fly line or the shooting line (SL) of a shooting taper (ST) system should be about 6 to 8 inches long. The loop must be large enough to accommodate the largest fly reel passing through it. If the shooting line (SL) is a single strand of nylon monofilament, a 6- to 8-inch loop can be formed using a Bimini Twist. Perform the following steps to secure a braided nylon monofilament loop to the end of a full-length fly line or the PVC-coated shooting line (SL) of a shooting taper (ST) system:

Step 1: Push the back end of the fly line or one end of the SL through the hollow core of the braided nylon monofilament and snug it flush against the doubled standing part of the braided loop.

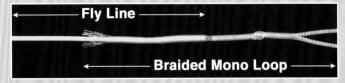

Fly Line

Braided Mono Loop

Step 2: Tie in a 6- to 8-turn nail knot using 8- to 12-pound semi-limp nylon monofilament line near the end of the braided nylon monofilament. An optional second nail knot between the first knot and the doubled standing part of the braided nylon monofilament loop is recommended for 6- to 13-weight fly line sizes. The step-by-step instructions for tying a nail knot are illustrated on pages 22-23.

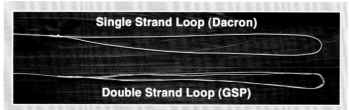

Single Strand Loop (Dacron)

Double Strand Loop (GSP)

Step 3: Remove any frayed strands of the braided nylon monofilament protruding from the first nail knot and partially coat only the wraps of both knots with cyanoacrylate (CA) glue, such as Krazy glue, or UV Knot Sense.

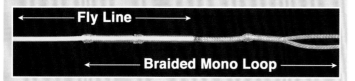

← Fly Line →

← Braided Mono Loop →

Connecting a Fly Line to Dacron Backing

Interchanging fly lines to braided Dacron backing is a quick and easy process. Perform the following steps to connect the loop formed in the braided Dacron backing by a Bimini Twist with the braided nylon monofilament loop at the end of a fly line or the shooting line (SL) of a shooting taper (ST) system. To complete Steps 4, 5 and 6 for a shooting taper (ST) system, the opposite end of the shooting line (SL) and one end of the shooting head (SH) must be rigged with 1/4-inch long braided nylon monofilament loops, which is illustrated on pages 19-20. If the shooting line (SL) is a single strand of nylon monofilament, both ends should be tied with a 6- to 8-inch loop for connection to the backing and a 1/4-inch loop should be formed at the other end for the shooting head (SH) using a Bimini Twist and Chermanski Loop knot as illustrated on pages 28-29 and 24-25 respectively. The step-by-step instructions for securing braided nylon monofilament loops to the shooting line (SL) and shooting head (SH) are illustrated on pages 19-20.

Step 1: Slip the braided nylon monofilament loop at the end of a fly line or SL over the Dacron loop. Pass the coils of the full-length fly line or shooting line (SL) through the 6- to 8-inch braided Dacron loop from behind or below.

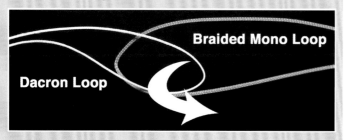

Braided Mono Loop

Dacron Loop

Step 2: Slowly pull the loops apart to form a tight square knot and wind the fly line or shooting line (SL) evenly onto the reel spool over the backing under moderate tension.

Dacron Loop

Braided Mono Loop

Step 3: To complete a shooting taper (ST) system, slip the braided nylon monofilament loop of the shooting head (SH) over the braided nylon monofilament loop of the shooting line (SL).

SL   SH

Step 4: Thread the front end of the shooting head (SH) through the braided nylon monofilament loop of the shooting line (SL) from behind or below and pull the entire length of the shooting head (SH) through the loop. Slowly draw the loops apart to form a tight square knot as shown in Step 2 and wind the shooting head (SH) evenly onto the reel spool over the shooting line (SL) under moderate tension.

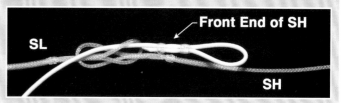

← Front End of SH

SL

SH

Joining a Fly Line to Gel-Spun Polyethylene (GSP) Backing

Interchanging fly lines to GSP backing material is also a quick and easy process. The process of joining the braided nylon monofilament loop at the end of a fly line with the loop formed in the GSP line by a Bimini Twist is modified slightly from braided Dacron backing. This modification is necessary to prevent the smaller diameter GSP line from severing the strands of the nylon monofilament loop, particularly under the extreme stress of a prolonged fight with a powerful fish.

Perform the following steps to interconnect the loop of the GSP backing material with the braided nylon monofilament loop at the end of a full-length fly line or the shooting line (SL) of a shooting taper (ST) system. To complete Steps 7, 8 and 9 for a shooting taper (ST) system, the opposite end of the shooting line (SL) and one end of the shooting head (SH) must be rigged with 1/4-inch long braided nylon monofilament loops, which are illustrated on pages 19-20. If the shooting line (SL) is a single strand of nylon monofilament, both ends should be tied with a 6- to 8-inch loop for connection to the backing and a 1/4-inch loop should be formed at the other end for the shooting head (SH) using a Bimini Twist and Chermanski Loop knot as illustrated on pages 28-29 and 24-25 respectively. The step-by-step instructions for securing braided nylon monofilament loops to the shooting line (SL) and shooting head (SH) are illustrated on pages 19-20.

Step 1: Slip the GSP loop over the braided nylon monofilament loop at the end of a fly line or the shooting line (SL). Pass the coils of the fly line or the shooting line (SL) through the braided nylon monofilament loop from below. Close the two loops slightly, but not too tightly. Pass the coils of the fly line or the shooting line (SL) through the braided nylon monofilament loop a second time.

Step 2: Rotate the GSP loop a complete revolution and pass the coils of the fly line or the shooting line (SL) through the braided nylon monofilament loop a third time.

Step 3: Slowly pull the loops apart to form a loop and cross-loop connection. Wind the fly line or shooting line (SL) evenly onto the reel spool over the backing under moderate tension. To complete a shooting taper (ST) system, interconnect the braided nylon monofilament loop of the shooting head (SH) and the braided nylon monofilament loop of the shooting line (SL) together as described in Steps 3 and 4 on page 59.

Forming a PVC fly line loop

I have tried numerous methods and connections to attaching a leader to the front, and backing material to the rear, of a fly line, but I was never totally satisfied with the results until I started forming a loop at the end of the fly line. Although the nail knot was adequate and the most commonly used method, it had two failings. First, a leader or backing material attached in this manner is permanent and can not be easily changed in the field. Second, some fly line coatings can be cut or severely abraded, compromising the strength and durability of the connection. My solution to the problem was to form a loop at the end of the fly line. I did not abandon the nail knot, however, I merely applied its use differently with much better results.

Forming a loop at the end of the fly line provides several advantages. The most significant advantage is the versatility of changing or modifying a leader system quickly and easily, because no one leader design can accommodate all fishing situations. An interchangeable loop system makes it easier to adapt to changing requirements, which are often dictated by changes in fishing conditions or strategies. In addition, a mini or instant sinking section can be looped between the fly line and the leader to change the sink rate and retrieval path of a fly. Equally important, a PVC fly line loop transfers the kinetic energy from the fly line to the leader butt section more smoothly and efficiently.

The following instructions apply to a right-handed person performing the steps to secure a loop at the end of any fly line.

Step 1: Fold the front taper of a fly line back about 1 inch from the end. Hold the tag end against the standing part with the thumb and index finger of the left hand, forming a wide loop about an inch long.

Step 2: Moisten one of the lines about half its length with cyanoacrylate (CA) glue, such as Krazy glue, and pinch the lines together with the thumb and index finger of the right hand. Continue to grip the lines for a few seconds until the glue cures and the lines remain bonded together.

Step 3: Tie a 6- to 8-turn nail knot, using 8- to 12-pound semi-limp nylon monofilament, on both lines to create a loop approximately 1/4- to 3/8-inch long. The step-by-step instructions for tying a nail knot are illustrated on pages 22-23. Tie a second 6- to 8-turn nail knot about 1/4- to 3/8-inch from the first knot.

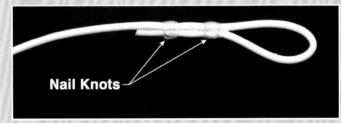

Step 4: Carefully trim the tag end on a tapered angle about an 1/8-inch from the second nail knot. For added strength, abrasion protection and enhanced passage through the rod guides, the wraps and doubled lines can be coated with Pliobond, Goop, Aquaseal, Softex, marine silicone or similar products.

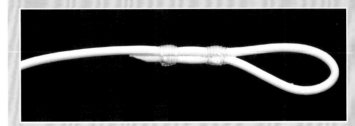

Assembling a Full-Length Fly Line

The first step in assembling a full-length fly line is rigging the shooting head (SH). The photo below illustrates the interlocking loop-to-loop connections between a full-length fly line, its backing and a leader system. A large braided nylon monofilament loop is secured at the back end of the fly line, which is interlocked with the large loop tied in the backing material. A PVC fly line loop is formed at the tip section of the fly line and it is interlocked with the small loop tied at the end of a leader butt section. The steps to create a large braided nylon monofilament loop are illustrated on page 20. The steps to form a PVC loop at the tip section of a fly line are shown on page 60. The steps to secure a large braided nylon monofilament loop to the end of a fly line are described on pages 58-59.

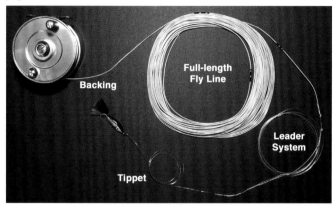

Assembling a Shooting Taper (ST) System

The first step in assembling a shooting taper (ST) system is rigging the shooting head (SH). The following photo illustrates the basic configuration of a shooting taper (ST) system with its interlocking loops. To begin the assembly process, secure a large braided nylon monofilament loop at one end of the shooting line (SL) and a small braided nylon monofilament loop at the other end. The large braided nylon monofilament loop is interlocked to a loop of similar size in the backing material already spooled on the reel. Next, a small braided nylon monofilament loop is secured to the front tapered end of the shooting head (SH) and a PVC fly line loop is formed at the other end. The small braided nylon monofilament loop is used to connect the shooting head (SH) with the shooting line (SL) and the loop at the end of the leader butt section is interlocked to the PVC loop at the end of a shooting head (SH). I prefer to attach the front taper section of the shooting head (SH) to the shooting line (SL), because this reversed configuration permits the line and leader to straighten more efficiently upon completion of a cast.

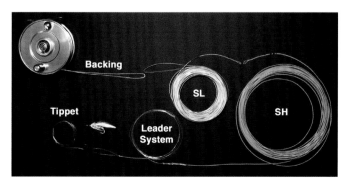

The steps to create a small braided nylon monofilament loop are illustrated on pages 19-20. The steps to form a PVC loop at the end of a shooting head (SH) are shown on page 60. The steps to secure a small braided nylon monofilament loop to the end of a shooting head (SH) or a PVC-coated shooting line (SL) are described on pages 19-20. These steps also apply for securing a large braided nylon monofilament loop to the end of a shooting line (SL).

To interconnect a shooting head (SH) with a shooting line (SL), slip the braided nylon monofilament loop at the end of the shooting head (SH) over the braided nylon monofilament loop of the shooting line (SL). Pass the PVC fly line loop or leader, if it is already attached, at the other end of the shooting head (SH) through the shooting line (SL) loop from below. Slowly pull the loops apart under moderate tension to form a tight square knot.

Customizing a Shooting Head (SH)

Most anglers purchase commercial shooting heads, which are generally manufactured in 30-foot lengths and in line weights designated to match their labeled rod weights. In reality, however, they may not be getting the optimum casting performance and distance when just the 30-foot head is extended beyond the rod tip. When casting a conventional, full-length weight-forward (WF) fly line, for example, most anglers are accustomed to extending more than 30 feet of fly line outside the rod tip for longer casts. In essence, when they extend more than the body of the fly line beyond the rod tip to generate the momentum needed for distant casts, they are casting a line size heavier. As a result, it is recommended a commercial, 30-foot shooting head (SH) one size heavier be used to compensate for the difference in line weight. This one size heavier head will enhance the load on a fly rod for producing increased line speeds required for longer casts.

To truly optimize the casting and fishing performance of a shooting taper (ST) system, I customize the major elements starting with the shooting head (SH). It is actually quite easy to do. To build a conventional floating or sinking shooting head (SH), I start with a double taper (DT) fly line of a weight matching the labeled line size of the intended fly outfit. A double taper (DT) fly line actually allows me to construct two shooting heads for different fly outfits since the body of a double taper (DT) fly line is level with exactly the same taper at each end.

The lengths of my shooting heads are generally 38 feet long, measured from either end of the double taper (DT) fly line. The length can be customized to match the casting skill of the angler. For example, a caster who can easily throw 70 feet with a weight-forward (WF) line, the optimum length of the shooting head (SH) will range between 35 and 38 feet. For less skilled casters, the best casting performance will probably occur between 32 and 34 feet. I would recommend starting at 38 feet and shortening the shooting head (SH) as required to achieve maximum casting performance.

To assemble the customized shooting head (SH), the small braided nylon monofilament loop is secured to the front tapered end of the shooting head (SH) and a PVC fly line loop is formed at the other end. The small braided monofilament loop is used to connect the shooting head (SH) with the shooting line (SL) and the loop of a leader system is interlocked to the loop at the end of shooting head (SH). I prefer to attach the front taper section of the shooting head (SH) to the shooting line (SL), because this reversed configuration permits the line and leader to straighten more efficiently upon completion of a cast. The steps to create a small braided nylon monofilament loop and to form a PVC fly line loop at the other end of a shooting head (SH) are shown on pages 19-20 and 60 respectively. The steps to secure the small braided nylon monofilament loop to the end of a shooting head (SH) is described on pages 19-20.

There are many specialized fishing situations where a customized shooting taper (ST) system is best suited to the task. One of my favorite types of fishing involves casting poppers, sliders and streamers to a variety of freshwater and marine species in confined areas infested with overhanging trees and other shoreline vegetation as well as under low bridges, docks, piers and culverts. Since the strike zone is usually the first 3 to 5 feet from the shoreline or structure, a specialized and unconventional approach in tackle selection is necessary to be efficient and consistently successful.

The most important key to success in these close-range fishing situations is the design of the fly line. Used with an 8-foot, 5-weight fly rod, for example, I built a shooting taper (ST) system consisting of a floating shooting head (SH) 18-1/2 feet long connected to a floating shooting line (SL). The overall length of the leader system is approximately 8 feet. Due to the relative shortness of the fly rod and, because the short shooting head (SH) and leader are closer to the fly, they will turn over faster, forming a narrower loop for easier and more accurate entry under the restrictive structure. In addition, the shooting taper (ST) configuration can consistently deliver the fly to the target area with no or one false cast.

Customizing a conventional shooting head (SH) for a specific fishing situation is a relatively easy process. If the purpose is to build a shorter shooting head (SH) than normal, the weight of the fly line must be heavier for a shorter length to be comparable to the conventional 30-foot length of the lighter line. To determine the length of a shorter shooting head (SH), follow these simple guidelines:

- Start by determining what line-weight fly rod is to be used with this specialized shooting taper (ST) system.
- Choose a weight-forward (WF) or double taper (DT) fly line two to three sizes heavier than the labeled line weight designated on the selected fly rod.
- Refer to the Fly Line Weight Standards table on page 42 to ascertain the average weight range in grains of the selected fly rod.
- As a starting point, choose the upper limit to the weight range of a line two times heavier.
- To ascertain the length in feet of the shooting head (SH), multiple the weight of the line determined to be twice as heavy by 30 and divide the results by the average weight range for the selected fly rod.
- Measure and cut the weight-forward (WF) or double taper (DT) fly line from its front taper.
- Secure a small braided nylon monofilament loop at the front tapered end of the shooting head (SH). The steps to form a small braided nylon monofilament loop and to secure it to the shooting head (SH) are illustrated on pages 19-20.

- Secure a PVC fly line loop at the other end of the shooting head (SH) as illustrated on page 60.
- Attach the shooting head (SH) to the shooting line (SL) and cast the shooting taper (ST) system to ascertain its performance qualities. If any adjustments are needed to be made, remove a foot of the back end of the shooting head (SH) on the first cut and 6 inches each subsequent cut until loop management and shootability are acceptable.

Using my favorite 8-foot, 5-weight outfit as an example, the average weight range for a 5-weight fly line is 140 grains. Since I wanted a very short shooting head (SH), I will built the shooting head (SH) from a DT8F line whose upper limit weight range is 218 grains. Multiplying 140 times 30, then dividing by 218, results in a shooting head (SH) length of 19 feet 3 inches. After some trial-and-error based on casting performance, I determined the optimum weight of the shooting head (SH) for my close-range fishing requirements was maximized at a length of 18 feet 8 inches.

Building a Specialized Sinking Shooting Head (SH)

Building a specialized, ultra fast-sinking shooting head (SH) is a similar process as the one described in the previous section for a conventional shooting head (SH). The ultra fast-sinking shooting head (SH), however, differs from the conventional sinking shooting taper (ST) and full-length sinking fly lines in length, weight, casting and handling. The modern alternatives to the traditional lead-core line, such as the Deep Water Express (DWE) and Kerboom fly lines, are impregnated with lead or tungsten in their PVC jackets. These products are more durable than a lead-core line and they are available in 30-foot lengths, ranging in weight from 400 to 850 grains. Due to their extreme weight, however, lead-core lines and their commercial alternatives usually require a modification of their length to achieve enhanced overall castability and manageability.

Ultra Fast-Sinking SH

Standard SH

When dealing with ultra fast-sinking fly lines, it is beneficial to establish some parity between the load capability of a fly rod and the weight of the shooting head (SH), which is concentrated in a much shorter length than a conventional shooting head (SH). Fly rods are designed to cast a specific weight of line measured in grains. The table shown on page 42 lists the various line sizes and the corresponding line weight in grains, which is based on a 30-foot section of fly line extended beyond the rod tip during the casting cycle. Non-conventional ultra fast-sinking fly lines, however, are generally much shorter and their casting dynamics are notably different. These lines are typically cast in a wide arc to achieve optimum casting performance as discussed on pages 47-48. Once the slight adjustments to the casting mechanics are mastered, it is possible to throw heavily weighted flies distances well beyond 100 feet.

Most fly rods can handle full-length and 30-foot shooting head (SH) fly lines two or three sizes heavier than specified on their labels. I suppose this logic can be extrapolated to the extreme by speculating my custom designed 17-weight fly rod could probably cast a coaxial cable into the next time zone, which is theoretically possible when fishing in the Florida Panhandle for instance. In reality, though, most fly rods are capable of handling an ultra fast-sinking shooting head (SH) about 1-1/2 times their labeled weight designation. The casting dynamics and consolidated weight in a much shorter length than a conventional shooting head (SH) exerts extreme loads on a fly rod and, therefore, requires slightly less than the maximum acceptable weight most fly rods can manage efficiently.

I try to build a specialized sinking shooting head (SH) to the maximum allowable length without exceeding the upper weight limit for a given size fly rod. The longer the length of the shooting head (SH), the more effectively it can be cast. As a result, I do most of my dredging near or on the bottom in water depths 30 feet or deeper primarily with four basic outfits: a 6-weight outfit rigged with a 20-foot 400-grain shooting head (SH), a 9-weight outfit rigged with a 30-foot 400-grain shooting head (SH); a 10-weight outfit rigged with a 24-foot 550-grain shooting head (SH), and a 12-weight outfit rigged with a 21-foot 850-grain shooting head (SH).

The table below is a recommendation to the lengths of various ultra fast-sinking fly lines for a given size fly rod. Start with one of the suggested lengths for a given fly rod size, and if it is too heavy to cast satisfactorily, cut 6-inch increments from the front of the line until the proper load on the fly rod and an acceptable castability of the shooting head (SH) are achieved. This trial-and-error process may be needed to be done once or twice after the initial setup. Granted, this task can be a labor-intensive effort, because a leader and fly should be reattached after each slight adjustment to ascertain the castability of the new length, but the effort is well worthwhile. To minimize the task, the PVC fly line loop at the front end of the shooting head (SH) can be secured with a single nail knot. After the final length is determined, a second nail knot should be tied, and both knots should be coated with a cement, to provide maximum strength and durability to the loop.

Fly Rod Size	Lead Core (13 gr./ft.)	DWE (400 gr.)	DWE (550 gr.)	DWE (700 gr.)	DWE (850 gr.)
6-wt.	20 ft.	20 ft.	14 to 14-1/2 ft.	n/a	n/a
7 -wt.	23-1/2 ft.	23 ft.	16 to 16-1/2 ft.	n/a	n/a
8 -wt.	27 ft.	26 ft.	18 to 18-1/2 ft.	14-1/2 to 15 ft.	n/a
9 -wt.	30 ft.	30 ft.	20-1/2 to 21 ft.	16-1/2 to 17 ft.	14 ft.
10 -wt.	36 ft.	35 ft.	23-1/2 to 24 ft.	18-1/2 to 19 ft.	16 ft.
12 -wt.	n/a	n/a	30 ft.	24-1/2 to 25 ft.	21 ft.
13 -wt.	n/a	n/a	30 ft.	30 ft.	24-1/2 ft.

To build a specialized ultra fast-sinking shooting head (SH), follow this simple procedure:

- Determine what line-weight fly rod is to be used with a specialized sinking shooting head (SH).
- Choose the type and weight of specialized SH to be used with the selected fly rod.
- Refer to the table on page 42 to ascertain the starting length of the shooting head (SH).

- Measure and cut the shooting head (SH) to the desired length. If a Deep Water Express (DWE) line is used, part of the front, rear or a combination of both tapered ends can be cut to attain the desired weight as shown in the drawing below.
- Secure a small braided nylon monofilament loop at both ends of the shooting head (SH). The steps to form a small braided nylon monofilament loop and to secure it to the shooting head (SH) are illustrated on pages 19-20. It is recommended the base of the front loop, to be connected to a leader system, be coated with Pliobond, Goop, Aquaseal, Softex, marine silicone or similar products for added rigidity and easier passage through the rod guides and tiptop.
- Attach the shooting head (SH) to the shooting line (SL) and cast the shooting taper (ST) system to ascertain its performance qualities. If any adjustments are needed to be made, remove a foot of the back end of the shooting head (SH) on the first cut and 6 inches each subsequent cut until the castability is acceptable.

Deep Water Express Shooting Tapers

550 Grains [Sink rate: 7.5 inches/second]
7 11 16 19 ———————— 21 grains per foot ———————— 19 15 12 9 7
Back Taper   Front Taper

700 Grains [Sink rate: 8.5 inches/second]
8 12 18 22 ———————— 28 grains per foot ———————— 22 18 16 14 10 9
Back Taper   Front Taper

850 Grains [Sink rate: 9.5 inches/second]
9 13 22 27 ———————— 33 grains per foot ———————— 31 27 22 18 15 12 9
Back Taper   Front Taper

Building a specialized ultra fast-sinking shooting head (SH) is the only occurrence where I use small braided nylon monofilament loops at both ends of the shooting head (SH). In extreme deepwater dredging for grouper, snapper and sea bass, for example, there is a common tendency for the front section of the shooting head (SH) to become chafed from being pulled across sharp rock ledges and other objects. Unless part of the shooting head (SH) is severely damaged affecting the breaking strength of the core material, this setup allows the shooting head (SH) to be reversed for extended use. When rigging a section of lead-core trolling line as a shooting head (SH), I recommend threading it through the hollow core of braided nylon monofilament for added protection and durability. The procedure to thread a continuous length of lead-core trolling line through a braided nylon monofilament line is similar to building a mini or instant sinking section as described on page 64.

Rigging a Shooting Line (SL)

The process for rigging a shooting line (SL) with end loops for connection to the backing and shooting head (SH) is generally similar to preparing a shooting head (SH). There are some slight variations in the process depending upon the type of shooting line (SL) material being rigged. The three most common types of shooting lines are: plastic-coated commercial, braided nylon monofilament and medium-stiff nylon monofilament. Each shooting line (SL) material has its advantages and disadvantages for a given fishing situation. In my opinion, the most durable and versatile of these shooting line (SL) materials is the braided nylon monofilament. I use the other two materials in more specific or specialized fishing situations.

With a plastic-coated commercial shooting line (SL), a braided nylon monofilament loop is secured at each end. A small braided nylon monofilament loop is used to connect the shooting head (SH) with the shooting line (SL) and a large braided nylon monofilament loop is used to interlock with the loop of the backing material. The instructions for forming a braided nylon monofilament loop are discussed on pages 19-20. The steps to secure these braided nylon monofilament loops to the ends of the shooting line (SL) are illustrated on pages 19-20. With braided nylon monofilament shooting line (SL), the loops are formed in the material at both ends.

In the assembly of a shooting taper (ST) system, the large loop of the shooting line (SL) is interlocked with the large loop of the backing material. The large loop of the shooting line (SL) is slipped over the large loop of the backing material and the other end of the shooting line (SL) is passed through the loop of the backing material. The loops are pulled apart and cinched tightly. The small loop at the other end of the shooting line (SL) is then connected to the small loop in the back end of the shooting head (SH) and secured as previously described. Finally, a leader system is looped to the PVC fly line loop at the front end of the shooting head (SH) in the same manner of connection and the shooting taper (ST) system is ready for use.

Nylon Monofilament Shooting Line (SL)

Medium-stiff nylon monofilament is the most difficult material to use and handle as a shooting line (SL), but it is has an application in some specialized fishing situations. Medium-stiff nylon monofilament must be stretched when pulled from the reel spool initially, because it will retain a memory set. In addition, the line can become tangled easily and influenced by wind, which usually necessitates the use of a stripping basket whenever possible. Finally, the line must be inspected frequently for any sign of a nick or abrasion that can be fatal to its integrity. As a result, I use a medium-stiff nylon monofilament shooting line (SL) in two specific fishing situations: reaching fish at depths 50 feet or greater with a 700- or 850-grain shooting head (SH) and pursuing IGFA world records with 2-, 4- and 6-pound class tippets.

To rig a nylon monofilament shooting line (SL), I form a 6- to 8-inch loop using a Bimini Twist at the end of the nylon monofilament shooting line (SL) to be joined to the large loop of the backing material. A small loop is formed at the other end by folding the tag end onto the standing part and holding both lines together with a cyanoacrylate (CA) glue, such as Krazy glue. The loop should be secured with two nail knots similar to forming a PVC fly line loop as described on page 60. I would recommend coating the knots of both loops with Pliobond, Goop, Aquaseal, Softex, marine silicone or similar products for easier passage through the rod guides. The loops are interlocked to the loops of the backing material and shooting head (SH) using the same method as described for other shooting lines previously mentioned in this chapter.

Mini or Instant Sinking Leader Sections

Short pieces of floating and sinking fly lines, including ultra fast-sinking lines such as lead core, Kerboom or Deep Water Express (DWE), can be used to make mini or instant leader sections. Adding a mini sinking section of various lengths to a full-length weight-forward (WF) or double taper (DT) floating fly line provides an increased versatility to adapt quickly and efficiently to varied fishing and water conditions. This interlocking loop system precludes the necessity of unstringing and restringing another line through the rod guides and switching reels or spare spools on the stream or in a boat. The process is much more convenient, faster and potentially less hazardous to the gear than interchanging reels or spare spools.

Mini or instant sinking sections are available commercially in lengths of 4, 5 and 6 feet with sink rates from 2 to 6 inches per second (ips). I prefer to make my own sinking sections of various lengths from 18 inches to 15 feet. I also make floating mini sections of 6 to 10 feet from old floating fly lines, which I attach to an intermediate or slow sinking shooting head (SH) for working flies and poppers on the surface when required. In some specific fishing situations, I will also use a short section of floating line with an ultra fast-sinking shooting head (SH) to keep a fly suspended over rough bottom structure. The small loops at both ends of a mini sinking or floating section are interlocked with the loops at the end of the fly line and leader butt.

With plastic-coated floating and sinking fly line sections, a small braided nylon monofilament loop is secured at each end. One of the small braided nylon monofilament loops is interlocked to the fly line loop and the other loop is connected to the small loop at one end of a short leader butt section. With this system of interlocking loops, pre-rigged tippet and fly assemblies can be interchanged with the larger loop at the other end of the leader butt section. The instructions for forming a braided nylon monofilament loop are discussed on pages 19-20. The steps to secure these braided nylon monofilament loops to the ends of the shooting line (SL) are illustrated on pages 19-20. With braided nylon monofilament shooting line (SL), the loops are formed in the material.

Traditionally, a lead-core shooting head (SH) was cut from the commercially available lead-core trolling lines. The braided, outer sheath of these lines determines their breaking strength (pound-test) and their weight, or sink rate, is predicated on the diameter of the lead core. Since the advent of plastic-coated sinking fly lines, however, I have relegated the lead-core line primarily for use as mini or instant sinking leader sections. To protect the braided Dacron outer sheath of a lead-core line section, thread the entire length of the lead-core section through the hollow core of a braided nylon monofilament line. Small connection loops are then formed at each end. The instructions for forming a braided nylon monofilament loop are discussed on pages 19-20.

Storing Shooting Heads & Mini Sinking Leader Sections

There are various methods for storing a shooting head (SH) and mini or instant sinking leader sections. In addition to the numerous commercial products available, the simplest and least expensive method is a plastic ziplock storage bag labeled with a permanent, waterproof marker or reproduced on a computer printer. Because I use many different fly outfits, I make my own customized wallets for specific fly line sizes or weights. Each wallet provides a compact system for storing shooting heads of different densities for the same line size as well as mini or instant sinking leader sections. In addition, the wallet protects the plastic bags, fly lines and mini sinking sections from heat, humidity and the damaging effects of direct sunlight.

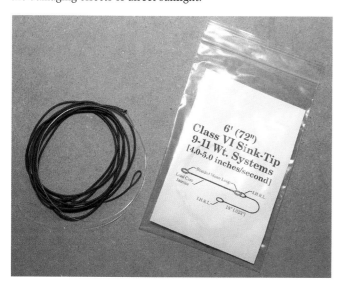

Building Storage Wallets

Constructing a customized storage wallet is easy and inexpensive. Start with heavyweight and sealable plastic bags with a two-part strip along the opening that can be pressed together and readily reopened. For durability and prolonged use, the thickness of the bags should be 4 Mil, which is four one-thousandths of an inch or 0.004 inches. The standard household ziplock sandwich bag sold in stores is 1.5 Mil and the heavier freezer bag is generally 1.75 Mil. The standard industry thickness, however, is 2 Mil and 4 Mil is considered heavy duty. The following steps will build a storage wallet for shooting heads and mini sinking leader sections:

- Use 4 Mil ziplock plastic bags 5 inches wide and 8 inches long. Choose a bag for each shooting head (SH) and one bag for two mini or instant sinking leader sections. A mini leader section can be stored in a single bag on each side of the labeled divider.
- Stack the ziplock bags on top of each other with the sealed ends even and flush.
- Sew a stitch across the width of the bags about 7 inches from their opened ends as shown in the photo below.

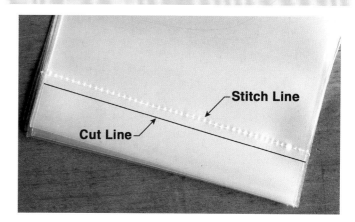

- Cut the bags with a pair of scissors about an 1/8-inch below the sewn stitch as shown in the photo above.
- Cut a piece of vinyl fabric 5-1/2 inches wide and 18 inches long.
- Cut a piece of strapping or heavy ribbon material, 1 to 1-1/2 inches wide, to a length of 5 inches.
- Lay the strapping or heavy ribbon material equidistant across the inside width of the vinyl fabric material and sew a stitch down the centerline of the strapping or heavy ribbon material about 3-1/4 inches from one end of the vinyl fabric material as shown in the photo below.

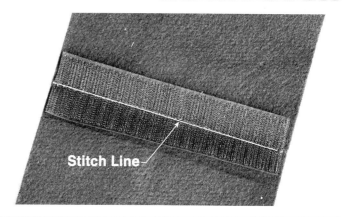

- Lay the edge of the stitched plastic bags along the sewn centerline and fold each side of the strapping or heavy ribbon material against the plastic bags.
- Sew a stitch across the top edges of the strapping or heavy ribbon material and through the plastic bags. Secure the ends of the sewing thread with a drop of glue to prevent fraying and unraveling with use.

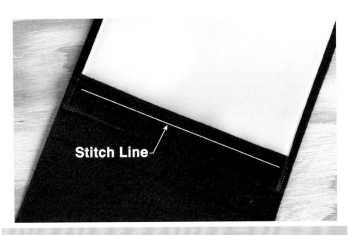

- Sew or glue a small piece of velcro loop material on the outside or front of the vinyl fabric material that is centered and about 3/4-inch from the edge.

- Sew or glue a longer piece of velcro hook material centered and near the front or outside edge of the other end of the vinyl fabric material. The velcro hook material can also be sewn on the inside of the vinyl fabric material if desired. The photos below show examples of velcro closing tabs secured internally and externally.

- Label the front of the storage wallet as desired with dimensional fabric paint.

To build a wallet with removable ziplock bags, substitute the strapping or heavy ribbon material with an adhesive-backed velcro loop material about 1-1/2 inches wide. After the ziplock bags are sewn together and the excess plastic is removed to within a 1/8-inch from the stitches, fold the adhesive-backed velcro hook material equidistant over the ends of the ziplock bags. Sew a stitch across the top edges of the velcro hook material and through the plastic bags.

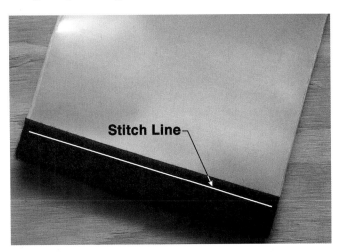

Heavier stock paper, such as 26-pound weight, should be used inside each ziplock bag. Cut the paper to approximately 4-5/8 inches wide and 5 inches high. Specific information regarding each shooting head (SH) or mini sinking leader section can be printed with a permanent, waterproof marker or reproduced on a computer printer. In addition to noting the length and type of density of each shooting head (SH) or mini sinking section, I also include information concerning the sink rate of the line and the duration for the line to reach specific depths. For example, the wallet on the left in the photo below is setup for 5-weight shooting heads, ranging in density from floating to extra-fast sinking. The sleeve for the ST5S Type I (intermediate) indicates the line has a sink rate of approximately 1.5 inches per second (ips). Since I would typically use this line in water depths ranging from 1 to 6 feet, I calculated the duration of the sink rate for depths of 2 feet (16 seconds), 3 feet (24 seconds) and 6 feet (48 seconds) as a guide for potential fishing strategies. The duration of the sink rate for a ST5S Type IV shooting head (SH), for example, is calculated for depths of 8 feet (26 seconds), 9 feet (29 seconds) and 20 feet (64 seconds).

Chapter 6
Leader System Theory & General Design

In terms of knots and leaders, there is no such thing as a second chance. If the thin web of line that spans the distance between the fly line and a hooked quarry fails, the fish has earned is freedom and another story about the one that got away is born. In essence, the leader is the critical link. The best rod, the finest reel or the most seductive fly are all unavailing if the knots will not stand the strain of hooking and battling a fish.

Importance and Function of a Leader System

The leader system is the most dynamic and subjective element of a balanced outfit. Its primary purpose is to reduce the visible connection between the fly line and fly as well as to turn over the fly properly for an effective presentation. The length and diameter of a leader are a compromise to most fishing conditions and the decreasing diameters of its taper filter the kinetic energy from the fly line for a proper turn over. Leader length and taper are often contingent on the wariness of the fish, the clarity of water and the weight and aerodynamic profile of the fly. Many species of fish, however, are not usually wary of striking a fly because of the tippet or shock trace size attached to it.

The basic approach in leader design is to build a tapered leader that turns over well, presents the fly with a minimum of surface disturbance and is invisible enough to deceive a fish into striking the fly. A fish credited with keen eyesight, such as a trout or a bonefish, may be somewhat suspicious of a meal being led by something opaque and bulky. While a nylon or fluorocarbon monofilament leader is not completely invisible to a fish, it is far less conspicuous than the end of a fly line. In addition, the translucency of nylon fluorocarbon monofilament tends to absorb and reflect the color of its background, making it less prominent to a fish.

Types of Leader Systems

There are five basic types of leaders with general and specialty variations within each type: level, knotless tapered, compound tapered, braided or furled, and shock trace. Each type has its own advantages and disadvantages. The simplest and most basic leader is the level leader, which is usually made from a single strand of 8- to 12-pound nylon or fluorocarbon monofilament. It is most commonly used in largemouth bass and panfish waters where the surface is cluttered with lily pads and other emerging aquatic plants. In these close-range situations, delicacy of presentation is not a factor and a knotted, tapered leader may snag the vegetation at the knots if they are not coated.

There are four basic types of tapered leader configurations: knotless, braided or furled, compound, and shock trace. These leader systems serve several important functions and the requirements of their construction can be critical in many fishing situations. A dry fly, for example, must float freely on the surface, as a natural insect does when it rests on the water. If the leader is not correctly designed, it will cause the fly to be dragged unnaturally in the current, alarming the fish to this abnormal behavior.

A commercial knotless tapered leader is extruded as a continuous length of nylon or fluorocarbon monofilament line that diminishes in size. Its butt section is heavy and its diameter gradually decreases as it reaches the tippet section. It is convenient to use, but it may not always be possible to obtain a leader with precisely the desired taper for the fishing situation. Once such a leader has been shortened by a few fly changes, a new tippet must be attached and the leader becomes a compound (knotted) type. As a result, based on expense and versatility, all of my leader systems for pursuing fish species from trout and bluegills to bonefish and billfish are compound tapered. The leaders are quick and easy to build, and, if needed, they can be customized promptly in real time on the water to meet specific fishing situations.

Braided or furled leaders generally consist of several feet of a braided butt section with one or more knotted tippet sections. They are made by twisting multiple strands of small diameter fiber, such as 4-pound nylon monofilament. Two or more lengths of these fibers are then twisted together to produce the desired taper and length. The braided lines tend to hold water that can spray out during a cast. To remedy this occurrence, some of the commercial leaders are subjected to a wax impregnation process, which significantly reduces the amount of spray over the water.

Braided or furled leaders are commercially available for trout, salmon and saltwater in various densities and standard lengths of 7-1/2, 9 and 12 feet. This type of leader is very effective at turning over long tippets or wind-resistant flies, because the kinetic energy transfer from the fly line to the braided leader is much more efficient. The floating and intermediate models, for example, can deliver a delicate presentation and the choice of using additional sinking densities provide possibilities not feasible with traditional tapered leaders.

Braided or furled leaders have many endearing qualities. The braided nylon monofilament construction is inherently elastic, providing excellent shock absorption to protect a very light tippet from breaking when setting a hook. This type of leader has considerably less memory or coiling than a knotless or compound tapered nylon monofilament leader due to its added suppleness. In addition, braided or furled leaders tend to resist wind knots more than tapered nylon monofilament leaders, but untying a knot when it occurs is more difficult.

Of the four types of tapered leaders, a compound tapered leader, which is also referred to as a knotted tapered leader, is the most versatile in my opinion. It is the leader system I have used since 1958 for every fishing situation. The system utilizes several strands of nylon or fluorocarbon monofilament line of successively decreasing diameters that are tied together to form a continuous tapered leader. For a compound tapered trout leader, as an example, the successive sections vary .003 inches or less in order to allow the proper transmission of kinetic energy for a delicate presentation and to maintain knot strength.

The real advantages of compound tapered leaders are twofold: cost and customized versatility. As the least expensive leader system to use, its construction can be customized or modified to deliver the optimum performance for any given fishing situation. The system I developed utilizes an interlocking loop design, which provides the capability to quickly change and adjust all the leader components to meet changing water and weather conditions as well as varied fly designs. Slight adjustments may be necessary to match prevailing conditions efficiently because calm mornings often become breezy afternoons before calming again towards sunset. Equally important, the species of fish pursued can change several times during a day, necessitating possible changes in leader design and fly configurations. The steps to building and customizing compound tapered leaders are detailed and illustrated in chapters 9 and 10.

A shock trace leader is a subset or specialized variation of a compound tapered leader. Its primary purpose is to protect a fragile tippet from the sharp teeth, gill plates and abrasive body parts of certain fish species such as northern pike, muskellunge, tarpon and sharks. It is also useful in fishing situations plagued by other line-cutting obstacles such as barnacles, coral and jagged structures. To prevent the tippet from being cut or abraded, a short section of wire or heavier nylon or fluorocarbon monofilament line is connected between the tippet and the fly. The basic rule is to use the shortest shock trace possible to enhance turn over on the final forward cast and to minimize visibility in the water. The steps to building and customizing compound tapered shock trace leaders

are detailed and illustrated in chapters 9 and 10.

The maximum length of a shock trace is typically 12 inches although 6 to 9 inches is generally more than sufficient and considerably easier to cast. If pursuing IGFA world records, the maximum length for a shock trace is 12 inches, which is measured from the single-strand tippet to the eye of the hook including all connecting knots. Fluorocarbon monofilament line should be the first choice as a shock trace material because it is less visible in the water than wire and it can be straightened if it becomes kinked or coiled. In addition, a nylon or fluorocarbon monofilament shock trace can be slightly longer because it is lighter and easier to cast than a wire shock trace. If pursuing an IGFA world record is not a consideration, a nylon or fluorocarbon monofilament shock trace of 12 to 15 inches works well in most fishing situations. This added length allows the fly to be retied a few times before the shock trace needs to be replaced.

This specialized section of a compound tapered leader is sometimes called a bite tippet or a shock tippet, but I believe the most accurate and less confusing term is shock trace. By definition, a shock is a sudden, violent collision of one object (the shock trace) striking against another (the teeth or a body part of a fish) and a trace is a very small quantity. The shortest section of this leader system is the shock trace and there are many species whose certain body parts, and not their teeth, require protection to the tippet section; therefore, I believe shock trace is a more applicable and universal term.

Although a shock trace is not absolutely necessary with most marine species, a 9- to 15-inch section of 20- or 25-pound fluorocarbon monofilament line is commonly used for added protection. Fish with small, fine teeth or sharp gill plates, such as snook, or species which jump repeatedly when hooked, such as ladyfish, as shown below, can be best handled on a shock trace of 25- to 40-pound fluorocarbon monofilament line. A shock trace of 60- to 100-pound fluorocarbon monofilament line is used for larger fish such as tarpon over 60 pounds or billfish. The heavy fluorocarbon monofilament shock trace is needed to counter the constant, abrasive resistance of the line rubbing against the mouth, gill plates or other body parts of large game fish during a lengthy battle.

When pursuing gamefish with extremely sharp teeth, such as a shark or a northern pike, the need for a wire shock trace of 6 to 9 inches

Tippet Section

Shock Trace

is unavoidable. There are two basic types of wire, which can be used as a shock trace: solid and cable. The latter type, also known as stranded or braided wire, is composed of numerous filaments of relatively soft wire which have been braided together to form a single strand. Cable is available either plain or coated with a nylon jacket. The nylon coating can be shredded easily by teeth and the tensile strength can be reduced when individual strands become severed. Cable is quite flexible and it can be knotted to the fly using a Chermanski Loop knot, for example. A wire trace of 30 and 40 pounds can be used in place of 25- and 40-pound nylon monofilament respectively for many species including pickerel, northern pike, Spanish mackerel, bluefish, little tunny, cero mackerel and small barracuda.

As an alternative to frming a loop using a Chermanski Loop knot, coated cable can be melted with a low-temperture flame from a match or lighter. The process of forming a small loop with melted coated cable is easy by following these simple steps:

- Tightly secure the bend of the hook to a fixed object such as a vise.

- Thread the coated cable through the hook eye and tightly secure the tag end and standing part of the coated cable about 2 inches from the hook eye with a pair of needle nose or vice grip pliers.

- Keeping the coated cable taut, rotate the needlenose or vise grip pliers 4 to 6 times to create twists in the tag end and standing part of the coated cable, forming a small loop directly in front of the hook eye.

- Pass a low-temperature flame from a match or lighter along the twists slowly until the plastic coating of the cable has melted together. Be carefull not to cause the plastic coating to burn into a flame.

- Allow the melted coating to cool before releasing pressure from the needlenose or vise grip pliers.

Solid wire is preferred as a metallic shock trace in anodized brown or black, especially for long battles with larger game fish including barracuda, king mackerel, sharks and wahoo, just to name a few species with razor-sharp teeth. It is stronger than cable because it will remain at the same tensile strength throughout a fight. It also has a smaller diameter for the same breaking strength and it provides an excellent sink rate to the fly. Solid wire kinks easily, however, often necessitating a change to a new shock trace after a catch.

Size	2	3	4	5	6	7	8	9	10
Diameter	.011"	.012"	.013"	.014"	.015"	.016"	.017"	.018"	.019"
Pounds	27	32	38	44	58	69	86	105	124
Kilograms	12	15	17	20	26	31	39	48	56

Solid wire has a size number designation. The table above shows the relationship between wire size and the corresponding breaking strength of solid, stainless steel wire. Most packaging of leader wire will specify the breaking strength, but the approximate breaking strength can be computed by multiplying the size number by 10. For example, consider a #4 solid stainless wire shock trace will have an estimated breaking strength of 40 pounds. Its actual strength is closer to 38 pounds.

For species such as pickerel, Spanish mackerel, cero mackerel, little tunny, bluefish, tripletail, dolphin and small barra-

cuda, #7 solid wire is suggested. For larger species such as king mackerel, wahoo, grouper, barracuda, cubera snapper, northern pike and sharks, #9 solid wirc is rccommended. The wahoo, for example, with its row of razor-sharp teeth and its scissor-type bite, can cut through nearly anything except solid stainless steel wire. This speedy game fish is also one of a few species where a slightly longer shock trace may be needed, because wahoo have a propensity for chewing their way up a shock trace and simply biting it off, at least in my experiences.

Solid fishing wire usually consists of two materials; single strand stainless steel or single strand Monel. Stainless steel is the older of the two materials and it is not as pliable, having a tendency to break relatively easy when kinked. Stainless steel wire is also much springier and more difficult to twist when attaching it to a fly using the Haywire Twist. Its prime advantage is essentially the price, which is considerably less expensive than Monel and the newer braided wires.

Monel is a nickel alloy that is considerably softer than stainless wire. As a result, it is much easier to manipulate in forming a Haywire Twist, which is illustrated on page 30. While it is more apt to kink due to its increased pliability, it is relatively simple to manage and to prevent from kinking. Its prime disadvantage, however, is its breaking strength, which is 20% to 30% lower than solid stainless steel wire of the same diameter. For example, for a diameter of 0.016 inches, #7 stainless steel wire has a breaking strength of 69-pound compared to 15-pound for soft Monel wire.

The latest innovation in shock leader wire is titanium. The BOA No-Kink Titanium shock leader, marketed by the Malin Company, is useful for all types of fly-fishing applications when the following advantages are desired:

- A corrosion proof titanium leader for maximum abrasion resistance.

- A titanium leader with a stretch value of 10% to 15% for increased hook setting ability, and protection against excessive shock.

- A titanium leader will rival fluorocarbon for invisibility in water because of its natural color and non-glare finish, and it combativeness to toothy fishes.

- A titanium leader is highly flexible and is virtually impossible to kink, although it can not be haywire twisted and it does not need to be crimped.

- A titanium leader can be tied using conventional knots, such as the Improved Clinch knot and the Chermanski Loop knot. Just pull the knot down snug using pliers, until it stretches and trim the tag end. The knot will appear to be loose and will not pack down like a nylon monofilament knot, but it will hold nevertheless.

Major Parts of Leader Systems

In general terms, a basic compound tapered leader is composed of the following three major parts, which diminish in diameter to the fly: the butt, the midsection and the tippet. The optional fourth major part, the shock trace, may be required in certain fishing situations. Typically, the elemental formula for the three major parts is 60%-20%-20% respectively. Leaders tied to this formula will turn over properly and present the fly effectively. Each section can be constructed of one or more nylon or fluorocarbon monofilament lines of similar diameters, depending upon the overall length of the leader. A short leader, for example, may require only a single section of nylon or fluorocarbon monofilament line to construct each major part.

The overall length for most types of tapered leaders is generally 7-1/2 to 12 feet with full-length floating fly lines and 3 to 6 feet with full-length sinking, dual density and shooting taper (ST)

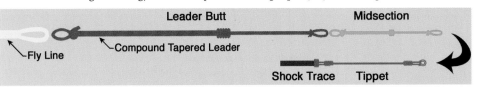

Leader Butt   **Midsection**

Fly Line

Compound Tapered Leader

Shock Trace   **Tippet**

fly lines. A short leader is preferred with sinking fly lines to ensure maximum depth penetration and sensitivity to subtle strikes. In contrast, casting to wary species such as trout, bonefish, permit and sheepshead in clear, shallow water may require a long leader ranging from 12 to 15 feet in overall length.

The leader butt is the heaviest section with the largest diameter and it is composed of medium-stiff nylon or fluorocarbon monofilament line for turning over the remainder of the leader at the completion of the cast. The length of the butt section is generally about 50% to 60% of the entire leader and its diameter is 60% to 75% of the fly line diameter. It is the strongest and most resistant part of a leader system. Its principal function is to receive the kinetic energy transmitted from the fly line during a cast and dissipate it more effectively to the other sections for an efficient turn over. The most common error in leader design is using too small a diameter or too short a length as the butt section. In most fishing and wind conditions, a longer and heavier leader butt section will turn over a greater range of flies more efficiently.

The leader butt section is attached to a fly line using an interlocking loop system. It can consist of more than one section of nylon or fluorocarbon line, depending upon the overall length and application of the leader system. Loops are formed at each end of the leader butt using a Chermanski Loop knot as described on pages 24-25. The loop interlocking to the PVC fly line loop can be made as small as possible, usually 1/4 to 1/2 inches long. If the leader butt section is intended to be used with a midsection, then the loop at the opposite end can be formed of similar size. However, with leader systems having no midsection in their design, the loop at the opposite end of the leader butt section should be large enough for the bulkiest fly to pass through it, which is usually 1 to 1-1/2 inches in length.

The midsection is used in leader systems for floating and intermediate fly lines. It serves as the transitional area of nylon or fluorocarbon monofilament line diameters connecting the heavier butt section to the smaller-diameter tippet section and its length is generally about 20% of the entire leader. It is an optional section in some saltwater fishing situations, particularly in bluewater applications. The midsection of a leader is added as a graduated section for handling lighter tippets or for extending the overall length of the leader. The sections forming the midsection are joined together using a blood knot and it is connected to the leader butt section using the interlocking loop system. The loop connecting the midsection to the leader butt can be formed as small as possible using a Chermanski Loop knot. The loop at the opposite end should be large enough for the bulkiest fly to pass through it, which is usually 1-1/12 inches in length.

The tippet is the lightest, weakest and least visible part of a

leader system and it is usually attached directly to the fly, except in some freshwater and many saltwater fishing situations where a shock trace may be required. The length of the tippet sections is about 20% to 25% of the entire leader depending upon the fishing situation. When a wary fish acts suspicious to what is believed to be the correct fly design, especially in clear water conditions, it generally means the tippet diameter or size is too large. Semi-limp nylon or fluorocarbon monofilament line is preferred as a tippet material, especially in freshwater applications. As a general rule, the lighter the tippet, the longer its length. To insure maximum strength and added shock absorption, the end of the tippet connecting to the rest of the leader is doubled using a Bimini Twist. A small double-stranded loop is formed at the end using the Chermanski Loop knot. For leader systems featuring a shock trace, the tippet material is doubled at both ends using a Bimini Twist and one end is attached to the shock trace material using the Albright Special. The steps to tying the Bimini Twist are illustrated on pages 28-29 and the instructions for tying the Albright Special are shown on pages 32-33.

Dynamics of a Leader during a Cast

When a fly line is unrolling forward during a cast, the unrolled section is the only portion pulling forward. As the loop unfolds and straightens, the front taper of the fly line ceases to pull entirely. If the applied kinetic energy exerted by the angler is executed properly, the front taper has sufficient momentum to straighten its own length and deliver the final impulse to straighten the leader. The leader and fly do not contribute to the cast. The leader and fly are merely pulled along by the unfolding fly line, ultimately being pushed forward by the momentum of the fly line. In actuality, the leader is an impediment. The longer its length, the less likelihood of its straightening and the more aerodynamic drag it adds to the unfolding fly line during a cast.

Willie Chermanski at age 10

Length & Weight of Leaders

To make a proficient and effective presentation, the leader must be designed correctly. The length and weight of a leader are an understanding to the fishing conditions and the taper design, which is a vital component, is responsible for the proper and efficient transmission of kinetic energy from the fly line to the fly. The length and weight of a leader are dependent to a certain degree upon the weather and water conditions as well as the size of the fish being pursued. The taper design of a leader is dependent primarily upon the size, weight and aerodynamic profile of the range of flies being used in addition to other mitigating factors. It is critically important in the presentation of a fly as it lands on the surface of the water.

The three most common lengths for commercial knotless tapered leaders are 7-1/2, 9 and 12 feet. A shorter leader is generally easier to turn over than a longer one. In most surface and near-surface fishing situations, particularly with floating fly lines, the greater the distance between the fly line and the fly, the more likely a fish is to strike the offering. Shorter leaders are easier to cast, but wary fish and crystalline water usually require smaller flies, longer leaders and finer tippets. A longer leader also presents a fly more delicately and, in many situations, allows for a longer and better drift of the fly. In general fishing situations, it is usually best to start with a 9-foot leader and extend the length of the tippet section as required.

The length of leaders will also be determined by the size, weight and aerodynamic profile of a fly. A dry fly, for example, does not have any appreciable weight, but its aerodynamic profile can provide considerable wind resistance during a cast. In this case, a 9-foot leader will probably provide better casting control and delivery than a 12-foot leader. Similarly, a big, bulky streamer can be presented more efficiently on a floating fly line with a leader as short as 6 feet than with a 12-footer.

While a shorter leader can make for easier casting with a streamer, it might not be the most effective and productive approach. With a floating line, a streamer or any subsurface fly will swim deeper on a 9-foot leader than on a shorter one. A weighted fly fished with a floating fly line, for example, may be easier to cast on a shorter leader, but a longer leader will allow the fly to descend and remain slightly deeper in the water column. At times, maintaining a slightly deeper retrieval path can prove beneficial, especially in circumstances associated with current flow.

The length of the leader can also be matched to the type of water being fished. As a general rule, floating fly lines commonly require longer leaders and sinking lines typically dictate shorter leaders in most water conditions. In extremely clear or very shallow water, for example, a leader system that does not alert wary or skittish fish is often required. In addition, many of these fishing situations usually necessitate the use of smaller flies. As a result, these circumstances will typically dictate the need for a longer leader and a lighter tippet. Common examples requiring longer leaders and finer tippets with floating fly lines include fishing calm pools in rivers and spring creeks, and windless days on shallow, tidal flats. In many of these extreme fishing situations, especially in crystal clear water under cloudless skies, leaders 15 feet or longer may be necessary.

When the surface of the water is agitated by the wind, however, there is usually no need for using an excessively long leader or the lightest tippet. Even with such wary quarry as bonefish, permit or tarpon, as well as skittish trout in spring creeks and tailwaters, a much shorter leader will generally suffice. On windy days, the splashdown of a fly line on the water is not as critical in most situations. Fish do not seem to be alerted or alarmed when a fly line crashes onto the water if the surface is rippled by the wind. It is much more difficult to properly turn over a fly with a long leader on a windy day. The presentation and delivery of the cast can be impeded if the aerodynamic profile of the fly resists being pulled by the leader and the wind diverts the leader from its intended target.

In windy conditions, a longer leader is prone to developing knots along its length that will weaken it. By shortening the leader, the fly will probably turn over much better in a breeze during a cast. And since the surface of the water is rippled, a fish is less likely to be alarmed as long as the splashdown of the fly line is not overly boisterous. This strategy is standard practice among most experienced anglers. Depending upon the fishing conditions, they will use a 9- to 15-foot leader on calm days. When a slight breeze intensifies, they will reduce the length of their leader to maintain control of the cast and to execute a smooth and accurate presentation.

A fundamental tenet to effective fishing success is maintaining complete control over the fly line and leader during a cast. No one leader design can satisfy every angling requirement even on the same body of water. In many fishing situations, therefore, experimentation is often necessary to assure proper turn over of a fly for an effective presentation. Most problems affecting the performance of a leader, however, are actually casting problems. It is far more advantageous and productive to manage a standard leader efficiently in diverse conditions than to struggle trying to turn over a long leader or making slight adjustments in its taper to compensate for deficient casting skills. Practicing to improve casting skills provides the control to handle any leader length more efficiently, and to execute specialized casts better for the more difficult fishing situations.

A 9-foot leader is the most versatile and manageable length when used with floating fly lines for general fishing situations in both freshwater and saltwater. It is short enough for throwing bulky flies in saltwater and long enough for most dry-fly, nymph and streamer fishing on freshwater lakes, rivers and streams. By using an interlocking loop system, a leader length can be customized to accommodate any fishing situation. For more delicate presentations with smaller flies, for example, additional length can be added to the tippet section when necessary. Conversely, the overall length of a leader can be shortened by changing to a shorter leader butt section or by eliminating the midsection.

The Use of Shorter Leaders

In many cases, using a shorter leader will actually help you catch more fish, particularly in some freshwater and most saltwater fishing situations. In fact, except for some specific fishing situations, the overall length of my leader systems rarely exceed the length of the fly rods they are being used with. A shorter leader provides more versatility and better performance to a diverse array of fishing situations, wind conditions and range of fly sizes. In general terms, a shorter leader is usually more efficient and effective when the size or weight of a fly is disproportionate to the diameter of the tippet, or a shock trace is attached between the tippet and a fly.

The three primary reasons for using a shorter leader are: to turn over heavy or bulky flies, to reach targets in areas restricted by structure or dense vegetation, and to keep a fly deeper in the water column or on the bottom with a sinking fly line. By my definition, a short leader is not any longer than the length of the fly rod being used with a floating fly line and not more than half the length of the fly rod being used with a sinking fly line. Whenever a shorter leader can be applied to a fishing situation, the casting performance will generally improve and the presentation will usually be more precise.

Since many freshwater and most saltwater species are not leader-shy, shorter leaders can often be used advantageously to deliver larger or heavier flies more efficiently and accurately, particularly with floating fly lines. Bulky flies and poppers commonly used with floating fly lines for largemouth, smallmouth and striped bass, pike, muskellunge, big trout and most marine species, for example, will turn over easier and more precisely at the completion of the cast. In many of these fishing situations, a fluent and proper turn over is often the key to success.

A shorter leader can also be effective in delivering a fly in confined surroundings in both freshwater and saltwater. On a fast and narrow mountain stream under a primeval canopied forest, for example, casts 20 feet or less are the most common approach. With a shorter leader, more fly line can be extended beyond the rod tip to load the rod and to better manage the cast. Similarly, when pursuing estuarine species, such as snook and baby tarpon in brackish and tidal creeks infested with overhanging shoreline brush, a shorter leader is a necessity to deliver the fly under the protruding vegetation. Because it is closer to the fly and fly line, a shorter leader will turn over quicker, forming a narrower loop for easier entry into a restrictive area. The same casting requirement pertains to docks, piers, culverts, low bridges and other confining structures.

At the end of the forward stroke in a cast, the rod tip stops and the fly line unrolls forward toward the target. A tight loop in the fly line will maintain its size as it unrolls but, when the leader begins to unroll, its loop often widens. Generally, the longer a leader, the wider a loop is formed. Although the fly line loop could easily unroll beneath confining structures and overhanging brush, a longer leader will usually rise upward and widen, causing the fly to strike the structure or vegetation. A shorter leader will ordinarily resolve this problem.

There is no incertitude to the premise the best advantage of using a short leader is when fishing with a sinking fly line. Only in situations with very clear water and exceptionally wary fish do I use a leader longer than 5 feet with a sinking fly line. A nylon monofilament leader sinks slowly and the longer the leader, the slower an unweighted fly will sink. The fly line may have descended down in the water column while an unweighted fly, attached to a long nylon monofilament leader, is actually traveling higher. I define this phenomenon affecting submerged fly lines and leaders as hydroplaning, and it is a definite impediment in many fishing situations.

To sustain an unweighted fly at the same relative depth as the sinking fly line, a shorter leader will be required. A short leader in this situation is comprised of a leader butt no longer than 18 to 24 inches. I simply interlock the loop at the end of the tippet, fly and optional shock trace assembly directly to the loop at the end of the

leader butt. There is no need to taper such a short leader with a midsection. As a result, the overall length of the leader system will usually range between 3-1/2 to 4-1/2 feet. In most fishing situations, a shorter leader system will provide better strike detection, which will result in more hooked fish.

There are many fishing situations in freshwater and saltwater where a short leader used with a sinking fly line will prove superior. Maintaining the sink rate of a fly comparable to the sink rate of the fly line in the same retrieval plane is very important when pursuing species suspended in the water column or over submerged structure, such as largemouth bass, striped bass, lake trout, white bass, king mackerel, bluefish, snapper and weakfish. Another important fishing zone is retaining a fly in a chum line, which is usually the most effective technique when tidal current is moderate to strong. The most prominent example, however, is keeping a fly near or on the bottom when using a lead-core or extra-fast-sinking shooting head (SH) in very deep water for species such as grouper, snapper, walleye, sauger, catfish, sea bass, pompano and flounder.

When using a short leader less than 6 feet in length, a simple adjustment to the forward casting stroke will be necessary to assure a proper turn over. Fly lines are aerodynes. In other words, they overcome the force of gravity and are kept airborne by their momentum. A longer leader acts somewhat like the tail on a kite, which acts as a drag and adds to the stability and balance of the unrolling fly line loop. A shorter leader often folds flat instead of turning over, particularly when using a heavily weighted fly, which can result in a tangled mess. To eliminate the problem, open the fly line loop wider by applying the power stroke a split-second longer on the final forward cast.

Fly Size versus Tippet Size

In theory, the longer the leader and finer the tippet, the more strikes should occur. In practice, however, the problem at times is getting a long tippet to turn over properly, particularly with the lightest tippets. Understanding the relationship between the size of a fly and a tippet can help to minimize this enigma. The virtual weightlessness of a dry fly, for example, will not travel far under its own momentum. The kinetic energy transferred from the fly line to the leader has to carry the fly almost all the way to its target.

The diameter of a tippet is described primarily for freshwater fishing applications with a X-number system, commonly ranging from 0X to 8X. The sizes of saltwater class tippets are usually expressed by their breaking strengths in pounds or pound-test. The X-number has no direct relationship with the breaking strength of a tippet, only its diameter, which is measured in thousandths of an inch. The higher the X-number, the thinner the tippet. For example, tippets designated as 6X, 7X and 8X are used on the most minuscule flies. Conversely, tippets rated as 2X, 1X and OX are applied to larger species including salmon, steelhead, muskellunge, northern pike and saltwater flies.

The X-number system is called the Rule of Eleven in which the X signifies 11, or more precisely .011 inches. For the correct diameter in inches of an X designation, subtract the X from 11. For example, a 6X tippet subtracted from 11 equals 5 and, therefore, should measure approximately .005 inches in diameter. A 3X leader subtracted from 11 equals 8, which means its approximate diameter is .008 inches. The following table shows the relationship of the X-number designation to the approximate diameter of the tippet material. The table also shows the correlation between the size of a tippet and the appropriate size of the fly. A simple method to ascertain the appropriate tippet size for a specific fly size is to divide the size of the fly by 3. For example, a #12 fly is most suitable with a 4X tippet. Dividing a #20 or #22 fly by 3, the closest tippet size is 7X. This system is an approximation and it is based on a tippet length of 24 to 30 inches.

Size Designation	Tippet Diameter	Breaking Strength	Range of Fly Sizes	General Types of Fly Designs
000X	.015"	20-25 lbs.	6/0 to 2/0	popper, slider, streamer
00X	.013"	16-20 lbs.	5/0 to 1/0	popper, slider, streamer
0X	.011"	12-16 lbs.	3/0 to 2	popper, slider, streamer
1X	.010"	8.5-12 lbs.	2/0 to 4	popper, slider, streamer
2X	.009"	7-12 lbs.	1 to 8	dry, wet, nymph, larvae, pupae, popper, slider, streamer
3X	.008"	6-8.5 lbs.	4 to 12	dry, wet, nymph, larvae, pupae, popper, slider, streamer, terrestrial
4X	.007"	5-7 lbs.	8 to 14	dry, wet, nymph, larvae, pupae, popper, slider, streamer, terrestrial
5X	.006"	4-5 lbs.	14 to 18	dry, wet, nymph, larvae, pupae, popper, slider, streamer, terrestrial
6X	.005"	3-3.7 lbs.	16 to 20	dry, wet, nymph, larvae, pupae, terrestrial
7X	.004"	2-2.8 lbs.	18 to 22	dry, wet, nymph, larvae, pupae
8X	.003"	1.2-1.8 lbs.	22 to 28	dry, nymph, larvae, pupae

My leader systems are made of both medium-stiff and semi-limp nylon monofilament: the stiffer leader butt section to turn over the midsection, tippet and fly; and the semi-limp tippet section for more movement of a fly or an extended float. The final determination to matching the correct tippet diameter to fly size

should be decided by the weight or aerodynamic profile, which is also referred to as the density, of a fly. If the fly collapses behind the leader or the tippet, then the fly is too dense for the length or diameter of the tippet or both. If the fly suddenly dives downward or hits the surface of the water prematurely, then the tippet is too short or its diameter is too large. Tippet length and diameter are not determined by hook size. It is possible to have three flies all tied on the same hook size, each with a different density and each requiring a different tippet length and diameter. A #16 Adams dry fly, for example, will be best suited with a long 5X tippet or a short 6X tippet, while a #16 Adams Irresistible will be better matched with a long 4X tippet or a short 5X tippet in most fishing conditions.

Unweighted subsurface flies, such as nymphs and pupae, can be cast effectively with a lighter tippet than a dry fly of the same size in most fishing situations. The turn over of the leader and the presentation of these flies are not as critical, especially with a 24-inch tippet. Extending the length of the tippet, however, may require using a tippet one size larger. Similarly, weighted subsurface flies may require a tippet one size larger than recommended for unweighted versions of the same hook size. For example, a heavily weighted #12 salmon fly will probably turn over more easily with a 3X tippet than a 4X tippet, although an unweighted version may be more productive on the lighter tippet. Generally, a tippet size of .001- or .002-inch larger in diameter will not affect the performance or the effectiveness of the fly in most fishing situations.

As shown in the table above, the breaking strength of nylon monofilament tippet material can vary for the same diameter. The X-number designation is, therefore, a little nebulous and confusing. The approximate breaking strength of a tippet can be estimated by subtracting the X-number from 9. For example, a 6X tippet subtracted from 9 equals 3 pound-test, and a 3X tippet subtracted from 9 means the breaking strength of the tippet is approximately 6 pounds.

Knotless versus Compound Tapered Leaders

I prefer to tie my own compound tapered leaders roughly conforming to the 60%-20%-20% formula for the butt, midsection and tippet components respectively regardless of the overall length of the leader. The butt section is approximately two-thirds the diameter of the fly line tip section. In most cases, this thickness will be .019 to .021 inches in diameter for fly line sizes of 4- to 9-weight. A leader butt of this diameter range will bend uniformly with the fly line, and it will not cause a collapsing hinge effect, which hinders a fly from turning over properly.

I connect the leader butt to the midsection with a blood knot, because the knot is in line with the joined sections, which are absolutely straight, and it will not catch on the rod guides when glued and trimmed close. I use interlocking loops throughout my leader systems. For floating fly lines, I form a 3/8- to 1/2-inch long loop at the end of the butt section, using a Chermanski Loop knot, for connecting it to the PVC fly line loop. The loop formed at the end of the midsection segment must be large enough, 1 to 1.5 inches, to allow for the bulkiest fly intended for use to pass through it. For sinking fly lines, a Chermanski Loop knot is formed at both ends of the butt section. The loop for attaching the butt section to the PVC fly line loop is 3/8- to 1/2-inch long. The opposite end must be large enough, 1 to 1.5 inches, to allow for the bulkiest fly intended for use to pass through it. For both float-ing and sinking fly lines, one end of the tippet section is doubled using a Bimini Twist and a double-stranded loop, 3/8- to 1/2-inch long, is formed using a Chermanski Loop knot. The complete steps for building a compound, tapered leader are discussed in chapters 9 and 10.

For maximum strength, the loops should come together to form a square loop-to-loop connection. Using the connection be-tween the tippet and leader butt sections as an example, slide the tippet section loop over the leader butt loop then thread the fly through the leader butt loop and pull the sections apart to close the loops. If there is a large discrepancy between the stiffness or line diameter size of the two loops being connected, pinch the stiffer loop flat with the thumb and index finger to form a tight square knot before pulling it tight against the other loop. Thread the opposite end of the section being connected through the loop of the standing section and then pass the end back through both loops before pulling it tight. The results should be a square loop-to-loop connection as shown below. The step-by-step instructions for tying a Chermanski Loop knot at the ends of the leader butt are illustrated on pages 24-25.

With knotless tapered leaders, it is almost imperceptible to determine where to replace the tippet section along the taper. For leaders 7-1/2 and 9 feet in length, measure back 24 inches and cut the line from the end. For a 12-foot leader, cut the line about 30 inches from the end. Tie a Chermanski Loop knot at the end of the leader, which is large enough, 1 to 1.5 inches, to allow for the bulkiest fly intended for use to pass through it. The tippet section can be tied in advance of various lengths, using a Bimini Twist and a Chermanski Loop knot at one end, and interchanged as needed. The method for modifying a knotless, tapered leader to inter-change tippet sections of various lengths and sizes is discussed in Chapter 9.

Leader Selections for Trout

Leader and tippet adjustments for trout fishing are probably more diverse in scope than any other fly-fishing discipline. In ad-dition, there are a plethora of leader formulas to further confuse and complicate the simplicity of the task. Some of the principles are necessary and justified while most of them are misleading and traditional nonsense. Ironically, all of them will work to some de-gree for many different reasons, which only adds perturbation to the issue. I have learned from experience and from various men-tors over the past 50 years to keep it as simple as possible while maintaining versatility. This sage advice is especially beneficial when it pertains to leader systems.

For most trout fishing situations, a leader 7-1/2 to 12 feet leader is preferred, providing the cast is executed properly. If the fly is heavy or bulky, such as a large streamer or weighted nymph, a leader 9 feet or less may be required. If the water is turbulent, such as in a riffle or ruffled by wind or current, then a short lead-er of 7-1/2 feet may be necessary. If the water is calm and glassy, a leader 12 feet or longer may be needed to keep the splashdown

of the fly line as far away from the fly as possible. The more wary the trout and the calmer the surface of the water, the longer the leader and tippet section will be required. Equally important, the smaller the flies used, the lighter the tippet needed to permit the fly to drift in a natural manner.

Tippet adjustment is often essential to angling success both on the surface with a dry fly and for an acceptable bottom roll in nymphing. Trying to control a long leader and an extended tippet when dry-fly fishing in windy conditions can prove to be challeng-ing and often frustrating. The problem is usually not loop control or turning over the leader, it is the combination of casting accu-racy and slack in the tippet section for a long, drag-free drift. As a result, a shorter or heavier tippet section, or both adjustments, may become necessary to enhance fishing success.

Adjusting to a slightly heavier tippet is acceptable as long as a drag-free drift can be maintained. There are some residual benefits to using a heavier tippet as well. For example, a fish can be landed more quickly on a heavier tippet with less stress for the fish and less lactic acid accertion for an improved survival rate of released fish. A heavier tippet can also hold bigger fish with fewer break offs and a stronger tippet will help buffer the force of setting a hook too powerfully, which can cause a tippet to snap prematurely. Since a heavier leader and tippet section can lift a nymph, pupae or larvae imitation off the bottom and possibly above the feeding zone of a fish, the tippet section may have to be lengthened. I use and recommend Orvis Super Strong tippet material for dry-fly fishing and Orvis Mirage pure fluorocarbon for everything else.

Every fly design has a different aerodynamic profile or density. There is no standard leader for every fishing situation and different types of water may require a change in leader length as well as a modification in the length and diameter of the tippet section. It may be a 6-foot leader in tight brush or a 12-footer in open water. If the tippet section is too long or the diameter too small, or both, for a specific fly density, it will collapse and not turn over properly. Conversely, when fishing a dry fly, if the tippet section is too short or the diameter too large, or both, the tippet will straighten without the necessary soft "S" curves to assure a drag-free float.

Dry fly fishing with small flies on a calm lake or river may require a 12-foot leader tapered to a 5X, 6X or 7X tippet section. On a windy day on the same lake or river when the surface is rippled by the breeze, a 9-foot leader may be needed to better manage casting accuracy and leader turn over. The same leader length may also be necessary on a smaller mountain stream where the water is calm and the pools are short. When the surface is rippled, however, a leader shorter than 9 feet may be best. Conversely, if there is sufficient space for casting, a 12-foot leader may prove more effective for fishing emerger or nymph imitations when the surface is calm or the water is deep.

When casting heavy streamers and weighted nymphs, a longer leader can make a proper turn over and presentation a difficult and frustrating task at times. An 8- to 9-foot leader will generally perform much better in most fishing situations. When fishing for larger trout, for instance, I would recommend using the strongest tippet section possible that still permits a fly to be drifted or worked appropriately. This advice also applies to poten-tially battling larger fish in heavy cover or around submerged obstructions. In these circumstances, I use a 4X or stronger section of Orvis Mirage pure fluorocarbon tippet material and to provide three-dimensional freedom of movement to the fly, I attach the fly to the tippet using a Chermanski Loop knot.

The Heretic Approach

I thought I was flaunting with conventional wisdom and traditional thinking in the late 1950s when I started looping 30-inch tippet sections to my 9-foot trout leaders. As a pre-teenager fishing almost every weekday morning throughout most of the summer with my great-uncle Andy Cremi, I could not afford replacing entire leaders every third or fourth day. But that excuse was really secondary to my ineptness at tying knots, especially the blood knot with 6X tippet material. Throughout each day of fishing, I constantly experimented with different fly designs and sizes so it became a real struggle for me to change a tippet section multiple times a day, especially when the fish were rising.

Uncle Andy was my mentor and his patience was saintly as he calmly showed me over and over again how to tie the blood knot, my worst nemesis of fishing knots. After a few weeks of futile effort, he devised a loop system so I could pretie tippet sections in advance and change them on the water when necessary without tying the horrific blood knot. I remember asking him how the name of the knot came about and he said with a hint of sarcasm, "Because it's guys like you that make the bloody knot so hard to tie correctly".

As a young kid, I felt like a heretic among my Uncle Andy's fishing cronies, because it was taboo to fish with a knotted leader for trout. It was particularly appalling to them when someone used such a system at the mouth of clear streams feeding the coldwater lakes where we did most of our fly fishing in Pennsylvania. As a result, I concealed my sin from them and I felt guilty about using my leader system adaptation until I met Joe Boyd many years later. Joe was a crop duster by trade in Alabama, but his lifelong vocation was dedicated to fly fishing, which he preferred to do alone and in secret. He was as cantankerous and opinionated as anyone I have ever met, but he was also the best fly fisherman and fly caster I have ever known.

As a fly caster, Joe had the ability of making a perfect delivery in which the fly always landed on the water before the fly line, regardless of the casting distance or the size of the fly. He also had an amazing knack of allowing only the fly to gently touch the surface of the water with repeated false casts, mimicking the actions of an adult aquatic insect laying its eggs. I was never upset that Joe would catch more fish than me most of the time, because he had 30-plus years more experience. What really annoyed me, though, was how he did it, because his methods were seemingly

Andy Cremi

contradictory to the traditional precepts I had learned growing up on Pennsylvania trout streams. In fact, I jokingly referred to Joe as "the Heretic".

Joe only cared about two types of fly fishing: dry-fly fishing for trout and popper fishing for panfish. In fact, he preferred to fish exclusively for brook, rainbow and cutthroat trout. He viewed the other coldwater species as trash fish; more specifically dumb and predictable. His opinions were not any different for the rest of the other freshwater fish species except for panfish. For the 50 years or more, he used only two leader systems: an 8-foot leader of 4X (6 pounds) nylon monofilament for trout and an 8-foot leader of 3X (8 pounds) line for panfish. Those riggings were his entire approach to any fishing situation. When I first asked him why he used such an unorthodox method, his reply was, "it's the (action of the) fly, stupid that catches the fish".

I could not really argue with Joe, because he almost always caught more fish than me and usually the biggest fish. Out of frustration, I took him to one of the famous spring creeks in Pennsylvania with the intent of showing him the inadequacy of his fishing methods. Before I was able to setup my outfit, Joe had hooked a nice trout on his second or third cast. As I hurried down to the river to see what he had caught, Joe was netting a 22-inch brown trout.

"What'd ya catch?" I asked.

"A dang ol' brown", he recanted, "they're the dumbest fish in the water. Hope there's something else in here than these dang things."

By the end of the day, Joe had hooked and released more than 40 fish, while I only managed to catch 6 small fish. Thankfully, most of the fish he caught were rainbow trout. At times, I thought we would surely be banned for life from fishing this hallowed stream, because much to my chagrin, every time he caught a brown trout, he would manifest into a tirade of loud rants and ravings about the stupidity of this species.

"I will say this," he said after releasing his last brown trout of the day, "they are tough".

"And ya know what I always say", he continued with a smirk. "Ya gotta be tough when you're dumb?", I quipped.

"That's right, my friend, and brown trout are the toughest fish I know".

I never questioned Joe Boyd's methods again. From that experience, I just enjoyed watching "the Heretic" in amazement as he clinically dissected every type of water we fished together with his two leader systems.

Deciding What Leader to Use in Freshwater

Freshwater leaders can be divided into two major uses: trout and general freshwater. While trout generally require the use of small flies on the lightest tippets, many other freshwater species will strike larger flies such as bass, pike, muskellunge, salmon, steelhead and panfish. As previously mentioned, trout leaders generally need to render a very delicate presentation and permit the fly to drift drag-free most of the time. A heavy freshwater leader, however, is used in a different manner for a variety of species and it must be capable of turning over larger, bulkier flies. In these instances, the fly line and leader is commonly used to manipulate the fly as well.

I have always believed that a fly with three-dimensional freedom of yaw, pitch and roll movement will produce more strikes, even when it is not being retrieved. As a result, I do not use a tightly cinched knot when attaching a fly to a tippet unless the breaking strength of the tippet is 4-pounds (5X) or weaker. Instead, I use the Chermanski Loop knot. I also believe this added freedom maintains a hook at an optimum angle-of-attack for improved hook penetration.

When fishing big or weighted flies, dressed on hooks ranging in size from 8 to 2/0, for largemouth or smallmouth bass in a lake or river with clear water conditions, for example, I will use a 9-foot leader with a 6- or 10-pound tippet section. When fishing amid heavy vegetation or around fallen timber and submerged obstructions, I will typically use a slightly shorter leader with a tippet of 12 pounds to help stop a fish from reaching the abrasive cover. When fishing for steelhead or salmon, I will use a 10-foot leader tapered to 8- to 12-pound tippet section. When throwing heavy streamers or fishing in water slightly roiled or muddied, I will use a 9-foot with a 12-pound tippet section. In all of these situations, the tippet section is approximately 24 inches long.

There are many times throughout a fishing experience when changes in weather and water conditions dictate a modification in tactics, which could also include a variation in leader length or tippet length and breaking strength. As a result, it is advantageous to have the ability to quickly change and adjust a leader system. This approach is paramount to success because calm mornings often become breezy afternoons, with the wind subsiding toward sunset. In addition, the species of fish targeted initially can differ several times during a day of fishing. For these reasons, I use small interlocking loops throughout all my leader systems, which are described in Chapters 9 and 10, to adapt quickly to the ever-changing conditions often introduced throughout a day of fishing.

Deciding What Leader to Use in Saltwater

Most freshwater leader principles do not apply efficiently and effectively in many saltwater fishing applications. The conventional tapered leader is appropriate for only a few marine species in clear, shallow water fishing situations, such as bonefish, permit, snapper, snook, spotted seatrout, redfish, sheepshead and tarpon, for example. In such cases, the use of a long, tapered leader is required to present the fly delicately, with minimum splashdown of the fly line and with as long of a less visible connection as possible.

When fishing in a light to medium breeze on clear, shallow water and especially with wary quarry, a 10- to 12-foot leader may be needed. For smaller flies, I use a 6- to 12-pound tippet of fluorocarbon tied to the fly using a Chermanski Loop knot. For flies larger than 1/0, I will use a 12- or 16-pound tippet to improve the turn over of the leader. On very calm, cloudless days, however, the leader may need to be extended as much as 14 or 15 feet by lengthening only the middle and tippet sections. This latter case, however, is typically uncommon and an extremely specialized approach for most marine species found on clear, shallow flats.

In general fishing situations, the total length and taper of the leader is usually unimportant and not alarming with most

marine species. In addition, most saltwater game fish seem to care less to the size of the tippet or shock trace attached to the fly, and neither component is a significant factor affecting casting performance. As a result, a saltwater leader is considered short in freshwater terms and it is usually composed of two to four sections. The overall length of the most basic saltwater leader is typically 8 to 9 feet. The butt section is attached to the fly line with interlocking loops and it is a semi-permanent fixture, inasmuch as it need not be changed unless it is damaged. The tippet section is looped to the butt section and the optional shock trace is looped to the tippet section. The leader can be lengthened by looping a midsection between the butt and tippet sections.

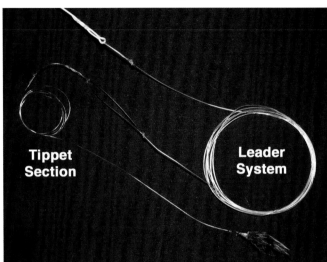

Tippet Section | Leader System

While the basic design of a general saltwater leader is relatively simple, its construction is more complex. The number and type of knots required are necessary for two reasons: to maintain maximum breaking strength in the tippet section and to allow a quick change of flies pretied to tippets and shock traces. Interchangeability of leader sections is very important and a definite asset to adapting quickly to the ever-changing conditions often introduced throughout a full day of fishing. It is achieved by preparing the desired number of tippet and shock trace combinations in advance, and affixing them to the butt section or midsection by interlocking loops as needed. The tippet and shock trace combinations not pretied to flies are coiled and stored in labeled ziplock bags or storage wallets. Consequently, no fishing time is wasted trying to tie knots hurriedly, especially when fish are actively feeding.

Protecting the tippet section and optimizing its breaking strength from the strain and other abusive forces associated with fishing in a marine environment is absolutely critical to angling success. To achieve maximum capability, an 18- to 24-inch section of tippet material is doubled at both ends using a Bimini Twist. A Chermanski Loop knot is then formed in the doubled line to connect the tippet to the leader at one end and the shock trace at the other end. If a permanent connection between the tippet and shock trace is desired, an Albright Special knot can be used. The step-by-step instructions for tying the Bimini Twist, Chermanski Loop and Albright Special are illustrated on pages 28-29, 24-25 and 32-33 respectively.

IGFA Leader Systems & Rules for World Record Pursuits

The International Game Fish Association (IGFA) has specific fly fishing rules and regulations for pursuing world records. Leaders, for example, must conform to generally accepted fly fishing customs as detailed in this book. By definition, a leader includes a class tippet and, optionally, a shock trace. A butt section of uniform diameter or multiple tapered sections, between the fly line and the class tippet, is also considered part of the leader and there are no limits on its length, material type or breaking strength.

A class tippet must be made of a nonmetallic material and either attached directly to the fly or to the shock trace if one is used. The class tippet must be at least 15 inches long, which is measured inside the connecting knots of the tippet section. With respect to knotless tapered leaders, the terminal 15 inches will also determine the tippet class. There is no maximum length limitation.

A shock trace, not to exceed 12 inches in length, may be added to the class tippet and tied to the fly. It can be made of any type of material, and there is no limit to its breaking strength. The shock trace is measured from the eye of the hook to the single strand of class tippet and includes any knots used to connect the shock trace to the class tippet. In the case of a tandem hook fly, the shock tippet shall be measured from the eye of the leading hook. A representation to the regulations pertaining to the tippet and shock trace sections is illustrated in the photo below. For complete information on the rules and regulations for fly fishing world records, contact the IGFA at 300 Gulf Stream Way, Dania Beach, Florida 33004; phone (954) 927-2628; web site: www.igfa.org.

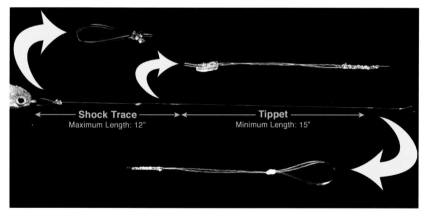

Shock Trace — Maximum Length: 12" — Tippet — Minimum Length: 15"

In addition to the shock absorption of a Bimini Twist at one or both ends of a tippet section, other precautions can be taken to safeguard a tippet from excessive strain. The most critical periods, that stress the elastic limits and breaking strength of a tippet section, occur when setting the hook, withstanding a long, fast and powerful run, and maneuvering a hooked fish the final few feet of the battle. The effort to defend against these stresses is further compounded when using an ultra light tippet, particularly in saltwater. Tippet strengths of 4 pounds or less require some specialized applications to thwart the power and speed of certain game fish from breaking the fragile connection they have with the angler.

The most damaging impact to the elasticity and breaking strength of a tippet section is the frictional forces acting upon the fly line and leader as they are pulled through the water at high speeds. Some inshore marine species found on shallow water flats, such as tarpon, bonefish, permit and sharks, for example, will usually sprint to deeper water at impressive speeds when hooked. Pelagic ocean species such as king mackerel, tuna, wahoo and billfish can easily generate speeds in excess of 40 mph. In freshwater, salmon and steelhead in large rivers can achieve formidable speeds during their frantic runs especially in strong currents. In all these cases, a tremendous amount of frictional forces are being exerted on the tippet section, which could quickly and easily exceed its breaking strength.

One solution to significantly reduce the frictional forces exerted in the water from high-speed runs or sudden bursts of velocity is to shorten the overall length of the fly line. Removing the running line from a full-length fly line, for example, will reduce the frictional resistance more than 40%. In addition, the smaller the diameter of the fly line, the less resistance it will generate traveling through the water. Consequently, using a sinking fly line with a smaller diameter than a comparable floating or intermediate density line of the same size or weight would be greatly beneficial in these extreme circumstances. In most highly specialized fishing situations of this nature, I generally use a shooting taper (ST) system and, in many instances, the overall length of the sinking shooting head (SH) is only 15 to 20 feet.

Surviving a long, high-speed run from a pelagic ocean species on a tippet strength of 2 to 6 pounds is one of the most ultimate challenges in fly fishing. The logistics alone are difficult and the entire process will test every facet of your angling skills to their fullest. In addition to reducing frictional forces, other techniques are needed to protect the elastic limits of the tippet from being exceeded. For example, 50 to 100 feet of 12- or 15-pound semi-limp nylon monofilament line can be attached with interlocking loops between a shortened fly line and the backing to enhance shock absorption. The nylon monofilament line functions analogous to a giant rubber band, stretching to absorb the frictional forces exerted against the fly line and leader traveling through the water.

When using a 2- or 4-pound class tippet in these exceptionally specialized fishing situations, providing added protection against the impact forces of a violent strike and the ensuing burst velocity from a departing hooked fish is imperative. The best approach to withstand these forces is the use of a stretchy material inserted between the tippet section and the leader to absorb sudden and accelerated shock. I call this section in a leader system the elasticity cord (EC). There are various materials that can provide this added elasticity. The key elements to choosing a material to serve as an elasticity cord (EC) is it must be rubbery in flexibility and stretches easily from a slight pulling force.

I have used various products as an elasticity cord (EC) with most of them obtained from craft stores. With the most fragile tippet sizes, 2 pounds or less in breaking strength, I use a clear, stretchy bead cord called Elasticity. For 2- and 4-pound tippets, I use a product marketed by Rio Products called Powerflex Shock Gum. It is available in two degrees of elasticity at 9- and 15-pound breaking strengths. The resiliency of the 9-pound strength is best suited for 2- and 4-pound tippet sections while the stronger material can be used with 6- and 8-pound class tippets. For 4- and 6-pound tippets, I also use a product with a hollow center called Loopie Cord, which is sold at most craft stores.

The specific use of an elasticity cord (EC) section in a leader system is applied as an option to Type P and Q leader systems, which are designed specifically for IGFA world record pursuits. These leader systems are discussed and illustrated in Chapter 10. The following instructions will build an elasticity cord (EC) for placement between the leader and tippet section of these leader systems.

Step 1: Starting about 4 to 6 inches from the tag end of the elasticity cord (EC), tie a 4- or 5-turn nail knot using 30-pound nylon monofilament. Pull the wraps snug, but do not cinch them tight so the shock gum is able to slide through the nail knot. Be careful to wrap the nylon monofilament firmly to avoid any overlap. The closer the wraps are made to each other, the easier it will be to tighten them evenly. The step-by-step instructions for tying the Nail knot are illustrated on pages 22-23.

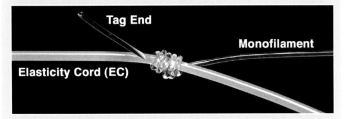

Step 2: With the tag end of the elasticity cord (EC), tie a 4- or 5-turn nail knot on the standing part of the 30-pound nylon monofilament. Pull the wraps snug, but do not cinch them tight so the nylon monofilament is able to slide through the nail knot. Be careful to wrap the EC firmly to avoid any overlap. The closer the wraps are made to each other, the easier it will be to tighten them evenly.

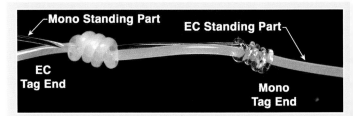

Step 3: Lubricate the knots and both lines between the knots. Pull the standing parts of the elasticity cord (EC) and nylon monofilament lines in opposite directions, cinching the two nail knots tightly together. Pull the tag end and standing part of each nail knot separately to tighten the wraps if needed. Trim the tag ends of the EC and nylon monofilament, leaving about a 1/16-inch excess.

Step 4: Perform Steps 1 to 3 on the opposite end of the elasticity cord (EC), creating a section about 10 to 12 inches between the two sets of nail knots.

Step 5: At one end of the elasticity cord (EC) section, about 1/2- to 3/4-inch from the nail knots, form a loop between 1 to 1-1/2 inches long in the 30-pound nylon monofilament using the Chermanski Loop knot. The tippet, optional shock trace and fly should be connected to this end of the EC section by interlocking loops. The step-by-step instructions for tying the Chermanski Loop knot are illustrated on pages 24-25.

Step 6: At the opposite end of the elasticity cord (EC) section, tie a loop as small as possible (3/8- to 1/2-inch long), about 1 inch from the nail knots, using the Chermanski Loop knot. This end of the EC section connects to the leader by interlocking loops.

Building Specialized IGFA Class Tippets

It has been suggested that originality demands a degree of lunacy. There is a fine line between obsession and lunacy as it applies to pursuing some fly fishing world records. Not all world records are equal in their degree of difficulty. Subduing a 2-pound fish on a 12-pound class tippet, for example, is not exactly the most challenging or Herculean angling feat unless the angler is an adolescent, at least chronologically. Pursuing a fish whose weight is many times more than the breaking strength of the tippet, however, is a completely different test of angling prowess. For these special pursuits, every conceivable possibility imaginative to reduce the degree of difficulty and to ensure success is extremely desirable.

In addition to a carefully planned strategy, the detailed

preparations to challenging certain world records can be vitally critical to success. The endeavor becomes progressively more difficult as the breaking strength of the class tippet is decreased. The crucial importance in the subtle details pertaining to tying knots, rigging preparations and fish-fighting techniques can reach critical mass when using 2- to 6-pound class tippets to subdue large, powerful game fish. Regardless of its breaking strength, protecting the tippet section from shock and impact forces is absolutely paramount with no margin for error. To ensure the maximum amount of shock absorption in the lightest tippet sections, I prepare my 2- to 6-pound IGFA class tippet sections in the following manner. I use and highly recommend Orvis IGFA-rated Mirage pure fluorocarbon tippet material for any world record pursuit.

Step 1: If a shock trace is to be used, tie a Bimini Twist at each end of the tippet material about 18 to 24 inches apart; otherwise tie a Bimini Twist at the tag end of the tippet material. The photo on the right shows a Bimini Twist tied in a 2-pound class tippet. The step-by-step instructions for tying the Bimini Twist are illustrated on pages 28-29.

Step 2: Form a small loop about 3/8- to 1/2-inch long in a piece of 20-pound Mirage pure fluorocarbon tippet material using the Chermanski Loop knot. If a shock trace is to be used, form a second, smaller loop about 1/4- to 3/8-inch long in a second piece of 20-pound line. The step-by-step instructions for tying the Chermanski Loop knot are illustrated on pages 24-25.

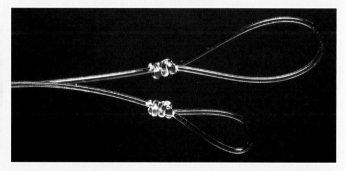

Step 3: Using the Albright Special knot, tie one end of the tippet section to the standing part of the larger loop about 1/2- to 3/4-inch from the Chermanski Loop knot. The step-by-step instructions for tying the Albright Special knot are illustrated on pages 32-33. The loop at the end of the tippet section is interlocked with either the loop at the end of an elasticity cord (EC) section, if one is used, or the main leader.

Step 4: If a shock trace is to be used, attach the other end of the tippet section to the standing part of the smaller loop using the Albright Special knot. The loop at the end of the tippet section is interlocked with the loop at the end of the shock trace. Tie this knot on the standing part as close as possible to the Bimini Twist and Chermanski Loop knot, because IGFA rules dictate the overall length between the Bimini Twist and the eye of the hook can not exceed 12 inches.

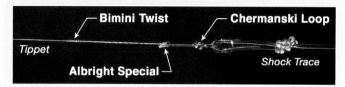

Stretching a Leader & Tippet

When a fly outfit is rigged but temporarily not in use, it is helpful to keep the leader stored in a relatively straight configuration. If the leader is longer than the length of the fly rod, it should be stored outside the rod tip by winding the leader around the perimeter of the reel and securing the fly on one of the rod guides as illustrated in the photo below. If the straightness of the leader

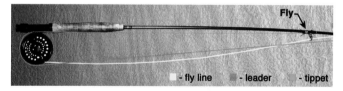

is not maintained properly, its stiff butt section will develop a memory set from being bent acutely around the wire frame of the tiptop guide, which can be difficult to remove. Conversely, when using a leader slightly shorter than the length of the fly rod and there is no hook keeper above the cork grip, secure the fly with a rubber band or an elastic hair band that is placed around the reel seat as shown below. The leader, which is secured entirely outside the tiptop guide, will remain absolutely straight under the slight tension of the elastic material.

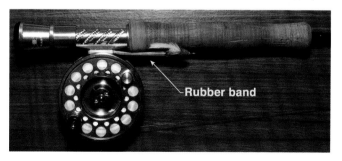

The best method to straighten the butt section and midsection of a leader system is to slowly pull the leader from a fixed object. Pictured in the photo on page 80 is a simple tool I built, which I call the Leader Stretcher, to straighten a leader system. It is basically a small, rectangular block of wood, 1/2 to 3/4 inches thick, with an open eye screw secured on the top and near one end of the wooden block. Any size of an open eye screw will work, but I would recommend using a heavier gauge model. I have a leader stretcher for use on my boat, another one for use at home and a third one stored in a travel bag.

Leader Stretcher

Stretching a leader before use is the first task I perform after an outfit has been assembled. The leader stretcher is quick and easy to use. Prior to interlocking a tippet section to a leader, I hook the leader butt or midsection loop to the open eye screw, step on the block of wood, grip the leader at the PVC fly line loop and slowly pull it vertically above my head as demonstrated in the photo on the right. I hold the stretched leader taut for about 5 seconds before releasing the tension. If a tippet is already attached to the leader, I still secure the leader butt or midsection loop to the open eye screw, stretching this leader section without affecting the tippet section.

The best method to straighten a coiled or twisted tippet section is to pull it slowly and steadily through two pieces of soft rubber once or twice until it is straight as shown in the photo below. Pulling the entire tippet through the line straightener is the prescribed approach. It takes only a few seconds to straighten a leader or tippet, but it often provides an increase in both casting and fishing performance.

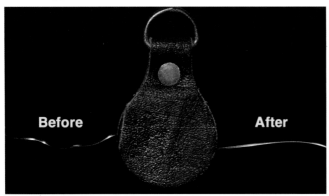

Before   After

Storage Systems for Pre-Rigged Flies

Having boxes setup with flies pre-tied to tippet or shock trace sections is a quick, easy and dependable way of spending more time fishing and less time tying knots. Although there are a plethora of boxes on the market for storing flies, there are virtually no models available that are designed for storing flies pre-tied to tippet sections. The only exception is the specialty boxes designed for keeping the shock traces straight on larger saltwater flies. There are simply no boxes available commercially where flies pre-tied directly to tippet sections can be stored. Consequently, I have had to build boxes of various sizes to meet my requirements or modify existing ones. It is actually a relatively simple procedure to modify an existing box to store flies pre-tied to tippet sections. For a given fishing situation, I generally carry at least two sets of the same box size with one box arranged with loose flies and the other box configured with flies pre-tied to tippet sections. In most cases with commercially available boxes, the same type and size can be used for freshwater, brackish water and marine species.

I use three different sets of box configurations for storing pre-rigged flies: commercially available plastic boxes modified for storing flies pre-tied to tippet sections, commercially available compartmental plastic boxes for storing flies pre-tied to shock traces and homemade boxes for storing flies pre-tied to tippet and shock trace sections. For flies not requiring a shock trace, which can be tied directly to the tippet section, I use commercially available plastic boxes ranging in three popular sizes approximately 4.25"(L) x 3"(W) x 1"(H), 5.75"(L) x 3.75"(W) x 1.25"(H) and 8.25"(L) x 4.5"(W) x 1.25"(H). I prefer the models that feature the rippled foam on the interior bottom half and the flat foam on the interior top half of the box.

To modify one of these commercially available plastic boxes for flies pre-tied to tippet sections, I cut one of the rippled foam strips flat from the bottom portion of the box and secure a 3/8-inch square piece of open-cell rubber-based foam. The foam strip is pre-slotted partially to hold a tippet section securely in position and it is bonded to the foam liner with a cement such as Goop, Aquaseal, marine silicone or similar products. The pre-slotted strip is about a 1/4-inch longer than the width of the box to create a compressive grip on each tippet strand. In the top portion of the box, I cement a block of closed-cell packing foam, which keeps the coiled tippet sections from tangling when the box is closed. Finally, I label it with a permanent, waterproof marking pen on the lid and on one of the narrow sides for identification. The smallest-sized box will hold 7 to 12 flies and the two larger sizes will store 9 to 18 flies, depending upon their length and bulk, which is usually a sufficient quantity for a full day of fishing.

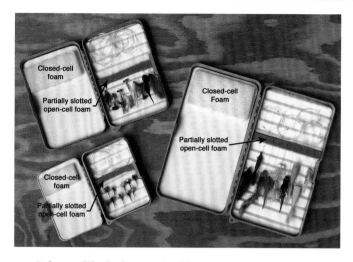

permit, striped bass, redfish, etc. The key feature to using these modified boxes is the fast, easy and reliable interchangeability of flies without the need to tie a knot. The valued importance of this system is fully appreciated and understood especially when the fish activity increases or a hastily tied knot results in a lost fish. This system of pre-rigged flies does not preclude the need to ever tie a knot in the field. It merely minimizes the need in most cases so more time can be spent enjoying the actual fishing experience.

I also modify the largest-sized box to accommodate flies dressed on inverted or keel-type hooks and pre-tied to tippet sections. In addition to the 3/8-inch square piece of open-cell rubber-based foam to hold the tippet sections in place, a second partially slotted foam strip is cemented in the bottom portion of the box about 1.75 inches from the first strip. This second strip is secured to the bottom portion of the box with a cement such as Goop, Aquaseal, marine silicone or similar products after the rippled foam is removed. Both pre-slotted strips are about a 1/4-inch longer than the width of the box to create a compressive grip on each tippet strand and fly. A block of closed-cell packing is glued to the top half of the box to prevent the coiled tippet sections from tangling when the box is closed. This box is designed to hold 7 flies, regardless of their bulk, to an overall length of 4.5 inches.

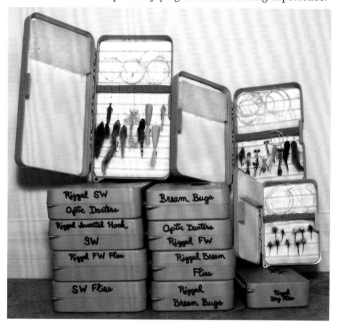

Storing Saltwater Flies

Because certain fish species require the use of a shock trace to protect the tippet from being abraded or cut, I use a second set of commercially available plastic boxes for storing flies pre-tied to shock traces. The two sizes of boxes I use are about 14" (L) x 8.75" (W) x 1.75" (H) and 10.75" (L) x 7" (W) x 1.5" (H). I selected these sizes and design for a number of reasons. Both boxes will accommodate a shock trace with an overall length of 9 inches relative to the size flies stored in them, which is the standard length I use excluding the connecting knots. A shock trace is attached to a fly at one end and a small loop is formed at the other end for interconnecting with the loop at the end of the tippet section. In essence, I can replace an abraded shock trace or mangled fly without the need for rigging a new shock trace or changing the tippet section. This method of interchanging tippet and shock trace sections is discussed in detail for Type D, G and J leader systems in Chapter 9 and for a Type Q leader system in Chapter 10.

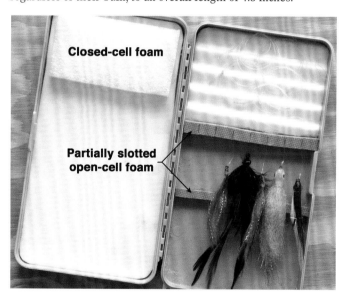

Storing Freshwater Flies

This set of modified commercially available plastic boxes is used as part of my standard equipment and taken on most freshwater and many saltwater fishing adventures along with a box of similar dimensions containing loose flies. These modified boxes and their sizes used are dedicated primarily to certain fish species or specific fishing situations in both freshwater and saltwater. A representation of some of the modified boxes I use is shown in the photo on the top right. Some of the other modified boxes are more specific to a fish species, such as carp, bonefish, trophy-sized trout,

Although these boxes are used primarily for storing pre-rigged flies for saltwater applications, I do have a box containing pre-rigged fly patterns dedicated for freshwater species such as muskellunge, pike and pickerel. The larger box has 4 compartments capable of holding 36 to 48 flies and the smaller box has 3 compartments for efficiently storing 24 to 48 flies, depending upon their length and bulk. Both boxes have adjustable dividers to minimize movement of the flies and their shock traces during transport.

Another important feature of these boxes is their semi-transparency, which allows the contents of each box to be viewed from all sides. As a result, multiple boxes can be stacked together for a given fishing trip and transported as a single unit. To achieve this purpose, as shown in the bottom right photo on page 81, strips of velcro hook material have been secured to the corners on the top of each lid and strips of velcro loop material have been fixed to the corners on the bottom of each box. In addition, any box in the cluster can be opened independently without detaching the boxes.

The third type and oldest form of storage system involves the use of homemade boxes for flies pre-tied to tippet and shock trace sections. There are some commercial products on the market, however, but they are expensive and limited in their applied use and capacity. Since the late 1970s, I have been making my own boxes, initially from 1/4-inch marine A/B grade plywood and, in the past 15 years, from high-impact ABS plastic attache-type cases, as shown in the photo to the right. The boxes are designed to keep the shock trace straight with the tippet section already attached. The models I build can handle a shock trace of any length to about 16 inches if desired and, over the years, I have customized boxes in various sizes for specific fish species or fishing situations, such as inshore, offshore, billfish, tarpon, grouper, etc.

The last two generations of wooden boxes I built measure about 18" (L) x 13.25" (W) x 3.25" (H) with a capacity of storing 36 pre-rigged flies. Some boxes also featured a removable foam platform for storing loose "backup" flies. More recently, I have switched to using plastic attache-type cases, as shown in the photo at the top right, because they are lighter, cheaper and less labor-intensive in building. These boxes will hold 32 pre-rigged flies and they measure approximately 18" (L) x 13.5" (W) x 4" (H). Both box designs use an open-cell rubber-based foam, which is partially slotted to hold the shock trace and tippet sections in position. The pre-rigged flies stored in this box design are compatible with the Type C, F and I leader systems discussed and illustrated in Chapter 9.

Chapter 7

Nylon Monofilament as a Leader & Tippet Material

In 1938, DuPont invented nylon and in 1939, they began marketing nylon monofilament fishing lines. In 1959, they introduced Stren, a thinner monofilament line that could be used with the newly introduced spinning and spin casting tackle. Modern fishing lines are almost entirely made from artificial substances, including nylon, polyethylene, Dacron and Dyneema (UHM-WPE). The most common type is monofilament that is made of a single strand. Recently, other alternatives to standard nylon monofilament lines have been introduced and they are made of copolymers or fluorocarbon, or a combination of the two materials. Fluorocarbon, in particular, is well regarded for its refractive index, which is similar to the refractive property of water and, as a result, it is less visible to fish. There are also cofilament and fused lines, also known as "super lines" for their small diameter, lack of stretch, and great strength relative to standard nylon monofilament lines.

Mono is a word meaning single. In terms of fishing line, the definition translates to meaning a single strand of line, and in sport fishing terms, it has become known generically as nylon fishing line. Nylon monofilament line is a single-component product formed through an extrusion process in which polyamide (nylon) pellets are liquefied in an extruder and subsequently pressed through a die under high pressure. After cooling in a water bath, the strands are expanded by a multiple of their length until they are stretched to their final diameter. Depending upon line quality, the strands receive special coatings in different immersion baths for surface hardness and UV resistance, for example. It is a polymetric byproduct of crude oil processing. Premium grade nylon monofilament line is more costly, because it is subjected to more additives, additional finishing processes and increased quality control in its manufacture, which results in better overall performance than standard nylon monofilament line.

Nylon monofilament is popular as a leader and tippet material because of its low memory and suppleness, which also makes it easy to handle. Furthermore, it boasts excellent knot strength and abrasion resistance. Nylon monofilament has an inherent stretch that makes it forgiving when subjected to sudden strain. But stretch can also be perceived as a disadvantage, since it may reduce the sensitivity needed to detect subtle strikes or limit the ability to set the hook solidly in certain situations. In addition, nylon monofilament absorbs water, and it can lose as much as 15% of its rated breaking strength when saturated. Lastly, it weakens considerably under repeated exposure to the ultraviolet (UV) rays of the sun.

There are only a handful of companies worldwide that actually manufacture nylon monofilament fishing line. Because of the standardized procedure in extruding nylon material into line, most manufacturers produce a fishing line that offers similar performance benefits. As a result, it is often difficult to distinguish between various lines because of their similarities. And even though a manufacturer can claim its product contains some or all of the same properties of a competitor, there is really no way of knowing how these properties have been balanced or how they will affect performance without testing a line in actual fishing conditions.

Types of Nylon Monofilament Leader & Tippet Materials

A leader system is arguably the single most important equipment item in fly fishing, and its weakest component, the tippet section, is the most vulnerable. A leader performs a key role in presenting a fly, in hooking a fish and in landing it. As a result, choosing the right material for each of its major components is essential, because it can significantly affect fishing success as well as the principal enjoyment of the overall fishing experience. Every angler must rely on the unique properties and characteristics of the selected leader and tippet materials to achieve the desired results. All of the properties associated with these lines affect their performance such as hardness or stiffness, breaking strength, stretch, tensile strength, elastic limits, knot strength, uniformity, abrasion resistance and color. Yet it is not surprising that varying fishing conditions subject these lines to different demands. The following 10 topics examine these attributes individually as they relate to specific fishing situations.

Stiffness of Nylon Monofilament

Nylon monofilament line is manufactured in specific grades of hardness, from very stiff to exceedingly limp. Except as a tippet material in some fishing situations, limp nylon monofilament is the poorest choice as a leader material for the remaining sections. In addition, the internal wraps comprising a knot tend to slip under moderate pressure, rendering it susceptible to failure. Stiff nylon monofilament, conversely, is more difficult to tie properly since it resists being drawn tight. It may not slip as easily or quickly as limp nylon monofilament, but its stiffness encourages slippage under extreme pressure, which can also result in knot failure.

In mechanical engineering terms, the bending stiffness of leader and tippet materials will vary according to a relationship that increases the diameter of the line to the fourth power. As an example, a 1X leader with a diameter of 0.010 inches is 16 times stiffer than a 6X leader with a diameter of 0.005 inches. The 1X leader is twice as big; therefore raising the factor 2 to the fourth power is 16. Another interesting comparison applies to the Chameleon and Ultragreen lines marketed by Maxima. On average, all Maxima leader materials are about 20% stiffer than the other comparable nylon monofilament materials I have tested. The conventional wisdom promoted by marketing leads the consumer to believe erroneously that Chameleon is stiffer than Ultragreen. It is simply not true, based upon my research and laboratory experimentation. Both nylon monofilament lines are essentially the same in stiffness although I prefer to use the Ultragreen line as a leader material.

When building leader systems, it is important to understand the relationship between the diameter of a line and its relative stiffness. Increasing the inherent stiffness of the material by 10% increases the leader stiffness by 10%. Increasing the diameter by 10% increases the leader stiffness by nearly 50%. The difference in stiffness or flexibility between a 4X tippet and a 6X tippet is nearly 4 times. A 5X tippet is about 5 times stiffer than a 7X tippet, but it is only 2 times stiffer than a 6X tippet of the same line grade.

At the conclusion of the forward cast, a leader butt section that is too limp will not transfer sufficient kinetic energy forward through the leader to properly present the fly. A fly line and leader deliver the fly to the target by unrolling, which starts at the rod tip and continues to unroll until the leader straightens. A stiff leader butt section does not unroll as easily as a softer one and it actually impedes the unrolling process. The solution is to use a butt section with a mass, or a large diameter, that has a medium-stiff hardness.

Medium-stiff nylon monofilament line is also the best choice for the leader midsection and shock trace portions of a leader system. It will turn over a fly more efficiently and, as a shock trace, it does not abrade as quickly as harder nylon monofilament. Also, medium-stiff nylon monofilament can be stretched straight more easily. I incorporate both semi-limp and medium-stiff nylon monofilament lines in a leader system. For the construction of a leader system, I use the Mirage pure fluorocarbon and medium-stiff Ultragreen nylon monofilament lines sold by Orvis and Maxima respectively. For the construction of a tippet section, I use the semi-limp nylon and fluorocarbon monofilament lines marketed by Orvis. I do not make leaders entirely of stiff or hard nylon monofilament, as the sections are too stiff and not in character with the casting characteristics of a fly line.

Breaking Strength of Nylon Monofilament

Nylon monofilament lines are sold by their breaking strength, but that is not the actual breaking strength of the line in most cases. Nationally known brands usually break above the rating on the packaging. The label designation for premium nylon monofilament lines is based on wet strength rather than dry strength, because all nylon monofilament lines lose their strength when they are immersed in water. Depending on the brand, some lines will be 10% weaker or more. Based on this fact, some manufacturers underrate their lines. They market them in a larger diameter and stronger breaking strength with a label designating the line as a lower pound-test rating than it really is. Underrated lines typically have larger diameters and excessive stiffness.

When a manufacturer states on the packaging a particular nylon monofilament line tests at 12 pounds, this disclosure usually means the line will not test less than 12 pounds. It may, in fact, test considerably higher. For example, Mason 12-pound hard nylon monofilament has been known to test as high as 15 pounds. The use of underrated tippet material is normally not a problem unless the intention is to pursue an IGFA world record in one of the seven class tippet categories. The solution to this problem is to purchase a tippet material that the manufacturer guarantees to be rated for submittals of potential IGFA world record catches.

Stretch in Nylon Monofilament

The stretch in the tippet and leader is a very important factor contributing to fishing success. The two most critical times the breaking strength of a tippet is tested occurs when a retrieved fly is explosively attacked in a surging assault and when a hooked fish is accelerating rapidly away from the angler in a frenzied run. Under these situations, the strength of the tippet and its ability to stretch are technically synonymous. The stretch serves as a shock absorber to keep the line from breaking, but once it is stretched to its elastic limit, the line will break.

Nylon monofilament line can be stretched repeatedly below the upper limits of its breaking strength without harm. Premium nylon monofilament line will stretch 20% to 30% or more before breaking. In fact, it is amazing how much slow, steady pressure can be exerted on a large fish with a relatively light tippet. Too much stretch in a line, however, can make it difficult to detect subtle strikes or to set the hook on a strike. Conversely, a tippet section with very little stretch has its disadvantages as well. This type of line may have a high breaking strength compared to its diameter, but it will lack shock absorption and be brittle. A good premium nylon monofilament line should have a proper balance of strength and stretch, with neither property being exaggerated. When one property is increased to the extreme, problems will usually occur.

To emphasize the amount of elasticity in nylon monofilament line and the aggregate of applied pressure a line can actually withstand, consider the challenge of hooking and landing a 29.2-pound Greater Amberjack (Seriola dumerili) on a 4-pound class tippet. Although the fish was teased to the surface and hooked a few feet below the surface, I was fishing in 50 feet of water in an area populated with rock formations jutting upwards to within 25 feet of the surface. In addition, this species is known for its relentless power and strong surges to the bottom or to nearby structure, so a special strategy and fish-fighting techniques were devised.

When the fish struck, I raised the rod tip at a slight angle momentarily and then dropped it almost immediately to create slack in the line. There is no margin for a sudden shock with a 4-pound class tippet from a powerful quarry, especially at such close striking range. If the fly has that magic ingredient, which I believe my fly designs possess, the fish will suck it in quickly and forcefully,

so setting the hook is actually not necessary. As I had anticipated, the hooked fish simply swam away at a moderate cruising speed. It felt no pressure or wild rod-bending pulls, just the hook in its mouth, which did not seem to bother it.

When the fish finally realized it was hooked, it made a really powerful surge to the bottom. I pointed the rod at the fish to prevent friction building up at the rod guides and I let the fish go. My playing strategy was to get the initial wildness out of the fish before it realized it was in real trouble. I wanted to keep the fish moving, expending energy. It is the combination of the reel drag, rod action and the amount of pressure you can safely put on a tippet that will eventually wear a fish down. My biggest concern was to prevent the fish from getting too much line out. If you get a large amount of line following the fish, just the cumulative resistance of the line running across the rod guides and through the water can easily break a fragile 4-pound class tippet. It was, therefore, critical to stay as close to the fish as possible at all times. Every time the fish would surge to the bottom, I partially submerged the tip section of the rod, pointed it at the fish and simply let the fish go wherever it wanted.

To bring the fish back to the surface, I utilized a technique I developed in the early 1970s, which has worked on all the really stubborn amberjack I have caught in the past. When I was able to lead the fish off its swimming course, I would instruct my son, Captain Willie, to move the boat directly ahead of the fish a few yards, then turn the boat perpendicular to the direction the fish was swimming and circle back parallel to the fish. This maneuver, which I call "walking the fish up the stairs", created a large bow in the line that angled down to the fish. The slight but constant pressure would lead the fish slowly up the water column. As the fish neared the surface, Captain Willie would run the boat directly to the fish as I retrieved the slack line. We repeated this process numerous times to keep the fish expending a lot of energy surging through the changing pressures in the entire water column.

During the nearly two-hour grueling battle, I kept the partially submerged rod tip pointed at the fish and the drag setting on the fly reel was preset to one pound. I fish with minimal mechanical drag because I have to vary the drag pressure constantly during an anticipated long fight. The overall maximum pressure I applied did not exceed 2.5 pounds, which was rendered with either finger pressure on the reel spool, palm pressure on the spool rim or slightly raising the angle of the fly rod. As a result, maintaining slow, steady and constant pressure on the fish was the key to success, because this technique utilizes the elasticity of a leader system, particularly the tippet section, without exceeding the breaking limit of the tippet. It is amazing how much pulling force can be generated effectively when it is applied smoothly and steadily.

Tensile Strength of Nylon Monofilament

Tensile strength is the common denominator used for comparing and measuring the strength of nylon monofilament lines against other types of materials, such as braided Dacron, solid wire, braided wire or copolymer super lines. Expressed in pounds per square inch (psi), tensile strength is the breaking strength of a line in pounds divided by the cross-sectional area in inches.

Premium quality nylon monofilament lines typically have a tensile strength about 100,000 psi. The smaller the line diameter, of course, the less force is required to break it. A nylon monofilament line with a diameter of 0.008 inches, for example, would be probably labeled as 6 pounds with a tensile strength of about 119,000 psi, but its actual breaking strength would be approximately 5.02 pounds. Inversely, a nylon monofilament line with a breaking strength of 12 pounds would be approximately 0.013 inches in diameter. The actual breaking strength would be about 13.2 pounds with a tensile strength of about 100,000 psi.

With regard to light tippet material, for example, 5X Maxima Chameleon measures 0.0075 inches in diameter while 5X Orvis Super Strong is 0.0061 inches in diameter. Both have similar breaking strengths of about 5 pounds, but the Maxima tippet material is almost three times as stiff. Conversely, the Maxima line has a tensile strength of 90,541 psi compared to the Orvis line of 136,869 psi. In comparison to other types of fishing lines, #3 solid wire, for example, has a breaking strength of 32 pounds, and a diameter of .012 inches. Its tensile strength is 282,935 psi. Spectra, one of the new copolymer super lines, has an incredible tensile strength of about 315,000 psi for a breaking strength of 30 pounds and a diameter comparable to 12-pound nylon monofilament line.

Elastic Limits of Nylon Monofilament

During a hard-fought battle with a powerful fish, the nylon monofilament leader, particularly the tippet section, will be subjected to the forces of stress and strain. In simple terms, stress is the breaking strength of the line measured in pounds and strain is the stretch or elongation of the line. When nylon monofilament line is initially pulled, all the force or stress is used to stretch the line. The total elongation of nylon monofilament ranges generally from 20% to 30% for medium-stiff to semi-limp grades.

In fighting a fish, the initial elongation of nylon monofilament serves as a safety buffer to the forces in setting the hook. For this reason, it is essential the barb and point of a hook are honed razor sharp as shown in the photo below. Once the initial stretch has been achieved, however, there is an immediate transfer of stress to the line, particularly the tippet section. The more force exerted on it, the more it continues to strain. When the tension is relaxed, the line recovers and the stress is again zero. These are the elastic limits of a line and, as long as these limits are not exceeded in holding and fighting a fish, there will be no damage or failure to the line. If the elastic limits are exceeded, however, permanent deformation will occur in which the molecules in the line will be displaced. The line will be irrevocably weakened and it must be replaced.

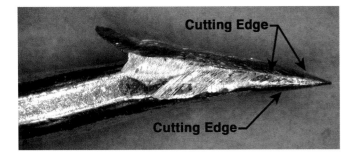

Cutting Edge

Cutting Edge

Impact Strength of Nylon Monofilament

Exceeding the elastic limits with a steady pull is one way to break a line, but impact force is another factor, occurring more frequently than most anglers realize. Impact resistance or the ability to withstand shock is termed as strain rate and it is defined as a percentage of how fast a load is being applied on the line. The standard laboratory test is to stretch a 12-inch line sample at the rate of 12 inches per minute. The strain rate in this case is 100% (the quotient of 12 divided by 12 multiplied by 100).

Under actual fishing conditions, however, the strain rate can be tremendous and the impact strength can be considerable. For example, a Little Tunny (Euthynnus alletteratus) can swim at a burst speed of at least 14 miles per hour or 20.5 feet per second, such as the one being held by my wife, Carol, in the photo below. If the fish was hooked on a 9-foot leader featuring a 24-inch tippet and it swam directly away from the angler at its burst speed, the strain rate would be slightly more than 600%, including the strain rate for the fly line and its backing. With a fish moving that swiftly for even a short distance, it only takes about a half-second for it to stretch the line and break it. More accurately, the actual time is 0.57 seconds in less than 100 feet of travel when considering 30% stretch in the 9-foot leader and 10% stretch in the fly line. That does not give an unprepared angler much reaction time to compensate for the impact.

Carol Chermanski

Consider another example when a three-pound largemouth bass lunges for a popping bug at its burst velocity and then immediately dives for cover in a surge of power away from the angler. The fish may be moving at a speed in excess of 1,000 feet per minute or 16.6 feet per second while the flyrod is sharply swinging from the horizontal to the vertical position in an attempt to set the hook. The strain rate is astonishing and the impact strength of the knots and each section of the leader definitely becomes a major consideration, especially when using a very light tippet.

In my opinion the ultimate challenge to withstand the strain rate and impact strength imposed by a fish is exemplified by my catch of a 8.8-pound King Mackerel (Scomberomorous cavalla), which is shown on the next page. The fish was landed on a 2-pound class tippet after being played for 2 hours and 5 minutes. The obvious difficulty of this task was compounded by the fact this streamlined marine species is one of the fastest swimming and swiftest striking fish in the ocean.

The biggest problem with using a 2-pound class tippet is teaching yourself not to set the hook. There is no margin for any sudden shock. When the fish struck, I raised the rod tip at a slight angle momentarily and then dropped it almost immediately to create slack in the line. I did not apply any added force to set the hook, because it is nearly impossible to set the hook on a speedster like a kingfish without breaking a 2-pound class tippet instantly. I simply allowed the fish to hook itself on the strike.

When the fish realized it was hooked, it reacted with a long, sizzling run. All I could do is point the rod at the fish to prevent frictional buildup along the rod guides and simply let the fish run with minimal resistance. I essentially employed the same slack-line, fish-fighting techniques I used to successfully capture the amberjack previously mentioned in this chapter. Slack is not the demon danger it is reputed to be when a fish is being played on fly tackle, because neither the fly nor the hook have any appreciable weight. The fly can not be shaken free by the fish or rubbed off if it is on the inside of its mouth. The fly will only fall out if there has been so much hard pulling by the angler that it has worn a hole big enough for the hook to slide back out. It is something that rarely occurs until late in a fight and where hard, sudden pressures have been used, which is not possible with a 2-pound class tippet.

There were times during the fight when it was impossible to give slack line to the fish, however. Every time the fish sped off, there was not a whole lot of fish-fighting tactics I could apply with a fast and powerful fish on a fragile tippet. It is mostly a matter of letting the fish go where it wants. I did my best to make certain the line did not touch any debris in the water. Even a thin clump of sargassum weed can break a 2-pound class tippet instantly.

Seeing no bend in my rod for more than an hour, my son, Captain Willie, finally asked, "Do you think it is still hooked?"

"Why don't you swim out and take a look", I suggested, "how in the hell should I know?"

How does anyone know? You really do not know except in bait fishing where there is some degree of certainty the bait has been swallowed and the hook has been lodged deep in the throat.

Whenever the fish ran, I fingered the spool just enough to prevent line from overrunning on the reel. Each time a run stopped, I raised the rod tip slightly and tried to encourage the fish to come my way by leading it within the elastic limit of the tippet. If the fish surged away, I released the line instantly and pointed the rod tip at the fish. Whenever I was able to retrieve any line, the large arbor Vortex reel allowed me to retrieve it as

fast as possible. This procedure leaves a wider margin for error, since the drag builds as the amount of line on a spool decreases. In essence, it is the combination of applying constant pressure, no matter how slight, keeping the fish moving and changing the direction of the force as much as possible that will eventually wear a fish down on a light class tippet. Knowing the elastic and breaking strength limits of the tippet is absolutely critical to success in these specialized situations.

The stretch in a nylon monofilament leader helps to absorb the impact of the strike, during the setting of the hook and any final surge at the end of the fight. The flexibly of a flyrod also acts as a buffer to absorb the shock. As an added precaution with some of my leader systems, I double the strands at one end of the tippet using the Bimini Twist. I then tie a double-stranded loop using the Chermanski Loop knot as shown in the photo below. With other leader systems utilizing a shock trace, both ends of the tippet are doubled with loops so that the connection between the fragile tippet and shock trace is strong, reliable and quick to replace. These techniques enhance the ability of a tippet section to withstand the sudden shock from a violent impact with a powerful quarry. As discussed in Chapter 6, I will also use an elasticity cord (EC) connected between the leader and tippet sections in extreme and specialized angling pursuits.

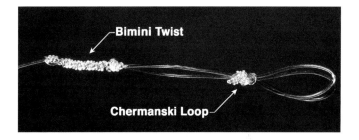

Knot Strength of Nylon Monofilament

Knot strength poses a more complex problem than breaking strength or impact strength, because there are more variables involved affecting this important property of a nylon monofilament line. For example, there are tippet materials featuring excessive stretch or extreme limpness coupled with excellent knot strength, yet both of these lines perform poorly under most fishing conditions. Getting maximum knot strength begins with the brand of line used and ends with the kind of knot tied in it. Even a premium quality line with the right balance of properties can be severely damaged by an improperly tied knot. Learning to tie a consistently strong knot is time well invested, because the dividends will be realized on the water with improved fishing success.

Some caution should be exercised when applied to knot strength, because the relevance of this property can be misleading. The most critical factor in determining knot strength is its breaking strength when submersed in water. Nylon monofilament absorbs a small amount of water and this absorption actually strengthens it. Dry tests for ascertaining knot strength, which were not submerged in water prior to testing, do not represent accurate results. Consequently, a knot should be tested only after it has been well lubricated. Remember, a knot will not fail until its turns or wraps start to slip internally. This photo was taken with a digital microscope at a magnifying power of 25 times the normal size of a blood knot. The wraps of the larger diameter line on the left were not cinched as tightly as the wraps of the smaller diameter line on the right. The telltale sign of internal slippage and subsequent knot failure is manifested by the small coil or curlicue, indicated by the two arrows on the right, where the breakage occurred. In addition, the arrow on the far left shows where frictional heat scored the smaller diameter line when the wraps were being cinched tight. The apparent result of the wraps not being lubricated properly.

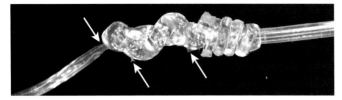

Abrasion Resistance of Nylon Monofilament

Abrasion resistance is the property of a line, which protects it from nicks, cuts and scrapes. It guards a line against damage inflicted by rocks, logs, pilings, raspy teeth and other underwater abrasive surfaces such as coral and barnacles. In essence, abrasion resistance in a line aids in keeping it from weakening. The importance of abrasion resistance must be judged with respect to the balance of the other critical properties affecting the performance of a line. Those other properties may be less effectual if abrasion resistance is the prime consideration to selecting a line.

Even a slight abrasion to a nylon monofilament line can have a catastrophic effect. A mildly frayed line may seem benign to the naked eye or to the touch, but the damage may be more extensive and grievous than perceived. The photo below was taken with a digital microscope at a magnification of 150 times the normal size of the line. It reveals just how severe a seemingly negligible abrasion can actually be.

The two major components of a leader system that require optimum abrasion resistance are the butt and shock trace sections. The importance of this property in these two leader sections justify the compromise or imbalance of the other attributes affecting nylon monofilament line, such as breaking strength, stiffness and elasticity. Enhanced abrasion resistance in a line, for example, will also increase its stiffness and lower its breaking strength and elasticity slightly. Nevertheless, a slight change to these properties does not drastically affect the function or performance of the butt and shock trace sections. A tippet section, however, can only benefit from a slight increase in abrasion resistance as long as the balance of the other properties in the formulation is not affected significantly.

Uniformity of Nylon Monofilament

If every inch of any nylon monofilament line on a spool was tested for breaking strength, some areas would be stronger and other sections would be weaker. Uniformity is the property of a line that evaluates the consistency of its diameter size for any given length. This property is extremely important, especially when applied to the quality of tippet material, because the homogeneity of line diameter is directly related to breaking strength. Consequently, a leader system is only as strong and dependable as the weakest part of its tippet section.

Economy-grade line is much less uniform than premium quality nylon monofilament. Even among the premium grades there is a difference, because uniformity varies with each brand of line. It takes additional costs and quality-control measures in the manufacturing process to produce a nylon monofilament line with consistent uniformity. It is important to note the most consistent and dependable nylon monofilament lines for uniformity and breaking strength are rated for IGFA usage.

Color of Nylon Monofilament

Color is one property in nylon monofilament lines that can be easily seen and measured. Some anglers believe a leader should be invisible underwater, while other anglers think at least a portion of the leader should be visible at all times to better track the fly or react quicker to a strike. Regardless of color, however, there is no such thing as an invisible nylon monofilament line. Most marine and freshwater fish species are capable of seeing any type fishing line including its color. Consequently, it is important to realize the appearance of a line is equally important above and below the surface of the water.

Nylon monofilament line can be colored three ways. The most economical method to simply dip the line in a dye solution, until it penetrates the surface of the nylon monofilament. The process is fast, but the color fades quickly when the line is exposed to natural sunlight. The second method is the addition of powdered colorants to the nylon pellets prior to melting. This process provides uniform color with good fade resistance. The third method involves a chemical reaction with the nylon molecules in which the color becomes chemically spliced into the nylon, producing high-visibility colors that are long-lasting and fade resistant.

The human eye can see some colors better than others. When looking at a rainbow of colors going from violet to red in the visible light spectrum, the human eye responds best to colors in the yellow and green spectrum, particularly as fluorescent colors. When fluorescence is added to a fishing line, it is easier to see and some anglers use a short section of fluorescent line as a strike indicator. The fluorescent pigments in the line absorb the sunlight and then discharges it at a higher frequency, making the line brighter and more visible. As a result, fluorescent fishing line seems to glow above the surface of the water. But contrary to common belief, a fluorescent fly line and leader continues to glow under the water as well. For that reason, a fluorescent line should be chosen carefully. While a fly dressed in fluorescent colors might be desirable in order to attract a fish, a glowing fluorescent fly line or leader can have the opposite effect. Fluorescent colors range from bright yellow and orange to more subdued blue shades. Research studies indicate fluorescent blue lines work better, even though they continue to glow underwater.

Surface	Clear	Black	White	Blue	Green	Yellow	Orange	Red
At 10 ft.	no change	no change	no change	no change	no change	no change	no change	rust
At 20 ft.	no change	no change	no change	no change	no change	no change	rust	brown
At 40 ft.	no change	no change	no change	no change	no change	pale yellow	dark brown	black
At 60 ft.	no change	no change	no change	no change	pale green	white	black	black

The color of the water is an important factor in the color selection of a nylon monofilament line. Water color can vary greatly, from crystal clear and a transparency with a blue or green tint to the opaqueness of pea soup green or chocolate. Over the many years dealing with a plethora of diverse water conditions, I have concluded the best color for a leader and tippet in almost all fishing situations is either clear or tinted a light olive color. Clear nylon monofilament works best in very clear water where fish have a tendency to be wary and alarmed easily. Leader and tippet sections tinted a light olive color are effective in most freshwater and inshore estuarine waters. Nevertheless, a clear line is always a wise selection when in doubt about water conditions.

Proper Care of Nylon Monofilament

There are many factors affecting the integrity of a nylon monofilament line and contributing to a lost fly or a lost fish, but none of them cause more trouble than a damaged line. Even premium nylon monofilament will become fatigued or weakened when subjected to intensive and strenuous use. Repeated stress, excessive abrasion, lengthy exposure to sunlight and improper storage can all damage a leader and tippet section. Knowing the condition of the leader and especially the tippet section, identifying the potential problem early and using some preventive measures, will enhance the success and enjoyment of the fishing experience.

All nylon monofilament lines, regardless of their grade and quality, are adversely affected by sunlight, heat, humidity, abrasion and chemicals. A nylon monofilament leader or tippet section that appears dull or fuzzy should be checked by running the suspect area slowly between moistened lips. This technique provides the sensitivity to detect even the slightest nick or fray spot. One slightly flawed spot becomes a focus point that can cause the breaking strength of the compromised area to drop by 50% or more. For example, an undetected nick or score in a 12-pound tippet could easily break at 6 pounds or less without the angler ever knowing it. The photos below were taken with a

digital microscope at a magnifying power of 100 times the normal size of the line. The line on the left was severely nicked on a sharp object and the line on the right was scored from the frictional heat generated by a grooved rod guide.

At times in many fishing conditions, getting snagged on structure or on the bottom and losing flies are unavoidable. In an attempt to work the fly free, the tippet section can be unknowingly stretched beyond its resiliency or elastic limit, thereby weakening it to the point of breaking. When this circumstance occurs or there is any doubt to the integrity of the line, the most prudent action is to replace the tippet section.

The best place to store spools and leaders of nylon monofilament line is in a location at room temperature, which is absent of direct sunlight, excessive moisture and chemicals. Ultraviolet (UV) light from the sun smashes nylon molecules, weakening the outer layer of the exposed line and causing its surface to appear dull and chalky. Nylon monofilament should not be stored where it can come in contact with chemical vapors, because they are absorbed in the line as quickly and easily as water. Similarly, areas with excessive moisture should also be avoided.

How Temperature Affects Nylon Monofilament

Nylon monofilament absorbs a small amount of water, which changes the strength, stretch and stiffness of a line. Water and air temperatures also have an effect on the performance of nylon monofilament line. The same leader system and tippet strength fished in the surf at Hatteras in August will perform differently when subjected to the near freezing waters in February. And the strength of the tippet in midsummer will break in freezing weather as easily as cotton sewing thread.

As the fishing temperature drops, expect most nylon monofilament lines to become stiffer and more brittle. In very cold temperatures, standard nylon monofilament becomes glassier and it will break much more easily. The line becomes wiry that coils and springs in loops and snarls. In warmer temperatures, nylon monofilament is more flexible and it behaves as expected. About the only recourse to minimize the effect of cold temperatures on a tippet section, especially stiffness, is to reduce the diameter to a smaller size.

How Odors Affect Fishing Line

Most fish species can detect and react to smaller traces of chemicals in their environment than many sophisticated laboratory instruments can recognize. Salmon, for example, navigate to the place of their birth by their acute olfactory senses alone and researchers have discovered most freshwater and saltwater fish species can discern a fractional drop of a chemical or foreign substance in the water. Through their keen sense of smell, fish not only find food and their way, but they can be alerted to enemies and conditions they instinc-

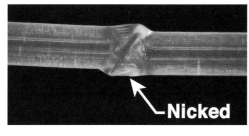

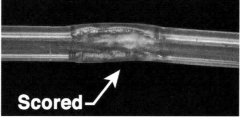

Nicked | Scored

tively know to avoid. Unless some care is taken, the odor emitted by a nylon monofilament leader may actually alarm a fish to take cover or maintain a cautious distance.

Anglers unknowingly transfer chemicals to their nylon monofilament leaders, particularly the tippet sections when attaching flies. Residue from suntan oil, bug repellant, aerosol lubricants, nicotine and many other foreign substances are often transferred to nylon monofilament unknowingly by the careless angler. In fact, simply handling nylon monofilament can prove offensive, because human skin contains a chemical ingredient called L-serine that is known to alarm fish. Keeping the hands clean by washing or wiping them and avoiding the transfer of chemicals to the line, especially the tippet section, are probably the simplest ways to minimize smell tracks.

Chapter 8
The Advantages of Fluorocarbon Line

Everyone has their favorite materials for leaders, tippets and shock traces, and mine is Mirage pure fluorocarbon line marketed by Orvis. As a leader and tippet material, particularly as a shock trace, pure fluorocarbon offers several advantages over nylon monofilament. I strongly believe more fly fishermen would choose fluorocarbon if they understood the unique attributes that make it superior to nylon monofilament.

Fluorocarbon line is a hybrid to the nylon monofilament line with similarities in the way it is manufactured. Small pellets of polyvinylidene fluoride (PVDF) are placed in a large bin where they are fed into a heating chamber. After they melt in the chamber, the liquid

material is extruded through a cone-shaped die, forming a long strand of line. It is then passed through a chamber of cold water for aligning the molecules into a uniform, straight line. After exiting the chamber, it is pulled across heated rollers and stretched to the desired diameter for a specific breaking strength (pound-test). It is wound onto a large spool to cool before being transferred to smaller spools for shipping. These steps constitute the basic general process for producing fluorocarbon line. Of course, each line manufacturer has its own proprietary augmentations to these production stages.

Fluorocarbon is available in two forms: pure and copolymer. The pure fluorocarbon line is the stiffer of the two lines and it is the preferred choice in fly fishing as a leader, tippet and shock trace material. Fluorocarbon tippet material is based on a different formula than fluorocarbon leader material. It is more supple and less prone to memory sets, characteristics similar to nylon monofilament. The copolymer fluorocarbon line has a nylon core to provide increased flexibility, but this blend minimizes the ben-

efits of this new technology in my opinion, primarily in the areas of abrasion resistance and low visibility.

The photo below shows the end views of 16-pound pure and copolymer fluorocarbon lines. The photo was taken with a digital microscope at a magnification of 230 times the normal size of the lines. Note the fused nylon monofilament in the core of the copolymer fluorocarbon line versus the uniform cross-sectional area of the pure fluorocarbon line. The pure fluorocarbon line also has a more uniform, symmetrical shape.

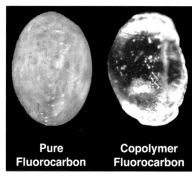

Pure Fluorocarbon   **Copolymer Fluorocarbon**

Refractive Index of Fluorocarbon

The most important characteristic of pure fluorocarbon line is its capability to blend in with the underwater environment more subtly than nylon monofilament line. The low visibility of fluorocarbon line is due to its refractory index, which is the degree light bends or refracts, as it passes through a substance such as water. Water has a refractory index of 1.33 and pure fluorocarbon, such as Orvis Mirage pure fluorocarbon, has a refractory index of 1.42 in comparison to clear nylon monofilament with a refractory index of 1.53 or higher. Since it has a refractory index very similar to water, pure fluorocarbon is considerably less visible to fish once it is immersed in water. This unique characteristic is especially advantageous in clear-water situations where fish are heavily pressured or more cautious to bite. Conversely, a nylon monofilament line is more detectable by fish regardless of its size or color.

Specific Gravity of Fluorocarbon

The ability of pure fluorocarbon to sink relatively fast is a very important advantage over nylon monofilament. Specific gravity is the ratio of the density of a substance to the density of water, which has a specific gravity value of 1.0. Water weighs 1 gram per cubic centimeter (g/cc), nylon weighs 1.21 g/cc and pure fluorocarbon weighs approximately 1.77 g/cc. Materials denser (heavier) than water will sink and those objects with less density than water will not readily sink. Even with a specific gravity of about 1.21, nylon monofilament line will not sink quickly unless it can overcome the surface tension of the water.

The following photo illustrates the relative sink rate of 20-pound Mirage pure fluorocarbon and nylon monofilament lines underwater. Since Mirage pure fluorocarbon line is more than twice as dense to break the tension of the surface of the water as nylon monofilament line, flies and leader systems will sink quicker and easier below the surface of the water. Conversely, nylon monofilament line is much slower to break the barrier of surface adhesion and to sink. Equally important, Mirage pure fluorocarbon line does not hydroplane, which can cause an un-weighted fly to rise slightly and unnaturally during a retrieve. It is also important to note pure fluorocarbon line is less visible in non-polarized light and, therefore, less detectable to a fish. This attribute is particularly helpful when using heavier tippets and shock traces.

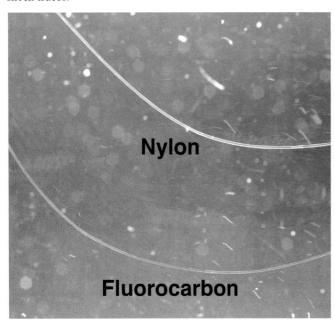

The cohesive forces between liquid molecules are shared with all neighboring atoms and they are responsible for the phenomenon known as surface tension. The molecules at the surface do not have other like molecules on all sides of them, and consequently, they cohere more strongly to those molecules directly associated with them on the surface. This forms a surface film or stretchy skin-like effect, which makes it more difficult to move an object through the surface than to move it when it is completely submersed. Surface tension plays an important role in the manner liquids behave. For example, if done slowly and carefully, a glass can be filled above the rim with water because of surface tension. The water strider walks and hunts its prey on the surface of still water. The stretchy skin-like surface of the water is depressed under the widely spaced feet of this small insect similar to the pads of a Lunar Lander used during the Apollo Space program. As shown in the photo below, the weight of a dressed hook is supported by the elastic tension of the surface film to keep the dry fly afloat.

With a specific gravity of 1.76, Mirage pure fluorocarbon breaks through the surface tension quickly and sinks faster than nylon monofilament, making it ideal when used for subsurface presentations. This property is very important in getting a fly to sink quicker as well as keeping it at the desired depth for a longer retrieval time. This aspect of fluorocarbon line also maintains a straight connection to the fly, because bows in the leader and tippet sections reduce the ability to detect subtle strikes. These bends and curves also decrease the time a fly is in the feeding zone and, in many cases, they cause the fly to act unnaturally by moving faster than intended or desired.

Abrasion Resistance & Stiffness of Fluorocarbon

Pure fluorocarbon is extremely abrasion resistant. This attribute is one of the most crucial aspects of this line when considering it for use in certain fishing situations or for specific game fish. The outer skin of this line is exceedingly hard, but it still retains its flexibility. This high degree of abrasion resistance can be advantageous in the more demanding situations, such as when fishing in and around razor-sharp structure, working flies on or near a rough bottom, or at other times when pursuing fish with raspy teeth, serrated gill plates or other abrasive body parts.

On average, pure fluorocarbon is about 30% stiffer than nylon, which helps ensure improved leader turnover and less tangles in windy conditions. Since fluorocarbon is also about 65% more dense than nylon, flies will sink quicker and easier below the surface of the water. Providing a drag-free drift to nymph, larvae and pupae fly imitations is more difficult to achieve, however, because the tippet section will be stiffer and more resistant to the movement of the water molecules. Conversely, the sensitivity, low stretch and stiffness should help in setting the hook, particularly when fish are feeding near the bottom, or when trying to maintain contact with a fly in a strong current. The limited stretch of fluorocarbon line, nevertheless, makes it less forgiving than nylon monofilament line.

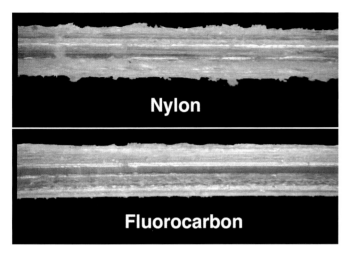

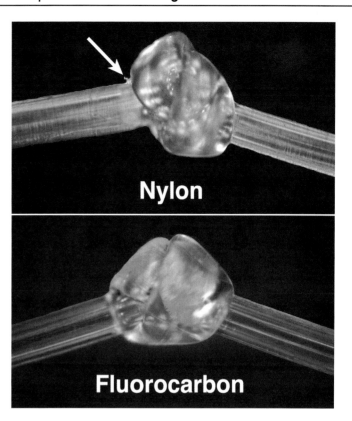

The above photo shows the abrasion resistance of 20-pound nylon monofilament and Mirage pure fluorocarbon lines. The photo was taken with a digital microscope at a magnification of 100 times the normal size of the 20-pound line samples. The nylon monofilament and Mirage pure fluorocarbon lines of 20-pound were abraded by pulling them only once across the edge of 80-grit sandpaper. The result of this action is similar to retrieving the line under the load of fighting a fish across a jagged rod guide or tiptop. This type of abrasion is considered minor in comparison to more severe abrasions produced from sharp objects. While this line would feel slightly rough to the touch, normal visual examination may not reveal how serious the damage or how close the line is to its breaking point.

Knot Strength of Fluorocarbon

Since it is nonporous and it does not absorb water, pure fluorocarbon maintains its rated breaking strength wet or dry. Some fluorocarbon copolymers will absorb as much as 3% water. By comparison, nylon monofilament absorbs water and it can lose as much as 15% of its rated breaking strength when submerged. Over time, water absorption will weaken a nylon monofilament line and loosen its knots when it is stretched. The less water the line soaks up, the longer it remains stronger. Because nylon monofilament line absorbs water, the line swells enough to tighten the knots tied, but they are not necessarily stronger, just tighter.

The photos on the top right show a simple overhand knot tied without lubrication in 6-pound Mirage pure fluorocarbon and nylon monofilament lines. The knots were cinched tight with 4 pounds of applied force and, during their tightening, a fracture occurred in the nylon monofilament line as indicated by the arrow. The photo was taken with a digital microscope at a magnification of 150 times the normal size of the 6-pound line samples.

Knots are traditionally tested by manufacturers both with dry line at normal temperatures and humidity content as well as with wet line, because water absorption will reduce the strength of nylon monofilament by approximately 15%. Since it is nonporous and it does not absorb water, Mirage pure fluorocarbon line maintains its rated breaking strength wet or dry. Since the knot represents the weakest link in the entire system, these attributes have an especially important meaning. Nylon monofilament line absorbs water and it can lose as much as 15% of its rated breaking strength when submerged. Over time, water absorption will weaken a nylon monofilament line and loosens its knots when it is stretched. The less water the line soaks up, the longer it remains stronger to its rated breaking strength.

To test the knot strength of a line, the simple overhand knot is the most destructive knot to tie in any type of fishing line. Pulled to the breaking point, an overhand knot will cut through monofilament line and break it at 50% or less of its rated pound-test. In contrast, the smooth and hard surface of Mirage pure fluorocarbon line will withstand the cutting of the overhand knot as much as 75% of the rating.

The arrow in the photo above shows a fracture in the nylon monofilament line on the standing part of the line where a cutting action occurred during the tightening of the knot, causing it to break. Due to a combination of the softness of its outer surface and the frictional heat generated when the knot was pulled tight, the nylon monofilament line is significantly weakened to a value below 50% of its breaking strength.

Also, depending upon the brand, pure fluorocarbon has a diameter generally smaller than nylon monofilament of the same breaking strength. This relatively small diameter and low refractivity can prove beneficial in the more demanding fishing situations, particularly when dealing with crystal clear water and wary fish. For less challenging circumstances, a slightly heavier line size can be used to increase abrasion resistance and to add strength.

The photo below shows the end views of 20-pound nylon monofilament and Mirage pure fluorocarbon line. The photo was taken with a digital microscope at a magnification of 150 times the normal size of the 20 pound-test line samples. The significance of the photo is two-fold. It shows the Mirage pure fluorocarbon line has a diameter smaller than the nylon monofilament line of the same breaking strength. Since Mirage pure fluorocarbon line is smaller in diameter than nylon monofilament line of the same breaking strength, it is considerably less noticeable to the fish. As a result, a fish can focus on a fly in terms of prey detection, recognition and capture without the distraction of unnatural elements such as the presence of a conspicuous tippet or shock trace.

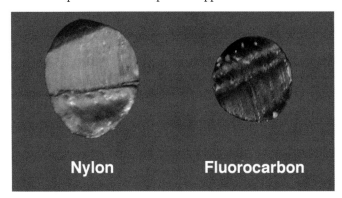

The second significant aspect of this photo is the uniform shape of the Mirage pure fluorocarbon line in the extrusion process during manufacturing. Pure fluorocarbon is a denser material than nylon and it extrudes more smoothly and more evenly. This aspect of the manufacturing process results in an improved overall line performance as well as more consistency to the breaking strengths of the line and its knots for any given length of line sample.

Mirage pure fluorocarbon line is chemically inert, so it is completely impervious to ultraviolet (UV) radiation of sunlight, gasoline, battery acid, DEET and other foreign substances. As illustrated in the photo, on the top right, the Mirage pure fluorocarbon line is unaffected by UV radiation after 9 days of continuous exposure. In addition, it is nontoxic, but it is not biodegradable and, therefore, it should not be discarded in the environment.

Nylon monofilament line starts to deteriorate and weaken over time from the prolonged exposure to heat, cold, sunlight, salt and other elements. When nylon monofilament line is damaged from UV radiation, its molecular structure is altered, causing its surface to become chalky, its translucency to be diffused, its elasticity to turn brittle and its breaking strength to be weakened considerably. These effects also cause the line to become more visible underwater, primarily because its opaque, chalky surface reflects more incident light.

The photo on the top right shows the result of 9 days of continuous exposure to ultraviolet radiation (UV) from direct sunlight to 12-pound Mirage pure fluorocarbon and nylon monofilament lines. The photo was taken with a digital microscope at a magnification of 100 times the normal size of the 12-pound lines. Note the opaqueness and chalky

surface of the nylon line exposed to 9 days of UV radiation. The fluorocarbon line, however, remained unchanged in its translucency, elasticity and relative suppleness.

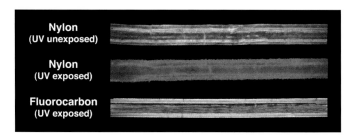

Early Experiments with Fluorocarbon Tippet Material

When I first started using fluorocarbon lines I was extremely skeptical to their effectiveness. A few weeks after using the Mirage pure fluorocarbon tippet material, I was running some computer analysis of data from my electronic fishing log when I noticed a marked increase in my strike-to-hookup ratio. At the time, the American and Hickory shad were running in the St. John's River in Florida, so I decided to experiment with the fluorocarbon line. I typically use a two-fly tandem rig for these anadromous species during their annual spawning run as shown in the photo below. I arranged three sets of tandem rigs in my experiment: one set entirely of fluorocarbon, another set entirely of nylon monofilament and a third set with the dropper section of fluorocarbon and the trailer section of nylon monofilament. The results were quite amazing as annotated in the table below.

After catching and releasing a total of 420 fish, there was a 64.5% increase in my overall catch rate using the Mirage pure fluorocarbon tandem rig in comparison to the success of using the nylon monofilament tandem rig. The Mirage pure fluorocarbon tandem rig accounted for 41.7% of the total number of fish caught and it yielded an astonishing 74% increase of double hookups versus the nylon monofilament tandem rig. Equally interesting, there was a 65% increase of fish caught on the pure fluorocarbon dropper fly versus the nylon trailer fly of the composite tandem rig. I used the same size, color and design of shad flies for all three tandem rigs. I did not expect the results to be as emphatic as indicated in the chart below because American and Hickory shad are not overly wary to tippet size or fly selection when they are in a spawning frenzy. Secondly, the visibility in the tannin-stained St. John's River is typically poor at best.

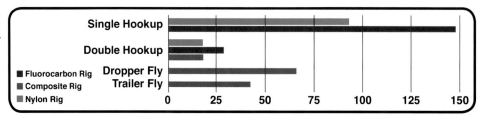

Essence to the Effectiveness of Fluorocarbon Tippet Material

After reviewing the data of the experiment, I wanted to know what specific properties of the Mirage pure fluorocarbon tippet material were actually creating these significantly improved results. The more I experimented with the line, the more confused I became. I was expecting a single characteristic to surface as conclusive evidence; namely, the refractive index of the line. Unfortunately, there was no smoking gun, so to speak. What I did discover, however, there is a combination of characteristics of the Mirage pure fluorocarbon tippet material, which contributed to my increased angling success; specifically, a significant increase in the number of strikes every 25 casts and in my strike-to-hookup ratio. This ratio indicates that the fish are more convinced my offering is the real thing and, therefore, strike it with abandon, resulting in more positive hookups. This discovery, nevertheless, did not explain why I was experiencing more strikes.

The first part of my investigation started with a visual inspection, because the line does not look all that different at a cursory glance. So, I launched a forensic investigation using a digital microscope and a specialized coaxial illumination lens with a magnification of 50 times the normal size of the line samples. The Mirage pure fluorocarbon tippet material looked significantly better than the nylon monofilament in both regular microscopic illumination and under polarized light. The Mirage pure fluorocarbon tippet material was clearer and extruded more smoothly than the nylon monofilament. Since the surface is much smoother, there are fewer reflective surfaces from the Mirage pure fluorocarbon than the nylon surfaces. Rough surfaces create more reflection.

The photo below shows a unique surface view of 20-pound nylon monofilament and Mirage pure fluorocarbon lines. The photo was taken with a digital microscope and a coaxial illumination lens at a magnification of 50 times the normal size of the line samples. The special coaxial illumination lens scans only the surface of a translucent or semi-translucent material such as monofilament line, showing the irregularities and imperfections specifically on the outer surface of the material.

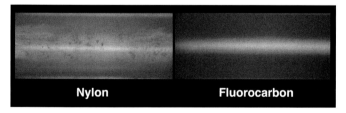

Nylon   **Fluorocarbon**

One of the most important characteristics of Mirage pure fluorocarbon line is its capability to blend in with the underwater environment more subtly than nylon monofilament. The low visibility of Mirage pure fluorocarbon line is due to its refractory index, which is the degree light bends, or refracts, as it passes through a substance such as water.

The significance of the photo above is the surface of the Mirage pure fluorocarbon line is much smoother and free of irregularities than the nylon monofilament line. The harder surface and higher density of the Mirage pure fluorocarbon line extruded more smoothly than the nylon monofilament line. Since the surface is much smoother, there are fewer reflective surfaces from

the Mirage pure fluorocarbon line than the nylon monofilament surface. Rough or irregular surfaces create more reflection of ambient light underwater and, therefore, are more visible to the fish.

Since the Mirage pure fluorocarbon line is clearer or more translucent, it is less visible to fish, although when viewing both materials side-by-side in water, they seem comparably visible. Given the turbidity of water and the fact fish do not have the visual acuity of humans, the issue is not whether the line is visible in the water or not, but how the visibility appears in context to a fish. Neither type of line casts a significant silhouette, but they do both reflect light and the smoothness of the Mirage pure fluorocarbon line reflects less polarized and non-polarized light than the irregular surface of nylon monofilament line. That revelation was a very important finding to me.

The smoother and harder outer surface of Mirage pure fluorocarbon line also provides a greater resistance to abrasion. Conversely, the softer and irregular outer skin of nylon monofilament line creates a surface area more easily susceptible to the shearing forces that cause line abrasions from fish and rough structure.

There are several ways light can be polarized. One method to polarize light is by reflection. Light reflecting off a surface will tend to be polarized, with the direction of polarization being parallel to the plane of the interface. I suspect polarized light reflection from fly lines, leaders, tippets and shock traces have been alarming fish of their presence since the beginning of their use. It is definitely a factor affecting our angling productivity, but not realized by most anglers. The polarized light theory as a means of prey enhancement and recognition should work for the angler and not in opposition. In essence, a fly imitation should reflect polarized light, not the leader and especially not the tippet or shock trace.

There are many natural and some synthetic materials used in fly design to dress hooks that reflect polarized light. The patterns utilizing these materials are more visible to the fish in widely diverse lighting conditions. The photo below, and the one on page 96, illustrate this important consideration in fishing strategy by revealing the visibility of each fly about 5 feet below the surface of very clear water and approximately 30 minutes after sunrise. The all-white fly in the photo below is seen under polarized light and it is considerably more visible when compared to the fly viewed under normal available sunlight in the photo on page 96. Note the prominent visibility of the silver braided Mylar body on the fly subjected to polarized light. During this time of day, the amount of light at the surface of the water is about 100 foot-candles of illumination. A foot-candle is a measure of the quantity of light or luminance which falls on a spherical surface 1 foot away from an ordinary wax candle. In comparison, the light penetrating the surface of the water when the sun is directly overhead would be more than a 100 times brighter.

Polarized

Non-polarized

In addition to light polarization, the photon reflection theory of light effects the colors and visibility of flies underwater, particularly those flies worked deep in the water column or near the bottom in deeper water. Photons from sunlight striking suspended particles and water molecules are reflected and scattered randomly, causing light to become diffused underwater. The effect of these actions provides a wide variation on light transmission and spectral irradiance at different depths. In essence, the deeper a fly is fished below the surface, the lower the photon density and the lower the reflective effect influencing its visibility. The lighter and brighter a fly pattern, the greater the number of reflected photons. Standard white reflects all light photons and black absorbs all light photons. In other words, a fly pattern is as bright as the available underwater illumination allows as illustrated in the above photo.

For a fish with polarization sensitivity, the relationship between the time of day and the angle of the sun could provide high visual acuity with increased contrast, which could determine feeding times. Fish are different from humans in that they never stop growing, and as they grow their eyes become bigger and their retinal packing density increases, which means their vision becomes more acute. Scientific studies have proved many fish species can sense polarized light, which is a particular and unique characteristic of ultraviolet (UV) light humans can not see. We do not have the ability to separate polarized from regular light. Human eyes are not designed to distinguish between different types of polarization, contrary to fish, insects, cephalopods, many amphibians and other animals, for which nature possesses a different class of colors. Even in human terms, common colors do not mean the same to everyone.

The colors we see depend on the wavelength sensitivities of the visual receptors within our eyes as well as the wavelengths of light entering them. In color vision, light excites different classes of photoreceptor cells, containing different visual pigments, and the brain compares their differential light absorption. Thus, in bright light, we see a colorful world because the cone cells in our retinas have three visual pigments, with maximal sensitivities in the red, green and blue (RGB) regions of the spectrum. The differential responses of these cells enable color vision. Human eyes are poor at sensing polarized light, but very good at sensing its color and brightness. In analogy to color vision, a key requirement for sensitivity to polarization is the excitation of two or more classes of visual pigments with differing alignments in the eye, which technically, are different axes of maximal excitation.

Many marine and freshwater fish species have retinal peculiarities. Trout, for example, have retinal rod and cone mosaic arrangements that allow for ultraviolet (UV) polarized light perception. Unlike humans, it is thought that trout identify prey, manage proximity to others, determine their orientation in water and even navigate with the use of their ultraviolet (UV) polarized light retinal machinery. The ability for a trout to perceive polarized light minimizes the guesswork out of prey selection. From the perspective of a fish, imagine viewing the underwater world as it might appear through infrared binoculars. Most of the background underwater is monochromatic shades of gray and the subjects that create heat seem to glow green in the foreground. Many marine and freshwater fish species have specialized retinal hardware that enables them to discern UV-reflecting surfaces. Not only can many marine and freshwater fish species see ultraviolet (UV) wavelengths, but they can also see a particular characteristic of it, which is polarized light.

Polarized light is important because it just may be the continuous thread of connection between the underwater world of fish and our understanding of what they see. Polarized light is impacted in many facets to the life of a fish. For example, it dictates how mayflies find water, and it is thought to help anadromous fish migrate such as salmon, steelhead and American shad. Some fish species, such as herring, use reflected polarized light to swim in formation with their fellow school mates while other species use it to discern what food is appropriate to eat in an environment where prey discrimination can be challenging.

When sunlight contacts the surface of the water, some polarized light is reflected or bounced upwards and some light is refracted downwards into the water column. The amount of polarized light refracted into the water is greatest when the sun is about 30 degrees above the horizon, which is known as Brewster's angle. The time of day the most polarized light is refracted into the water column is during the crepuscular times of dawn and dusk. When polarized light is reflected by a leader, tippet or shock trace, it causes them to become luminous and more easily seen by the fish. Interestingly, a natural quirk in the structure of the human eye gives us the ability to tell apart different states of polarization. Thanks to this small aberration or defect of the eye we are not completely blind to polarization; nevertheless, we cannot see the full effects of polarized light as fish do and there lies the significance.

The subtlety of polarization vision in humans makes it difficult for us to appreciate the fact that polarized light is common and prevalent throughout nature. In general, the sensitivity to polarization enhances contrast vision, and this is particularly important for predatory fish species, since underwater objects such as baitfish generally have lower contrast. Polarization sensitivity, however, allows a predator to better see many of the fish upon which it preys. For example, the silvery sides of many species of baitfish, such as minnows, dace and herring, strongly reflect polarized light.

In general, even in the clearest water, 99% of the light is filtered out in the first 30 feet below the surface. In murky or riffled water, most of the light is absent in the first 10 feet. Still, if sunlight is illuminating the surface of the water at 1000 foot-candles, there will be 10 foot-candles of illumination at the depth where only 1% of the light remains, which is plenty of light for certain fish species to feed by. Most colors, such as violet, indigo, blue, green and yellow, are significantly attenuated. Illumination is limited to a depth of approximately 16 feet. The spectral irradiance 5% level of available light, which is normal to the direction of flow of radiant energy through water, occurs at about 5 feet. Consequently, the total amount of light that arrives from a clear, brightly-lit sky at noon only 45% remains at about a 3-foot depth and 15% remains at about 32 feet of depth in the clearest water conditions. In addition, ultraviolet (UV) and infrared (IR) light are severely attenuated at about 3 feet, while red and orange light are absent at about 30 feet.

I also think there might be a few other substantial reasons why Mirage pure fluorocarbon catches more fish than nylon monofilament line. It might be that because it is stiffer, it makes the fly behave differently. In clear water, I have noticed a fly tracks more linearly in the retrieval path, which is a more natural movement of swimming or escaping prey. I think this observation is the least likely, however, unless this phenomenon is coupled with another possibility; namely, specific gravity. The combination of the relative stiffness and the specific gravity of the Mirage pure fluorocarbon line definitely improve strike detection and hook-setting response. These two properties, therefore, explain why my hookup-to-strike ratio had improved significantly.

But there is still another factor that aroused my attention; namely, the refractive index of fluorocarbon line. I have concluded this property, in combination with the fact the line is smaller in diameter than nylon monofilament of the same breaking strength and reflects less polarized light, makes it considerably less noticeable to the fish. As a result, a fish can focus on a fly in terms of prey detection, recognition and capture without the distraction of unnatural elements such as the presence of a conspicuous tippet or shock trace. This conclusion, therefore, would explain why the number of strikes for every 25 casts rose so sharply in both clear and discolored water conditions.

When attaching a fly directly to a tippet, I do not use a tightly cinched knot, such as the improved clinch knot, unless the breaking strength of the tippet material is 4 pounds (5X) or less. Instead, I use the Chermanski Loop knot because it allows complete freedom of movement to a fly. I firmly believe a fly with three-dimensional freedom of yaw, pitch and roll movement will produce more strikes, even when it is drifting in the current without any action being induced externally by the angler. I also believe this added freedom maintains a hook at an optimum angle-of-attack for improved hook penetration. Note the two underwater views of size 18 caddis emergers attached to a 5X tippets and the air bubbles trapped in their thorax areas. The Chermanski Loop knot allows a fly to swim in a more natural and realistic manner

as shown in the photo on the top right. Notice the different

angle of drift for the fly in the photo below. It was secured to a 5X tippet using an improved clinch knot. Regardless of how a fly is attached to a tippet, however, it is my opinion the low-stretch attribute of the Mirage pure fluorocarbon line enhances hook penetration, based upon my research and experiments in the field.

Since my initial experiments on the St. John's River, I have used tandem rigs with similar results on a variety of marine species. From my experiments and analysis, I have discovered a 35% increase in my overall hookup-to-strike ratio whenever I attach the fly directly to the Mirage pure fluorocarbon tippet material, and a 45% increase when using a fluorocarbon shock trace. I have also observed the clearer the water, the better the results of using pure fluorocarbon leader and tippet materials versus nylon monofilament lines. In addition to its low visibility, it has very little stretch and a hard, smooth finish that is extremely abrasion resistant. Its tough finish stands up better to the abuse of structure and the raspy jaws, gill plates and scales of certain game fish.

Because pure fluorocarbon monofilament line does not absorb water, it will not weaken or increase in stretch like nylon monofilament line. Less stretch means increased sensitivity to detect subtle strikes and to feel the performance of a fly, including any contact it makes with submerged structure or the bottom. Minimal stretch also promotes positive hook sets. As a result, I have become a believer to the effectiveness of pure fluorocarbon monofilament line as a leader, tippet and shock trace material, because it has definitely contributed to a significant increase in my overall angling success.

Chapter 9

General Freshwater & Saltwater Leader Systems

In applying the principles of leader design discussed in Chapter 6 and the attributes of nylon and fluorocarbon lines explained in Chapters 7 and 8, I have developed a series of general and specialty leader systems for freshwater and saltwater fishing applications. The leader systems described and illustrated in this chapter are basic, modular setups that utilize a network of interlocking loops designed for efficiency, quickness and dependability in virtually any fishing situation. This chapter features two general categories of leader systems that I have used since the early 1960s: commercial knotless tapered leaders and compound tapered leaders.

For example, the commercial knotless tapered leader, which I classify as a Type A leader system, is the simplest and most basic configuration. It is recommended for the novice to the sport until an experience base dealing with knots and diverse fishing situations can be established. Also, an angler who does not want to tinker with knots, or simply does not have a need or desire to customize a leader system, will want to use a Type A leader system. The remaining 9 leader systems defined in this chapter, Types B through J, are essentially a progression of leader system designs I have developed over the past 40 years. I started using a leader system similar to the Type B when I was about 12 years old, primarily for economical reasons. Trout fishing almost every week day throughout the summers with my great uncle Andy Cremi in the 1960s, and on weekends with my dad, became a costly concern since I was constantly changing flies. In addition, my ineptness at tying knots and splicing leader sections together quickly and securely prompted me to design a better system. With the inspiration and innovation of my great uncle Andy, I started using the Type B system with an interchangeable tippet section he had developed for me.

Once I became proficient at tying strong and reliable knots, I experimented with making the Type B leader system more modular and versatile to accommodate my expanding fishing opportunities. For the past 30 years, I have been using Type E & G leaders for floating fly lines and Type H & J leaders for sinking fly lines. I also use more specialized and customized leader systems for specific fishing situations or for certain species, such as a trout and bonefish, which are discussed and illustrated in Chapter 10.

At first glance, these commercial knotless and homemade compound tapered leader systems appear to be confusing and complicated. In actuality, however, they are really quite simple to build and easy to maintain. For example, the Type B, C and D leaders are simply derivatives of the basic Type A commercial knotless tapered leader design. As a knotless tapered leader is concerned, Type B and D systems are the most versatile, efficient and cost effective. With regard to compound tapered systems, Types F and G leaders are options of the Type E system for floating fly lines and Types I and J configurations are alternatives of the Type H system for sinking fly lines. The most important point to remember is only one or two types of leader systems are required to satisfy most or all fishing needs in both freshwater and saltwater. It is simply a matter of deciding which system to use. The recommended approach is to first examine each leader system carefully to better understand its advantages and disadvantages. Next, select a leader system type for floating and intermediate fly lines that is the most accommodating to your present knot tying skills and the perceived fishing situations you most likely will encounter. If certain fishing situations require the use of a sinking fly line, then select a second leader system type comparable to the one chosen for a floating or intermediate fly line. As a result, all the other types of leader systems become irrelevant to your needs, allowing you to focus specifically on only the leader systems you have selected.

Building Leader Sections by Strength or Diameter

All the leader systems discussed in this book are designed to use a medium-stiff leader butt section. The moderate flexibility of the leader butt section is important to the fluid transfer of the kinetic energy from the fly line and the decreasing progression of energy along the remaining leader sections to the tippet. The Type E through J leader systems are built entirely by the angler. Construction of these leader systems by the angler will provide the maximum effectiveness in adjusting to the size of the fish, the size of the fly as well as to specific fishing situations. The Type B through J leader systems permit a fly to be pretied to the tippet or shock trace section in advance of a planned fishing trip for quick and reliable replacement changes. These systems allow an angler to spend more time fishing and less time tying knots.

As you study each leader system, you will note that I apply line strength (pound-test) rather than diameter as the primary criterion. Some leader sections are defined by their diameter while other sections, primarily tippets, are defined by line strength. Line diameter for a given breaking strength is not consistent among manufacturers for various reasons. For example, a 20-pound nylon monofilament line from one manufacturer can have a diameter of .018", while a competitor can market a comparable 20-pound line with a diameter of .023". Whatever brand of nylon monofilament line I choose, I try to use it throughout the construction of the entire leader. If you use the same brand of nylon monofilament line constructing a leader system, then it really becomes irrelevant which criterion you choose. The exception to this rule, however, occurs if I want to utilize a more abrasion-resistant tippet section of either nylon or fluorocarbon monofilament line. This material will generally have a stiffer flexibility, but it does not significantly affect the overall performance of the leader system.

Achieving Optimum Leader Performance with Floating Fly Lines

When a floating fly line is used exclusively for surface or near-surface fishing applications, the complete system can be optimized and the fishing experience can be enhanced with the use of a floating leader butt section. A leader greased with a silicone paste or liquid is only a temporary fix. It also magnifies the visibility of the leader to a fish especially in clear water fishing conditions. The solution is to use of a leader butt material that permanently floats, such as Orvis Hy-Flote. The elliptical or flattened shape of this material features a core comprised of six hollow chambers for superior and permanent buoyancy. As a result, this leader butt material is the ideal transition from a floating fly line to a leader system.

The advantages of a floating leader butt are smooth, easy and quieter pickups for improved casts, easier mends of a floating fly line, better floatation and sensitivity of strike indicators, and finally, enhanced control of surface flies and poppers. In addition, Orvis Hy-Flote leader butt material is particularly effective for skating caddis, hoppers or big dry-fly attractors across the surface of the water. It is also ideal for nymphing and for use in tricky currents. I use a floating leader butt with Type E, F and G leader systems in this chapter and exclusively with Type K and M systems in Chapter 10. It is available in two sizes: the 30-pound line is 0.019" in diameter and the 40-pound line is 0.021" in diameter.

Storing Leaders & Tippets

There are various commercial products available for storing leaders and tippet sections. I prefer, however, to make my own wallets, because I can customize them for specific fly lines or for certain fishing applications. For example, I have a wallet dedicated to trout fishing, one for general freshwater, one for general inshore saltwater and another for bluewater. I make individual wallets for freshwater and saltwater even though many of the sleeves contain the same leader or tippet section. As a result, even if I pack the wrong wallet for a fishing trip, the leader and tippet sections are essentially the same for either freshwater or saltwater. The wallets can store an ample supply of pre-tied leaders and tippets of various lengths and sizes for use on many fishing trips. The detailed steps to building leader and tippet wallets are illustrated in Chapter 5.

Fly Fishing Knots & Leader Systems

The table below explains the symbols used in the drawings of all the leader system variations discussed and illustrated in this chapter.

Symbol	Legend for Leader System Configurations Description of Symbol	Photo Illustration
1	PVC Fly Line Loop. See page 60 for illustrated step-by-step tying instructions.	
2	Chermanski Loop knot. See page 24 for illustrated step-by-step tying instructions.	
1 2	The connection between the fly line and the leader butt section of a leader system.	
3	Improved Clinch knot. See page 26 for illustrated step-by-step tying instructions.	
4	Double Chermanski Loop knot. See page 24 for illustrated step-by-step tying instructions.	
5	Bimini Twist knot. See page 28 for illustrated step-by-step tying instructions.	
4 5	Double Chermanski Loop knot (r) formed from a Bimini Twist (l)	
5 6	The connection between an Albright Special knot (r) and a Bimini Twist (l).	
6	Albright Special knot. See page 32 for illustrated step-by-step tying instructions.	
7	Haywire Twist. See page 29 for illustrated step-by-step tying instructions.	
8	Haywire Twist Loop. See page 31 for illustrated step-by-step tying instructions.	
9	Twisted & burned plastic-coated wire. See page 69 for step-by-step tying instructions.	
10	Blood knot. See page 25 for illustrated step-by-step tying instructions.	
11	Tandem blood knot. See page 25 for illustrated step-by-step tying instructions.	
12	Tandem Bimini Twist knot. See page 28 for illustrated step-by-step tying instructions.	
13	Double Nail knots in elasticity cord (l) and 30-pound mono (r). See page 78 for detailed instructions.	

Type A: Knotless Leader System for Floating & Intermediate Fly Lines

Commercial Knotless Tapered Leader (7.5', 9', 10' & 12')

The Type A leader system is a versatile rig for nearly all freshwater fishing situations requiring a floating or intermediate fly line. This leader system can also be used effectively in certain saltwater situations where a shock trace is not required such as fishing the clear, shallow flats for bonefish or permit. It is the simplest of the leader systems, requiring only a maximum of two knots for construction and usage.

2 3 interconnection between the PVC Fly Line Loop (about 0.5 inches long) and the leader butt loop (about 0.5 inches long) formed by a Chermanski Loop knot.

2 Chermanski Loop knot.

3 Improved Clinch knot.

A small loop of about 0.5 inches or less is formed using the Chermanski Loop knot for interconnection to the PVC fly line loop at the end featuring the largest diameter. At the opposite end, a fly can be attached to the tippet section using either a Chermanski Loop or an improved clinch knot. Technically, an angler can effectively utilize this leader system in a diverse range of fishing situations using just one knot, the Chermanski Loop knot.

Once the tippet section becomes too short, a Type A leader can easily be converted to a Type B system if desired. The remaining length of tippet section is removed by measuring the length of the leader from the opposite end to the length (L) specified in the Type B Leader Specifications table corresponding to the overall leader length being used.

Type B: Knotless Leader System with an Interchangeable Tippet Section for Floating & Intermediate Fly Lines

The Type B leader is the most versatile, efficient and cost effective system when using a commercial knotless tapered leader. It is designed to save the frequent angler time and money in building new leaders or in purchasing them. The Type B leader system features a semipermanent section that interconnects with a replaceable, pre-tied tippet section as required. As a result, the only knot required to be tied in the field is the one attaching a fly to the tippet, such as the Chermanski Loop or improved clinch.

When using a commercial knotless tapered leader, the Type B leader is the most versatile system for general freshwater fishing with a floating fly line. It is also used for general saltwater situations with a floating fly line where a shock trace is not required. When a shock trace is required, however, this leader system can be transformed into a Type C or D leader system for more specific fishing applications with fly line sizes ranging from 4- to 13-weight.

Modified Commercial Knotless Tapered Leader

1 2 interconnection between the PVC Fly Line Loop (about 0.5 inches long) and the leader butt loop (about 0.5 inches long) formed by a Chermanski Loop knot.

2 Chermanski Loop knot.

3 Improved Clinch knot.

4 5 double Chermanski Loop knot formed with the lines created from a Bimini Twist.

Type B Leader Specifications						
OAL	L	A	B	C + Loop	T1	T2
6' (72")	52"	0.25"-1.5"	0.25"-0.5"	n/a	20" (12-20 lb.)	n/a
6' (72")	52"	0.25"-1.5"	n/a	≤2" OAL + 0.25"-0.5"	n/a	20" (7X-3X)
7.5' (90")	66"	0.25"-1.5"	0.25"-0.5"	n/a	24" (12-20 lb.)	n/a
7.5' (90")	66"	0.25"-1.5"	n/a	≤2" OAL + 0.25"-0.5"	n/a	24" (7X-3X)
9' (108")	78"	0.25"-1.5"	0.25"-0.5"	n/a	30" (12-20 lb.)	n/a
9' (108")	78"	0.25"-1.5"	n/a	≤2" OAL + 0.25"-0.5"	n/a	30" (7X-3X)
10' (120")	88"	0.25"-1.5"	0.25"-0.5"	n/a	32" (12-20 lb.)	n/a
10' (120")	88"	0.25"-1.5"	n/a	≤2" OAL + 0.25"-0.5"	n/a	32" (7X-3X)
12' (144")	108"	0.25"-1.5"	0.25"-0.5"	n/a	36" (12-20 lb.)	n/a
12' (144")	108"	0.25"-1.5"	n/a	≤2" OAL + 0.25"-0.5"	n/a	36" (7X-3X)

OAL = *overall length;* ≤ = *less than or equal to;* lb. = *pound;* n/a = *not applicable*

Note: Leader design is not an exact science and, therefore, the dimensions specified in the table above do not have to be met precisely to assure maximum performance. A variance of an inch or less in length is acceptable. The overall length (OAL) of the leader and tippet section specified in the table above does not include a loop of 0.25 inches or larger at the end of the T1 tippet section or the 2.5 inches or less between the Bimini Twist and the Chermanski Loop knot of the T2 tippet section.

A Type B leader system requires a maximum of four knots for construction and usage. In its simplest form with heavier tippets, however, the entire system can be built and fished using only one knot, the Chermanski Loop knot. It is recommended this leader system be built from a previously used commercial knotless tapered leader whose tippet section has been shortened from repeated fly changes. Remove the remaining tippet section by measuring the length of the leader from the opposite end to the length (L) specified in the table above and corresponding to the overall length (OAL) of the leader being used.

After the leader is cut to the specified length, a small loop of about 0.5 inches or less is formed using the Chermanski Loop knot at the end of semipermanent leader section L featuring the largest diameter for interconnection to the PVC fly line loop. A second loop is formed at the thinnest end of semipermanent leader section L using a Chermanski Loop knot. The size of the loop at the end of semipermanent leader section L can be small (about 0.25" to 0.5" long) for

interchanging tippet sections only or large (about 1" to 1.5" long) for exchanging tippet sections pretied to flies.

It is recommended flies are pretied to tippet sections for quick and reliable substitution. The connecting loop in tippet sections T1 and T2 can be made as small as possible (0.25" to 0.5" long) using a Chermanski Loop knot. For tippet strengths ranging from 3X to 7X, the loop should be formed from two lines created from a Bimini Twist. A fly can be attached to the tippet section using either a Chermanski Loop knot or an improved clinch knot.

A Type B leader system generally can handle a range of at least two tippet sizes, which is advantageous when using an assortment of flies, poppers and streamers pretied to tippet sections. In many fishing situations, flies pretied to tippet sections will provide the most optimum performance in terms of delivery and presentation. In dry-fly trout fishing, for example, a size 16 Parachute Adams can be pretied to a 5X tippet for best efficiency while the increased casting resistance of a size 16 Wulff Adams can be tied to a 4X tippet for comparable proficiency.

Type C: Knotless Leader System with an Interchangeable Tippet & Shock Trace (ST) for Floating & Intermediate Fly Lines

The Type C leader is the most versatile, efficient and practical system when using a commercial knotless tapered leader that requires a shock trace section. This system is essentially a modified Type B leader with a shortened tippet section to accommodate an added shock trace. It uses a maximum of only 3 knots for construction and usage.

Modified Commercial Knotless Tapered Leader

①② interconnection between the PVC Fly Line Loop (about 0.5 inches long) and the leader butt loop (about 0.5 inches long) formed by a Chermanski Loop knot.

② Chermanski Loop knot.

④⑤ double Chermanski Loop knot formed with the lines created from a Bimini Twist.

⑤⑥ double lines formed from a Bimini Twist and attached to a shock trace (ST) by an Albright Special.

⑥ Albright Special knot.

⑦ Haywire Twist.

⑨ twisted and burned plastic-coated stainless steel wire.

Type C Leader Specifications								
OAL	L	A	B	C + Loop	T1	T2	T3	ST
7.5' 90"	66"	0.25"-1.5"	n/a	≤2" OAL + 0.25"-0.5"	n/a	n/a	15" 2-6 lb.	9"-11"
7.5' 90"	66"	0.25"-1.5"	n/a	≤2" OAL + 0.25"-0.5"	n/a	15" 8-12 lb.	n/a	9"-11"
7.5' 90"	66"	0.25"-1.5"	0.25"-0.5"	n/a	15" 12-20 lb.	n/a	n/a	9"-11"
9' 108"	78"	0.25"-1.5"	n/a	≤2" OAL + 0.25"-0.5"	n/a	n/a	18" 2-6 lb.	9"-11"
9' 108"	78"	0.25"-1.5"	n/a	≤2" OAL + 0.25"-0.5"	n/a	18" 8-12 lb.	n/a	9"-11"
9' 108"	78"	0.25"-1.5"	0.25"-0.5"	n/a	18" 12-20 lb.	n/a	n/a	9"-11"
10' 120"	88"	0.25"-1.5"	n/a	≤2" OAL + 0.25"-0.5"	n/a	n/a	20" 2-6 lb.	9"-11"
10' 120"	88"	0.25"-1.5"	n/a	≤2" OAL + 0.25"-0.5"	n/a	20" 8-12 lb.	n/a	9"-11"
10' 120"	88"	0.25"-1.5"	0.25"-0.5"	n/a	20" 12-20 lb.	n/a	n/a	9"-11"
12' 144"	108"	0.25"-1.5"	n/a	≤2" OAL + 0.25"-0.5"	n/a	n/a.	24" 2-6 lb.	9"-11"
12' 144"	108"	0.25"-1.5"	n/a	≤2" OAL + 0.25"-0.5"	n/a"	24" 8-12 lb.	n/a	9"-11"
12' 144"	108"	0.25"-1.5"	0.25"-0.5"	n/a	24" 12-20 lb.	n/a	n/a	9"-11"

OAL = overall length; ST = shock trace; ≤ = less than or equal to; lb. = pound; n/a = not applicable

Note: Leader design is not an exact science and, therefore, the dimensions specified in the table on the previous page do not have to be met precisely to assure maximum performance. A variance of an inch or less in length is acceptable. The overall length (OAL) of the leader and tippet sections specified in the table does not include the negligible distance between the Bimini Twist and the Chermanski Loop knot of the T2 and T3 tippet sections. The overall length of the shock trace (ST) includes all the connecting knots at both ends in compliance with the rules regulated by the IGFA, which are discussed in Chapter 6.

It is recommended this leader system be built from a previously used commercial knotless tapered leader whose tippet section has been shortened from repeated fly changes. Remove the remaining tippet section by measuring the length of the leader from the opposite end to the length (L) specified in the table on the previous page and corresponding to the overall leader length of the leader being used.

After the leader is cut to the specified length, a small loop of about 0.5 inches or less is formed using the Chermanski Loop knot at the end of semipermanent leader section L featuring the largest diameter for interconnection to the PVC fly line loop. A second loop is formed at the thinnest end of semipermanent leader section L using a Chermanski Loop knot. The size of the loop at the end of semipermanent leader section L can be small (about 0.25" to 0.5" long) for interchanging tippet sections only or large (about 1" to 1.5" long) for exchanging tippet sections pretied to flies.

It is recommended flies are pretied to tippet and shock trace sections for quick and reliable substitution. The connecting loop in tippet sections T1, T2 and T3 can be made as small as possible (0.25" to 0.5" long) using a Chermanski Loop knot. For tippet

strengths ranging from 2 to 12 pounds, the loop should be formed from two lines created from a Bimini Twist. A fly can be attached to the shock trace section using either a Chermanski Loop, a Haywire Twist or plastic-coated stainless steel wire that is twisted and burned.

Type D: Knotless Leader System with Interchangeable Tippet & Shock Trace (ST) Sections for Floating & Intermediate Fly Lines

The Type D leader is a modified Type C leader with inter-changeable tippet and shock trace sections for maximum versatility when using a commercial knotless tapered leader.

Modified Commercial Knotless Tapered Leader

①② interconnection between the PVC Fly Line Loop (about 0.5 inches long) and the leader butt loop (about 0.5 inches long) formed by a Chermanski Loop knot.

② Chermanski Loop knot.

④⑤ double Chermanski Loop knot formed with the lines created from a Bimini Twist.

⑦ Haywire Twist.

⑧ Haywire Twist Loop.

⑨ twisted and burned plastic-coated stainless steel wire.

				Type D Leader Specifications						
OAL	L	A	B	C + Loop	D	T1+Loop	T2+Loop	T3+Loop	ST+Loop	
7.5'-8' 90"-96"	66"	0.25"-1.5"	n/a	≤2" OAL + 0.25"-0.5"	1"-1.5"	n/a	n/a	15"+0.25" 2-6 lb.	9"-11" + 0.25"-0.375"	
7.5'-8' 90"-96"	66"	0.25"-1.5"	n/a	≤2" OAL + 0.25"-0.5"	n/a	n/a	15"+0.25" 8-12 lb.	n/a	9"-11" + 0.25"-0.375"	
7.5'-8' 90"-96"	66"	0.25"-1.5"	0.25"-0.5"	n/a	n/a	15"+0.25" 12-20 lb.	n/a	n/a	9"-11" + 0.25"-0.375"	
≈9' 108"	78"	0.25"-1.5"	n/a	≤2" OAL + 0.25"-0.5"	1"-1.5"	n/a	n/a	18"+0.25" 12-20 lb.	9"-11" + 0.25"-0.375"	
≈9' 108"	78"	0.25"-1.5"	n/a	≤2" OAL + 0.25"-0.5"	n/a	n/a	18"+0.25" 12-20 lb.	n/a	9"-11" + 0.25"-0.375"	
≈9' 108"	78"	0.25"-1.5"	0.25"-0.5"	n/a	n/a	18"+0.25" 12-20 lb.	n/a	n/a	9"-11" + 0.25"-0.375"	
≈10' 120"	88"	0.25"-1.5"	n/a	≤2" OAL + 0.25"-0.5"	1"-1.5"	n/a	n/a	20"+0.25" 12-20 lb.	9"-11" + 0.25"-0.375"	
≈10' 120"	88"	0.25"-1.5"	n/a	≤2" OAL + 0.25"-0.5"	n/a	n/a	20"+0.25" 12-20 lb.	n/a	9"-11" + 0.25"-0.375"	
≈10' 120"	88"	0.25"-1.5"	0.25"-0.5"	n/a	n/a	20"+0.25" 12-20 lb.	n/a	n/a	9"-11" + 0.25"-0.375"	
≈12' 144"	108"	0.25"-1.5"	n/a	≤2" OAL + 0.25"-0.5"	1"-1.5"	n/a	n/a	24"+0.25" 12-20 lb.	9"-11" + 0.25"-0.375"	

Type D Leader Specifications									
OAL	L	A	B	C + Loop	D	T1+Loop	T2+Loop	T3+Loop	ST+Loop
≈12' 144"	108"	0.25"-1.5"	n/a	≤2" OAL + 0.25"-0.5"	n/a	n/a	24"+0.25" 12-20 lb.	n/a	9"-11" + 0.25"-0.375"
≈12' 144"	108"	0.25"-1.5"	0.25"-0.5"	n/a	n/a	24"+0.25" 12-20 lb.	n/a	n/a	9"-11" + 0.25"-0.375"

OAL = overall length; ≈ = approximately; ST = shock trace; ≤ = less than or equal to; lb. = pound   n/a = not applicable

Note: Leader design is not an exact science and, therefore, the dimensions specified in the table above do not have to be met precisely to assure maximum performance. A variance of an inch or less in length is acceptable. The overall length (OAL) of the leader and tippet sections specified in the table above does not include the negligible distance between the Bimini Twist and the Chermanski Loop knot of the T2 and T3 tippet sections or the small loop formed in the shock trace section. The overall length of the shock trace (ST) includes all the connecting knots at both ends in compliance with the rules regulated by the IGFA, which are discussed in Chapter 6.

It is recommended this leader system be built from a previously used commercial knotless tapered leader whose tippet section has been shortened from repeated fly changes. Remove the remaining tippet section by measuring the length of the leader from the opposite end to the length (L) specified in the table above and corresponding to the overall leader length of the leader being used.

After the leader is cut to the specified length, a small loop of about 0.5 inches or less is formed using the Chermanski Loop knot at the end of semipermanent leader section L featuring the largest diameter for interconnection to the PVC fly line loop. A second loop is formed at the opposite end of semipermanent leader section L using a Chermanski Loop knot for attaching tippet and shock trace sections. The size of the loop at the end of semipermanent leader section L can be small (about 0.25" to 0.5" long) for interchanging tippet and shock trace sections only or large (about 1" to 1.5" long) for exchanging shock traces pretied to flies. The loop size in tippet sections T1, T2 and T3 connecting to semipermanent leader section L should range between 0.25" and 0.5" in length. The loop at the other end of the tippet sections should be as small as possible (0.25" to 0.375") to interlock with the loop of similar size formed in the shock trace.

It is recommended flies are pretied to shock traces for quick and reliable substitution. The tippet section is connected to the loop of the shock trace section and both assemblies are then interlocked to the loop at the end of the semipermanent leader section L. For tippet strengths ranging from 2 to 12 pounds, the loop should be formed from two lines created from a Bimini Twist. A fly can be attached to the shock trace section using either a Chermanski Loop, a Haywire Twist or plastic-coated stainless steel wire that is twisted and burned.

Type E: Compound Leader System for Floating & Intermediate Fly Lines

The Type E leader system is used in general freshwater situations and in certain saltwater applications where a shock trace is not required. For a more specific leader system designed for trout, salmon and steelhead fishing with 2- to 7-weight floating fly lines, refer to the Type K leader system illustrated in Chapter 10. A Type E leader system requires a minimum of 3 knots for construction and usage.

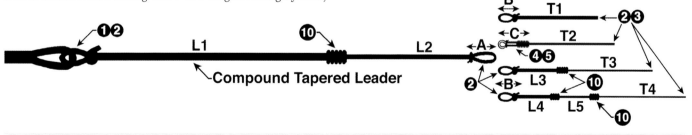

❶❷ interconnection between the PVC Fly Line Loop (about 0.5 inches long) and the leader butt loop (about 0.5 inches long) formed by a Chermanski Loop knot.

❷ Chermanski Loop knot.

❸ Improved Clinch knot.

❹❺ double Chermanski Loop knot formed with the lines created from a Bimini Twist.

❿ Blood knot.

Type E Leader Butt Specifications				
Fly Line	OAL	L1 + Loop	L2	A
2-4 wt. F/I	5' (F/I)	36"(F)/36"(I) (.021")+0.5"	24" (.019")	0.25"-1.5"
5-6 wt. F/I	6' (F) or 5' (I)	48"(F)/36"(I) (.023")+0.5"	24" (.021")	0.25"-1.5"
7-8 wt. F/I	6' (F) or 5' (I)	48"(F)/36"(I) (.025")+0.5"	24" (.023")	0.25"-1.5"
9-10 wt. F/I	6' (F) or 5' (I)	48"(F)/36"(I) (.026")+0.5"	24" (.025")	0.25"-1.5"
12-13 wt. F/I	6' (F) or 5' (I)	48"(F)/36"(I) (.032")+0.5"	24" (.026")	0.25"-1.5"

OAL = overall length; wt. = weight; F/I = floating or intermediate; F = floating; I = intermediate

Type E Specifications for T1 & T2 Tippets					
Fly Line	OAL	B	C + Loop	T1	T2
2-4 wt.	≈7' (F/I)	n/a	≤2" OAL + 0.25"-0.5"	n/a	24" 4-8 lb.
2-4 wt.	≈7' (F/I)	n/a	n/a	24" 8-12 lb.	n/a
5-6 wt.	≈8' (F) ≈7' (I)	n/a	≤2" OAL + 0.25"-0.5"	n/a	24" 4-8 lb.
5-6 wt.	≈8' (F) ≈7' (I)	0.25"-0.5"	n/a	24" 8-12 lb.	n/a
7-10 wt.	≈8' (F) ≈7' (I)	n/a	≤2" OAL + 0.25"-0.5"	n/a	24" 4-8 lb.
7-10 wt.	≈8' (F) ≈7' (I)	0.25"-0.5"	n/a	24" 8-16 lb.	n/a
12-13 wt.	≈8' (F) ≈7' (I)	0.25"-0.5"	n/a	24" 10-20 lb.	n/a

OAL = overall length; wt. = weight; ≤ = less than or equal to; lb. = pound; ≈ = approximately; F/I = floating or intermediate; n/a = not applicable; F = floating; I = intermediate

Type E Specifications for T3 & T4 Tippets							
Fly Line	OAL	B	L3	T3	L4	L5	T4
2-8 wt.	≈8.5' (F) or 9.5' (F) ≈8.5' (I)	0.25"-0.5"	18" 8 lb.	24" 4 lb.	n/a	n/a	n/a
2-8 wt.	≈9' (F) or 10' (F) ≈9' (I)	0.25"-0.5"	n/a	n/a	12" 12 lb.	12" 8 lb.	12" 4 lb.
2-9 wt.	≈8.5' (F) or 9.5' (F) ≈8.5' (I)	0.25"-0.5"	18" 12 lb.	24" 6 lb.	n/a	n/a	n/a
2-9 wt.	≈9' (F) or 10' (F) ≈9' (I)	0.25"-0.5"	n/a	n/a	12" 12 lb.	12" 8 lb.	12" 6 lb.
2-10 wt.	≈8.5' (F) or 9.5' (F) ≈8.5' (I)	0.25"-0.5"	18" 12 lb.	24" 8 lb.	n/a	n/a	n/a
2-10 wt.	≈9' (F) or 10' (F) ≈9' (I)	0.25"-0.5"	n/a	n/a	12" 16 lb.	12" 12 lb.	12" 8 lb.
4-10 wt.	≈9.5' (F) ≈8.5' (I)	0.25"-0.5"	18" 16 lb.	24" 10 lb.	n/a	n/a	n/a
4-10 wt.	≈9.5' (F) ≈8.5' (I)	0.25"-0.5"	n/a	n/a	12" 16 lb.	12" 12 lb.	12" 10 lb.
6-13 wt.	≈9.5' (F) ≈8.5' (I)	0.25"-0.5"	18" 16 lb.	24" 12 lb.	n/a	n/a	n/a
6-13 wt.	≈9.5' (F) ≈8.5' (I)	0.25"-0.5"	n/a	n/a	12" 20 lb.	12" 16 lb.	12" 12 lb.
7-13 wt.	≈9.5' (F) ≈8.5' (I)	0.25"-0.5"	18" 20 lb.	24" 16 lb.	n/a	n/a	n/a
9-13 wt.	≈9.5' (F) ≈8.5' (I)	0.25"-0.5"	18" 25 lb.	24" 20 lb.	n/a	n/a	n/a

OAL = overall length; wt. = weight; lb. = pound; n/a = not applicable; ≈ = approximately; F = floating; I = intermediate

Note: Leader design is not an exact science and, therefore, the dimensions specified in the table above do not have to be met precisely to assure maximum performance. A variance of an inch or less in length is acceptable. The overall length (OAL) of the leader and tippet sections specified in the two Specifications table does not include the negligible distance between the Bimini Twist and the Chermanski Loop knot of the T2 tippet section.

To assemble the system, L1 and L2, L3 and T3, and L4, L5 and T4 sections are joined together using a blood knot. A small loop of about 0.5 inches or less is formed using the Chermanski Loop knot at the end of semipermanent leader section L1 for interconnection to the PVC fly line loop. A loop is also formed at the end of semipermanent leader section L2 using a Chermanski Loop knot for connecting pretied tippet sections. The size of the loop at the end of semipermanent leader section L2 can be small (about 0.25" to 0.5" long) for interchanging tippet sections only or large (about 1" to 1.5" long) for exchanging tippet sections pretied to flies.

It is recommended flies are pretied to tippet sections for quick and reliable substitution. The connecting loop in all four tippet sections can be made as small as possible (0.25" to 0.5" long) using a Chermanski Loop knot. For tippet strengths ranging from 4 to 12 pounds, the loop should be formed from two lines created from a Bimini Twist. A fly can be attached to the tippet section using either a Chermanski Loop knot or an improved clinch knot.

Type F: Compound Leader System with a Shock Trace (ST) for Floating & Intermediate Fly Lines

The Type F leader system is used in certain freshwater situations and in many saltwater applications where a shock trace is required. A Type F leader system requires a minimum of 4 knots for construction and usage.

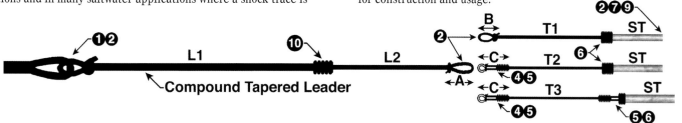

1 2 interconnection between the PVC Fly Line Loop (about 0.5 inches long) and the leader butt loop (about 0.5 inches long) formed by a Chermanski Loop knot.

2 Chermanski Loop knot.

4 5 double Chermanski Loop knot formed with the lines created from a Bimini Twist.

5 6 double lines formed from a Bimini Twist and attached to a shock trace (ST) by an Albright Special.

6 Albright Special knot.

7 Haywire Twist.

9 twisted and burned plastic-coated stainless steel wire.

10 Blood knot.

Type F Leader Specifications										
Fly Line	OAL	L1 + Loop	L2	A	B	C + Loop	T1	T2	T3	ST + Loop
2-4 wt. F/I	≈7'-8' (F/I)	36"+0.5" .021"	24" .019"	0.25"-1.5"	n/a	≤2" OAL + 0.25"-0.5"	n/a	n/a	15"-24" 2-6 lb.	9"-11" + 0.25"-0.375"
2-4 wt. F/I	≈7'-8' (F/I)	36"+0.5" .021"	24" .019"	0.25"-1.5"	n/a	≤2" OAL + 0.25"-0.5"	n/a	15"-24" 8-12 lb.	n/a	9"-11" + 0.25"-0.375"
2-4 wt. F/I	≈7'-8' (F/I)	36"+0.5" .021"	24" .019"	0.25"-1.5"	0.25"-0.5"	n/a	15"-24" 12-16 lb.	n/a	n/a	9"-11" + 0.25"-0.375"
5-6 wt. F/I	≈8'-9' (F) ≈7'-8'(I)	48"(F)/36"(I)+0.5" .023"	24" .021"	0.25"-1.5"	n/a	≤2" OAL + 0.25"-0.5"	n/a	n/a	15"-24" 2-6 lb.	9"-11" + 0.25"-0.375"
5-6 wt. F/I	≈8'-9' (F) ≈7'-8'(I)	48"(F)/36"(I)+0.5" .023"	24" .021"	0.25"-1.5"	n/a	≤2" OAL + 0.25"-0.5"	n/a	15"-24" 8-12 lb.	n/a	9"-11" + 0.25"-0.375"
5-6 wt. F/I	≈8'-9' (F) ≈7'-8'(I)	48"(F)/36"(I)+0.5" .023"	24" .021"	0.25"-1.5"	0.25"-0.5"	n/a	15"-24" 12-16 lb.	n/a	n/a	9"-11" + 0.25"-0.375"
7-8 wt. F/I	≈8'-9' (F) ≈7'-8'(I)	48"(F)/36"(I)+0.5" .025"	24" .023"	0.25"-1.5"	n/a	≤2" OAL + 0.25"-0.5"	n/a	n/a	15"-24" 2-6 lb.	9"-11" + 0.25"-0.375"
7-8 wt. F/I	≈8'-9' (F) ≈7'-8'(I)	48"(F)/36"(I)+0.5" .025"	24" .023"	0.25"-1.5"	n/a	≤2" OAL + 0.25"-0.5"	n/a	15"-24" 8-12 lb.	n/a	9"-11" + 0.25"-0.375"
7-8 wt. F/I	≈8'-9' (F) ≈7'-8'(I)	48"(F)/36"(I)+0.5" .025"	24" .023"	0.25"-1.5"	0.25"-0.5"	n/a	15"-24" 12-20 lb.	n/a	n/a	9"-11" + 0.25"-0.375"
9-10 wt. F/I	≈8'-9' (F) ≈7'-8'(I)	48"(F)/36"(I)+0.5" .026"	24" .025"	0.25"-1.5"	n/a	≤2" OAL + 0.25"-0.5"	n/a	n/a	15"-24" 4-6 lb.	9"-11" + 0.25"-0.375"
9-10 wt. F/I	≈8'-9' (F) ≈7'-8'(I)	48"(F)/36"(I)+0.5" .026"	24" .025"	0.25"-1.5"	n/a	≤2" OAL + 0.25"-0.5"	n/a	15"-24" 8-12 lb.	n/a	9"-11" + 0.25"-0.375"
9-10 wt. F/I	≈8'-9' (F) ≈7'-8'(I)	48"(F)/36"(I)+0.5" .026"	24" .025"	0.25"-1.5"	0.25"-0.5"	n/a	15"-24" 12-20 lb.	n/a	n/a	9"-11" + 0.25"-0.375"
12-13 wt. F/I	≈8'-9' (F) ≈7'-8'(I)	48"(F)/36"(I)+0.5" .032"	24" .026"	0.25"-1.5"	n/a	≤2" OAL + 0.25"-0.5"	n/a	15"-24" 8-12 lb.	n/a	9"-11" + 0.25"-0.375"
12-13 wt. F/I	≈8'-9' (F) ≈7'-8'(I)	48"(F)/36"(I)+0.5" .032"	24" .026"	0.25"-1.5"	0.25"-0.5"	n/a	15"-24" 12-20 lb.	n/a	n/a	9"-11" + 0.25"-0.375"

OAL = overall length; ST = shock trace; F/I = floating or intermediate; F = floating; I = intermediate; wt. = weight; ≈ = approximately; ≤ = less than or equal to; lb. = pound; n/a = not applicable

Note: Leader design is not an exact science and, therefore, the dimensions specified in the table above do not have to be met precisely to assure maximum performance. A variance of an inch or less in length is acceptable. The overall length (OAL) of the leader and tippet sections specified in the table above does not include the negligible distance between the Bimini Twist and the Chermanski Loop knot of the T2 and T3 tippet sections. The overall length of the shock trace (ST) includes all the connecting knots at both ends in compliance with the rules regulated by the IGFA, which are discussed in Chapter 6.

To assemble the system, L1 and L2 leader sections are joined together using a blood knot. A small loop of about 0.5 inches or less is formed using the Chermanski Loop knot at the end of semipermanent leader section L1 for interconnection to the PVC fly line loop. A loop is also formed at the end of semipermanent leader section L2 using a Chermanski Loop knot for attaching a pretied tippet and shock trace section. The size of the loop at the end of semipermanent leader section L2 can be small (about 0.25" to 0.5" long) for interchanging tippet and shock trace sections only or large (about 1" to 1.5" long) for exchanging tippet and shock trace sections pretied to flies.

It is recommended flies are pretied to tippet and shock trace sections for quick and reliable substitution. The connecting loop in all three tippet sections can be made as small as possible (0.25" to 0.5" long) using a Chermanski Loop knot. For tippet strengths ranging from 2 to 12 pounds, the loop should be formed from two lines created from a Bimini Twist. A fly can be attached to the shock trace section using a Chermanski Loop, a Haywire Twist or plastic-coated stainless steel wire that is twisted and burned.

Type G: Compound Leader System with an Interchangeable Shock Trace (ST) for Floating & Intermediate Fly Lines

The Type G leader is a modified Type F leader system with interchangeable tippet and shock trace sections for optimum adaptability to sudden or unexpected changes in fishing strategy and tactics. In most fishing situations, it is usually the shock trace section that needs to be replaced. As a result, this leader system allows one of these components to be quickly exchanged, if it becomes unusable, without the need to replace the other element.

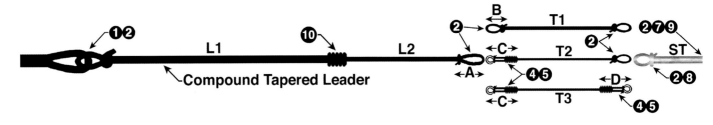

1 2 interconnection between the PVC Fly Line Loop (about 0.5 inches long) and the leader butt loop (about 0.5 inches long) formed by a Chermanski Loop knot.

2 Chermanski Loop knot.

4 5 double Chermanski Loop knot formed with the lines created from a Bimini Twist.

7 Haywire Twist.

8 Haywire Twist Loop.

9 twisted and burned plastic-coated stainless steel wire.

10 Blood knot.

Type G Leader Specifications											
Fly Line	OAL	L1 + Loop	L2	A	B	C + Loop	D	T1 + Loop	T2 + Loop	T3 + Loop	ST + Loop
2-4 wt. F/I	≈7'-8' (F/I)	36"+0.5" .021"	24" .019"	0.25"-1.5"	n/a	≤2" OAL + 0.25"-0.5"	1"- 1.5"	n/a	n/a	15"-24" + 0.25" 2-6 lb.	9"-11" + 0.25"- 0.375"
2-4 wt. F/I	≈7'-8' (F/I)	36"+0.5" .021"	24" .019"	0.25"-1.5"	n/a	≤2" OAL + 0.25"-0.5"	n/a	n/a	15"-24" + 0.25" 8-12 lb.	n/a	9"-11" + 0.25"- 0.375"

Type G Leader Specifications

Fly Line	OAL	L1 + Loop	L2	A	B	C + Loop	D	T1 + Loop	T2 + Loop	T3 + Loop	ST + Loop
2-4 wt. F/I	≈7'-8' (F/I)	36"+0.5" .021"	24" .019"	0.25"-1.5"	0.25"-0.5"	n/a	n/a	15"-24" + 0.25" 12-16 lb.	n/a	n/a	9"-11" + 0.25"- 0.375"
5-6 wt. F/I	≈8'-9' (F) ≈7'-8'(I)	48"(F)/36"(I)+0.5" .023"	24" .021"	0.25"-1.5"	n/a	≤2" OAL + 0.25"-0.5"	1"- 1.5"	n/a	n/a	15"-24" + 0.25" 2-6 lb.	9"-11" + 0.25"- 0.375"
5-6 wt. F/I	≈8'-9' (F) ≈7'-8'(I)	48"(F)/36"(I)+0.5" .023"	24" .021"	0.25"-1.5"	n/a	≤2" OAL + 0.25"-0.5"	n/a	n/a	15"-24" + 0.25" 8-12 lb.	n/a	9"-11" + 0.25"- 0.375"
5-6 wt. F/I	≈8'-9' (F) ≈7'-8'(I)	48"(F)/36"(I)+0.5" .023"	24" .021"	0.25"-1.5"	0.25"-0.5"	n/a	n/a	15"-24" + 0.25" 12-16 lb.	n/a	n/a	9"-11" + 0.25"- 0.375"
7-8 wt. F/I	≈8'-9' (F) ≈7'-8'(I)	48"(F)/36"(I)+0.5" .025"	24" .023"	0.25"-1.5"	n/a	≤2" OAL + 0.25"-0.5"	1"- 1.5"	n/a	n/a	15"-24" + 0.25" 2-6 lb.	9"-11" + 0.25"- 0.375"
7-8 wt. F/I	≈8'-9' (F) ≈7'-8'(I)	48"(F)/36"(I)+0.5" .025"	24" .023"	0.25"-1.5"	n/a	≤2" OAL + 0.25"-0.5"	n/a	n/a	15"-24" + 0.25" 8-12 lb.	n/a	9"-11" + 0.25"- 0.375"
7-8 wt. F/I	≈8'-9' (F) ≈7'-8'(I)	48"(F)/36"(I)+0.5" .025"	24" .023"	0.25"-1.5"	0.25"-0.5"	n/a	n/a	15"-24" + 0.25" 12-20 lb.	n/a	n/a	9"-11" + 0.25"- 0.375"
9-10 wt. F/I	≈8'-9' (F) ≈7'-8'(I)	48"(F)/36"(I)+0.5" .026"	24" .025"	0.25"-1.5"	n/a	≤2" OAL + 0.25"-0.5"	1"- 1.5"	n/a	n/a	15"-24" + 0.25" 4-6 lb.	9"-11" + 0.25"- 0.375"
9-10 wt. F/I	≈8'-9' (F) ≈7'-8'(I)	48"(F)/36"(I)+0.5" .026"	24" .026"	0.25"-1.5"	n/a	≤2" OAL + 0.25"-0.5"	n/a	n/a	15"-24" + 0.25" 8-12 lb.	n/a	9"-11" + 0.25"- 0.375"
9-10 wt. F/I	≈8'-9' (F) ≈7'-8'(I)	48"(F)/36"(I)+0.5" .026"	24" .026"	0.25"-1.5"	0.25"-0.5"	n/a	n/a	15"-24" + 0.25" 12-20 lb.	n/a	n/a	9"-11" + 0.25"- 0.375"
12-13 wt. F/I	≈8'-9' (F) ≈7'-8'(I)	48"(F)/36"(I)+0.5" .032"	24" .026"	0.25"-1.5"	n/a	≤2" OAL + 0.25"-0.5"	n/a	n/a	15"-24" + 0.25" 8-12 lb.	n/a	9"-11" + 0.25"- 0.375"
12-13 wt. F/I	≈8'-9' (F) ≈7'-8'(I)	48"(F)/36"(I)+0.5" .032"	24" .026"	0.25"-1.5"	0.25"-0.5"	n/a	n/a	15"-24" + 0.25" 12-20 lb.	n/a	n/a	9"-11" + 0.25"- 0.375"

OAL = overall length   ST = shock trace   F/I = floating or intermediate   wt. = weight   F = floating
I = intermediate   ≈ = approximately   ≤ = less than or equal to   lb. = pound   n/a = not applicable

Note: Leader design is not an exact science and, therefore, the dimensions specified in the table above do not have to be met precisely to assure maximum performance. A variance of an inch or less in length is acceptable. The overall length (OAL) of the leader and tippet sections specified in the table above does not include the negligible distance between the Bimini Twist and the Chermanski Loop knot of the T2 and T3 tippet sections or the small loop formed in the shock trace section. The overall length of the shock trace (ST) includes all the connecting knots at both ends in compliance with the rules regulated by the IGFA, which are discussed in Chapter 6.

To assemble the system, L1 and L2 leader sections are joined together using a blood knot. A small loop of about 0.5 inches or less is formed using the Chermanski Loop knot at the end of semipermanent leader section L1 for interconnection to the PVC fly line loop. A loop is also formed at the end of semipermanent leader section L2 using a Chermanski Loop knot for attaching pretied tippet and shock trace sections. The loop size in all three tippet sections connecting to semipermanent leader section L should range between 0.25" and 0.5" in length. The loop at the other end of a tippet section should be as small as possible (0.25" to 0.375") to interlock with the loop of similar size formed in the shock trace.

It is recommended flies are pretied to shock traces for quick and reliable substitution. The tippet section is connected to the loop of the shock trace section and both assemblies are then interlocked to the loop at the end of the semipermanent leader section L2. For tippet strengths ranging from 2 to 12 pounds, the loop should be formed from two lines created from a Bimini Twist. A fly can be attached to the shock trace section using either a Chermanski Loop, a Haywire Twist or plastic-coated stainless steel wire that is twisted and burned.

Type H: Compound Leader System for Sinking Fly Lines

A Type H leader system is a modified version of the Type E leader for sinking fly lines. The shortness of semipermanent leader section L1 and the overall length of the system, permits a fly to be fished deeper in the water column and in a more lateral alignment with a sinking fly line. It requires a maximum of 3 knots for construction and usage.

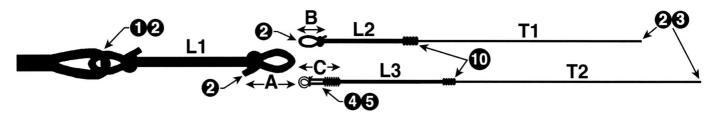

❶❷ interconnection between the PVC Fly Line Loop (about 0.5 inches long) and the leader butt loop (about 0.5 inches long) formed by a Chermanski Loop knot.

❷ Chermanski Loop knot.

❸ Improved Clinch knot.

❹❺ double Chermanski Loop knot formed with the lines created from a Bimini Twist.

❿ Blood knot.

Type H Leader Specifications										
Fly Line	**OAL**	**L1 + Loop**	**A**	**B**	**C + Loop**	**L2**	**L3**	**T1**	**T2**
4-6 wt.	≈4.5'	24"+0.5" .023"	0.25"-1.5"	n/a	≤2" OAL + 0.25"-0.5"	n/a	12" 8 lb.	n/a	18" 4 lb.
4-6 wt.	≈4.5'	24"+0.5" .023"	0.25"-1.5"	n/a	≤2" OAL + 0.25"-0.5"	n/a	12" 10 lb.	n/a	18" 6 lb.
4-6 wt.	≈4.5'	24"+0.5" .023"	0.25"-1.5"	n/a	≤2" OAL + 0.25"-0.5"	n/a	12" 12 lb.	n/a	18" 8 lb.
4-6 wt.	≈4.5'	24"+0.5" .023"	0.25"-1.5"	0.25"-0.5"	n/a	12" 12 lb.	n/a	18" 10 lb.	n/a
4-6 wt.	≈4.5'	24"+0.5" .023"	0.25"-1.5"	0.25"-0.5"	n/a	12" 16 lb.	n/a	18" 12 lb.	n/a
7-9 wt.	≈4.5'	24"+0.5" .025"	0.25"-1.5"	n/a	≤2" OAL + 0.25"-0.5"	n/a	12" 8 lb.	n/a	18" 4 lb.
7-9 wt.	≈4.5'	24"+0.5" .025"	0.25"-1.5"	n/a	≤2" OAL + 0.25"-0.5"	n/a	12" 10 lb.	n/a	18" 6 lb.
7-9 wt.	≈4.5'	24"+0.5" .025"	0.25"-1.5"	n/a	≤2" OAL + 0.25"-0.5"	n/a	12" 12 lb.	n/a	18" 8 lb.
7-9 wt.	≈4.5'	24"+0.5" .025"	0.25"-1.5"	0.25"-0.5"	n/a	12" 12 lb.	n/a	18" 10 lb.	n/a
7-9 wt.	≈4.5'	24"+0.5" .025"	0.25"-1.5"	0.25"-0.5"	n/a	12" 16 lb.	n/a	18" 12 lb.	n/a
7-9 wt.	≈4.5'	24"+0.5" .025"	0.25"-1.5"	0.25"-0.5"	n/a	12" 20 lb.	n/a	18" 16 lb.	n/a
10-13 wt.	≈4.5'	24"+0.5" .026"	0.25"-1.5"	n/a	≤2" OAL + 0.25"-0.5"	n/a	12" 10 lb.	n/a	18" 6 lb.
10-13 wt.	≈4.5'	24"+0.5" .026"	0.25"-1.5"	n/a	≤2" OAL + 0.25"-0.5"	n/a	12" 12 lb.	n/a	18" 8 lb.
10-13 wt.	≈4.5'	24"+0.5" .026"	0.25"-1.5"	0.25"-0.5"	n/a	12" 12 lb.	n/a	18" 10 lb.	n/a

Type H Leader Specifications									
Fly Line	OAL	L1 + Loop	A	B	C + Loop	L2	L3	T1	T2
10-13 wt.	≈4.5'	24"+0.5" .026"	0.25"-1.5"	0.25"-0.5"	n/a	12" 16 lb.	n/a	18" 12 lb.	n/a
10-13 wt.	≈4.5'	24"+0.5" .026"	0.25"-1.5"	0.25"-0.5"	n/a	12" 20 lb.	n/a	18" 16 lb.	n/a
10-13 wt.	≈4.5'	24"+0.5" .026"	0.25"-1.5"	0.25"-0.5"	n/a	12" 25 lb.	n/a	18" 20 lb.	n/a

OAL = overall length   wt. = weight   ≈ = approximately   ≤ = less than or equal to   lb. = pound   n/a = not applicable

Note: Leader design is not an exact science and, therefore, the dimensions specified in the table above do not have to be met precisely to assure maximum performance. A variance of an inch or less in length is acceptable. The overall length (OAL) of the leader and tippet sections specified in the table above does not include the negligible distance between the Bimini Twist and the Chermanski Loop knot of the L3 section or the small loop formed in the L2 and L3 sections.

To assemble the system, a small loop of about 0.5 inches or less is formed using the Chermanski Loop knot at the end of semipermanent leader section L1 for interconnection to the PVC fly line loop. A loop is also formed at the opposite end of semi-permanent leader section L1 using a Chermanski Loop knot for connecting pretied tippet sections. The size of the loop at the end of semipermanent leader section L1 can be small (about 0.25" to 0.5" long) for interchanging tippet sections only or large (about 1" to 1.5" long) for exchanging tippet sections pretied to flies. L2 and T1, and L3 and T2 sections are joined together using a blood knot.

It is recommended flies are pretied to tippet sections for quick and reliable substitution. The connecting loop in tippet sections T1 and T2 can be made as small as possible (0.25" to 0.5" long) using a Chermanski Loop knot. For tippet strengths ranging from 4 to 12 pounds, the loop should be formed from two lines created from a Bimini Twist. A fly can be attached to the tippet section using either a Chermanski Loop knot or an improved clinch knot.

Type I: Compound Leader System with a Shock Trace (ST) for Sinking Fly Lines

A Type I leader system is a modified version of the Type F leader for sinking fly lines. The shortness of semipermanent leader section L1 and the overall length of the system, permits a fly to be fished deeper in the water column and in a more lateral alignment with a sinking fly line. It requires a maximum of 4 knots for construction and usage.

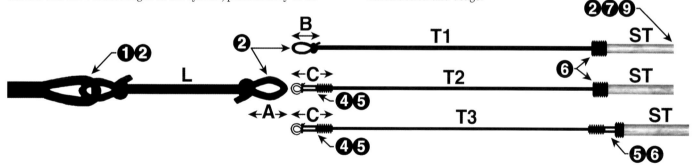

①② interconnection between the PVC Fly Line Loop (about 0.5 inches long) and the leader butt loop (about 0.5 inches long) formed by a Chermanski Loop knot.

② Chermanski Loop knot.

④⑤ double Chermanski Loop knot formed with the lines created from a Bimini Twist.

⑤⑥ double lines formed from a Bimini Twist and attached to a shock trace (ST) by an Albright Special.

⑥ Albright Special knot.

⑦ Haywire Twist.

⑨ twisted and burned plastic-coated stainless steel wire.

⑩ Blood knot.

Type I Leader Specifications									
Fly Line	OAL	L1 + Loop	A	B	C	T1	T2	T3	ST
4-6 wt.	≈4.5'	24"+0.5" .023"	0.25"-1.5"	n/a	≤2" OAL + 0.25"-0.5"	n/a	n/a	15"-24" 2-6 lb.	9"-11"
4-6 wt.	≈4.5'	24"+0.5" .023"	0.25"-1.5"	n/a	≤2" OAL + 0.25"-0.5"	n/a	15"-24" 8-12 lb.	n/a	9"-11"
4-6 wt.	≈4.5'	24"+0.5" .023"	0.25"-1.5"	0.25"-0.5"	n/a	15"-24" 12-16 lb.	n/a	n/a	9"-11"
7-9 wt.	≈4.5'	24"+0.5" .025"	0.25"-1.5"	n/a	≤2" OAL + 0.25"-0.5"	n/a	n/a	15"-24" 4-6 lb.	9"-11"
7-9 wt.	≈4.5'	24"+0.5" .025"	0.25"-1.5"	n/a	≤2" OAL + 0.25"-0.5"	n/a	15"-24" 8-12 lb.	n/a	9"-11"
7-9 wt.	≈4.5'	24"+0.5" .025"	0.25"-1.5"	0.25"-0.5"	n/a	15"-24" 12-20 lb.	n/a	n/a	9"-11"
10-13 wt.	≈4.5'	24"+0.5" .026"	0.25"-1.5"	n/a	≤2" OAL + 0.25"-0.5"	n/a	n/a	15"-24" 6-8 lb.	9"-11"
10-13 wt.	≈4.5'	24"+0.5" .026"	0.25"-1.5"	n/a	≤2" OAL + 0.25"-0.5"	n/a	15"-24" 10-12 lb.	n/a	9"-11"
10-13 wt.	≈4.5'	24"+0.5" .026"	0.25"-1.5"	0.25"-0.5"	n/a	15"-24" 12-20 lb.	n/a	n/a	9"-11"

OAL = overall length   ST = shock trace   wt. = weight   ≈ = approximately   ≤ = less than or equal to   lb. = pound   n/a = not applicable

Note: Leader design is not an exact science and, therefore, the dimensions specified in the table above do not have to be met precisely to assure maximum performance. A variance of an inch or less in length is acceptable. The overall length (OAL) of the leader and tippet sections specified in the table above does not include the negligible distance between the Bimini Twist and the Chermanski Loop knot of the T2 and T3 tippet sections. The overall length of the shock trace (ST) includes all the connecting knots at both ends in compliance with the rules regulated by the IGFA, which are discussed in Chapter 6.

To assemble the system, a small loop of about 0.5 inches or less is formed using the Chermanski Loop knot at the end of semipermanent leader section L for interconnection to the PVC fly line loop. A loop is also formed at the opposite end of semipermanent leader section L using a Chermanski Loop knot for connecting pretied tippet and shock trace sections. The size of the loop at the end of semipermanent leader section L can be small (about 0.25" to 0.5" long) for interchanging tippet sections only or large (about 1" to 1.5" long) for exchanging tippet and shock trace sections pretied to flies.

It is recommended flies are pretied to tippet and shock trace sections for quick and reliable substitution. The connecting loop in all three tippet sections can be made as small as possible (0.25" to 0.5" long) using a Chermanski Loop knot. For tippet strengths ranging from 2 to 12 pounds, the loop should be formed from two lines created from a Bimini Twist. A fly can be attached to the shock trace section using either a Chermanski Loop, a Haywire Twist or plastic-coated stainless steel wire that is twisted and burned.

Type J: Compound Leader System with an Interchangeable Shock Trace (ST) for Sinking Fly Lines

The Type J leader is a modified Type G leader system with interchangeable tippet and shock trace sections for sinking fly lines. In most fishing situations, it is usually the shock trace section that needs replacement. Consequently, this leader system allows one of these components to be quickly exchanged, if it becomes unusable, without the need to replace the other element.

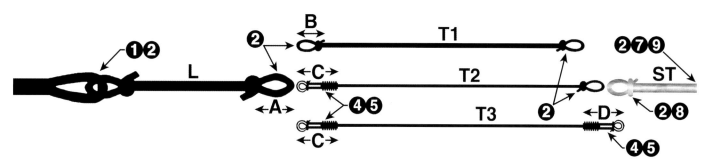

1 2 interconnection between the PVC Fly Line Loop (about 0.5 inches long) and the leader butt loop (about 0.5 inches long) formed by a Chermanski Loop knot.

2 Chermanski Loop knot.

4 5 double Chermanski Loop knot formed with the lines created from a Bimini Twist.

7 Haywire Twist.

8 Haywire Twist Loop.

9 twisted and burned plastic-coated stainless steel wire.

Fly Line	OAL	L + Loop	A	B	C + Loop	D	T1 + Loop	T2 + Loop	T3 + Loop	ST + Loop
4-6 wt.	≈4.5'	24" + 0.5" .023"	0.25"-1.5"	n/a	≤2" OAL + 0.25"-0.5"	1"- 1.5"	n/a	n/a	15"-24" + 0.25" 2-6 lb.	9"-11" + 0.25"-0.375"
4-6 wt.	≈4.5'	24" + 0.5" .023"	0.25"-1.5"	n/a	≤2" OAL + 0.25"-0.5"	n/a	n/a	15"-24" + 0.25" 8-12 lb.	n/a	9"-11"+ 0.25"-0.375"
4-6 wt.	≈4.5'	24" + 0.5" .023"	0.25"-1.5"	0.25"- 0.5"	n/a	n/a	15"-24" + 0.25" 12-16 lb.	n/a	n/a	9"-11"+ 0.25"-0.375"
7-9 wt.	≈4.5'	24" + 0.5" .025"	0.25"-1.5"	n/a	≤2" OAL + 0.25"-0.5"	1"- 1.5"	n/a	n/a	15"-24" + 0.25" 4-6 lb.	9"-11"+ 0.25"-0.375"
7-9 wt.	≈4.5'	24" + 0.5" .025"	0.25"-1.5"	n/a	≤2" OAL + 0.25"-0.5"	n/a	n/a	15"-24" + 0.25" 8-12 lb.	n/a	9"-11"+ 0.25"-0.375"
7-9 wt.	≈4.5'	24" + 0.5" .025"	0.25"-1.5"	0.25"- 0.5"	n/a	n/a	15"-24" + 0.25" 12-20 lb.	n/a	n/a	9"-11"+ 0.25"-0.375"
10-13 wt.	≈4.5'	24" + 0.5" .026"	0.25"-1.5"	n/a	≤2" OAL + 0.25"-0.5"	1"- 1.5"	n/a	n/a	15"-24" + 0.25" 6-8 lb.	9"-11"+ 0.25"-0.375"
10-13 wt.	≈4.5'	24" + 0.5" .026"	0.25"-1.5"	n/a	≤2" OAL + 0.25"-0.5"	n/a	n/a	15"-24" + 0.25" 10-12 lb.	n/a	9"-11"+ 0.25"-0.375"
10-13 wt.	≈4.5'	24" + 0.5" .026"	0.25"-1.5"	0.25"- 0.5"	n/a	n/a	15"-24" + 0.25" 12-20 lb.	n/a	n/a	9"-11"+ 0.25"-0.375"

Type J Leader Specifications

OAL = overall length   ST = shock trace   ≈ = approximately   wt. = weight

≤ = less than or equal to   lb. = pound   n/a = not applicable

Note: Leader design is not an exact science and, therefore, the dimensions specified in the table above do not have to be met precisely to assure maximum performance. A variance of an inch or less in length is acceptable. The overall length (OAL) of the leader and tippet sections specified in the table above does not include the negligible distance between the Bimini Twist and the Chermanski Loop knot of the T2 and T3 tippet sections or the small loop formed in the shock trace section. The overall length of the shock trace (ST) includes all the connecting knots at both ends in compliance with the rules regulated by the IGFA, which are discussed in Chapter 6.

To assemble the system, a small loop of about 0.5 inches or less is formed using the Chermanski Loop knot at the end of semipermanent leader section L for interconnection to the PVC fly line loop. A loop is also formed at the opposite end of semipermanent leader section L using a Chermanski Loop knot for attaching pretied tippet and shock trace sections. The loop size in all three tippet sections connecting to semipermanent leader section L should range between 0.25" and 0.5" in length. The loop at the other end of the tippet sections should be as small as possible (0.25" to 0.375") to interlock with the loop of similar size formed in the shock trace.

It is recommended flies are pretied to shock traces for quick and reliable substitution. The tippet section is connected to the loop of the shock trace section and both assemblies are then interlocked to the loop at the end of the semipermanent leader section L. For tippet strengths ranging from 2 to 12 pounds, the loop should be formed from two lines created from a Bimini Twist. A fly can be attached to the shock trace section using either a Chermanski Loop, a Haywire Twist or plastic-coated stainless steel wire that is twisted and burned.

Chapter 10

Specialty Leader System Configurations

The leader systems featured in this chapter are, for the most part, specialized variations of the leaders illustrated in Chapter 9 for more specific fishing applications. The table below

explains the symbols used in the drawings of all the leader system variations discussed and illustrated in this chapter.

Symbol	Description of Symbol	Photo Illustration
Legend for Leader System Configurations		
1	PVC Fly Line Loop. See page 60 for illustrated step-by-step tying instructions.	
2	Chermanski Loop knot. See page 24 for illustrated step-by-step tying instructions.	
1 2	The connection between the fly line and the leader butt section of a leader system.	
3	Improved Clinch knot. See page 26 for illustrated step-by-step tying instructions.	
4	Double Chermanski Loop knot. See page 24 for illustrated step-by-step tying instructions.	
5	Bimini Twist knot. See page 28 for illustrated step-by-step tying instructions.	
4 5	Double Chermanski Loop knot (r) formed from a Bimini Twist (l)	
5 6	The connection between an Albright Special knot (r) and a Bimini Twist (l).	
6	Albright Special knot. See page 32 for illustrated step-by-step tying instructions.	
7	Haywire Twist. See page 29 for illustrated step-by-step tying instructions.	
8	Haywire Twist Loop. See page 31 for illustrated step-by-step tying instructions.	

Legend for Leader System Configurations		
Symbol	Description of Symbol	Photo Illustration
9	Twisted & burned plastic-coated wire. See page 69 for step-by-step tying instructions.	
10	Blood knot. See page 25 for illustrated step-by-step tying instructions.	
11	Tandem blood knot. See page 25 for illustrated step-by-step tying instructions.	
12	Tandem Bimini Twist knot. See page 28 for illustrated step-by-step tying instructions.	
13	Double Nail knots in elasticity cord (l) and 30-pound mono (r). See page 78 for detailed instructions.	

Type K: Compound Leader System for Dry Fly Trout, Salmon & Steelhead

The Type K leader is the system I use exclusively with 2- to 7-weight fly lines when fishing trout, salmon and steelhead flies on or near the surface of the water. With the potential of interchanging flies pretied to tippet sections, the leader system is versatile in handling any fishing application quickly and efficiently. For example, I will use pretied flies when fishing an evening hatch to preclude the need to tie flies to a 5X, 6X or 7X tippet under low-light conditions. A fly is simply exchanged by removing the present fly-tippet configuration with a different one. The last thing I want to do is try to calmly fasten a fly to an ultra-thin tippet in waning light, especially when fish are rising and actively feeding.

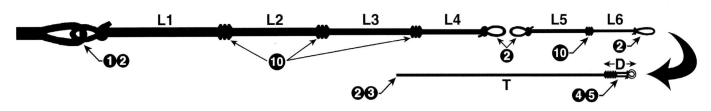

❶ ❷ interconnection between the PVC Fly Line Loop (about 0.5 inches long) and the leader butt loop (about 0.5 inches long) formed by a Chermanski Loop knot.

❷ Chermanski Loop knot.

❸ Improved Clinch knot.

❹ ❺ double Chermanski Loop knot formed with the lines created from a Bimini Twist.

❿ Blood knot.

OAL	L1 + Loop	L2	L3	L4 + Loop	L5 + Loop	L6 + Loop	T + D + Loop
9' (108") 5X/6X tippets	.021" .019" HF 24"+0.25"	.017" 16"	.015" 12"	.012" 9"+0.25"	.010" 7"+0.25"	.008" 6"+0.75"-1"	.006" (5X) or .005" (6X) 30"+2"+0.25"
9.5' (114") 5X/6X tippets	.021" .019" HF 24"+0.25"	.017" 16"	.015" 12"	.012" 9"+0.25"	.010" 7"+0.25"	.008" 6"+0.75"-1"	.006" (5X) or .005" (6X) 30"+2"+0.25"
9.5' (114") 7X tippet	.021" .019" HF 24"+0.25"	.017" 16"	.015" 12"	.012" 9"+0.25"	.010" 7"+0.25"	.008" 6"+0.75"-1"	.004" (7X) 36"+2"+0.25"
12' (144") 5X tippet	.021" .019" HF 35"+0.25"	.017" 24"	.015" 16"	.012" 12"+0.25"	.010" 10"+0.25"	.008" 8"+0.75"-1"	.006" (5X) 36"+2"+0.25"
12' (144") 6X tippet	.021" .019" HF 35"+0.25"	.017" 24"	.015" 16"	.012" 12"+0.25"	.009" 10"+0.25"	.007" 8"+0.75"-1"	.005" (6X) 36"+2"+0.25"
12' (144") 7X tippet	.021" .019" HF 35"+0.25"	.017" 24"	.015" 16"	.012" 12"+0.25"	.009" 10"+0.25"	.006" 8"+0.75"-1"	.004" (7X) 36"+2"+0.25"

Table title: **Type K Leader Specifications for Fly Line Sizes 2- to 7-weight**

OAL = overall length   HF = Orvis Hy-Flote

Note: Leader design is not an exact science and, therefore, the dimensions specified in the table above do not have to be met precisely to assure maximum performance. A variance of an inch or less in length is acceptable. The overall length (OAL) of the leader and tippet sections specified in the table above does include the connecting loops formed by the Chermanski Loop knot. Leader and tippet sections L4, L5, L6 and D include various loop sizes, as specified in the table, for interconnection with other segments.

Since I use this system exclusively for fishing flies on or near the surface of the water, I use Orvis Hy-Flote leader material for the semipermanent leader section L1. This line, with six hollow chambers, provides permanent floatation at the tip section of a fly line as well as increased freedom of movement to the remaining leader and tippet sections. In addition, the fly line and leader can be lifted from the water more smoothly and efficiently with less resistance and disturbance.

To assemble the system, leader sections L1 through L4, and L5 and L6 are joined together using a blood knot. A small loop of about 0.5 inches or less is formed using the Chermanski Loop knot at the end of semipermanent leader section L1 for interconnection to the PVC fly line loop. A small loop (about 0.25" long) is formed at the end of semipermanent leader sections L4 and L5 using a Chermanski Loop knot. The size of the loop at the end of semipermanent leader section L6 can be small (about 0.25" to 0.5" long) for interchanging tippet sections only or large (about 0.75" to 1" long) for exchanging tippet sections pretied to flies.

It is recommended flies are pretied to tippet sections for quick and reliable substitution. The connecting loop in tippet section T can be made as small as possible (0.25" to 0.5" long) using a Chermanski Loop knot. The loop should be formed from two lines created from a Bimini Twist. A fly can be attached to the tippet section using either a Chermanski Loop or an improved clinch knot.

Type L: Compound Leader System for River Nymph & Streamer

The Type L leader is a specialized system designed for use with 2- to 7-weight fly lines when fishing flies near or below the surface of the water. In addition to fishing for trout, salmon and steelhead, I use this system when pursuing largemouth bass, smallmouth bass, striped bass, panfish, American shad, hickory shad and a variety of other fish species in freestone streams and rivers. With the potential of interchanging flies pretied to tippet sections, the leader system is adaptable in handling any fishing situation or fish species quickly and efficiently without the need for tying any knots in the field. A fly is simply exchanged by removing the present fly-tippet configuration with a different one.

This leader system is also designed to accommodate the use of a 2-fly tandem rig. The possible tandem combinations are: popper/wet fly or streamer (weighted or unweighted) and wet fly or streamer/wet fly or two streamers (weighted or unweighted). To minimize the two tippet sections from becoming tangled, the fly attached to the lead section (L) should be slightly heavier than the fly tied on the trailer section (T) whenever possible. In most cases, a hook size larger or a fly slightly weighted on the lead section is usually sufficient to make the difference in preventing tangles.

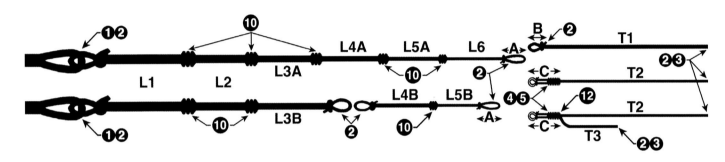

① ② interconnection between the PVC Fly Line Loop (about 0.5 inches long) and the leader butt loop (about 0.5 inches long) formed by a Chermanski Loop knot.

② Chermanski Loop knot.

③ Improved Clinch knot.

④ ⑤ double Chermanski Loop knot formed with the lines created from a Bimini Twist.

⑩ Blood knot.

⑫ lead section of a tandem rig produced by a Bimini Twist.

Type L Leader Specifications for Fly Line Sizes 2- to 7-weight									
OAL	L1 + Loop	L2	L3A or L3B + Loop	L4A or L4B + Loop	L5A or L5B + A	L6 + A	T1 + B	T2 + C + Loop	T3 + C + Loop
8.5' (102") 2X tippet	.022" 18"+0.5"	.020" 16"	.017" 14"+0.25"	.015" 12"+0.25"	.013" 10"+0.25"-1.5"	.010" 8"+0.25"-1.5"	.009" (2X) 24"+0.25"	n/a	n/a
8.5' (102") 2X tippet	.022" 18"+0.5"	.020" 16"	.017" 14"+0.25"	.015" 12"+0.25"	.013" 10"+0.25"-1.5"	.010" 8"+0.25"-1.5"	n/a	.009" (2X) 24"+2"+ 0.25"	n/a
8.5' (102") 2X tippet	.022" 18"+0.5"	.020" 16"	.017" 14"+0.25"	.015" 12"+0.25"	.013" 10"+0.25"-1.5"	.010" 8"+0.25"-1.5"	n/a	.009" (2X) 24"+2"+ 0.25"	.009" (2X) 8"+2"+ 0.25"
8.5' (102") 3X tippet	.022" 18"+0.5"	.020" 16"	.017" 14"+0.25"	.015" 12"+0.25"	.013" 10"+0.25"-1.5"	.010" 8"+0.25"-1.5"	.008" (3X) 24"+0.25"	n/a	n/a

Type L Leader Specifications for Fly Line Sizes 2- to 7-weight									
OAL	L1 + Loop	L2	L3A or L3B + Loop	L4A or L4B + Loop	L5A or L5B + A	L6 + A	T1 + B	T2 + C + Loop	T3 + C + Loop
8.5' (102") 3X tippet	.022" 18"+0.5"	.020" 16"	.017" 14"+0.25"	.015" 12"+0.25"	.013" 10"+0.25"-1.5"	.010" 8"+0.25"-1.5"	n/a	.008" (3X) 24"+2"+ 0.25"	n/a
8.5' (102") 3X tippet	.022" 18"+0.5"	.020" 16"	.017" 14"+0.25"	.015" 12"+0.25"	.013" 10"+0.25"-1.5"	.010" 8"+0.25"-1.5"	n/a	.008" (3X) 24"+2"+ 0.25"	.008" (3X) 8"+2"+ 0.25"
8' (96") 4X tippet	.020" 23.5"+0.5"	.017" 18"	.015" 15"+0.25"	.013" 12"+0.25"	.010" 9"+0.25"-1.5"	n/a	.007" (4X) 24"+0.25"	n/a	n/a
8' (96") 4X tippet	.020" 23.5"+0.5"	.017" 18"	.015" 15"+0.25"	.013" 12"+0.25"	.010" 9"+0.25"-1.5"	n/a	n/a	.007" (4X) 24"+2"+ 0.25"	n/a
8' (96") 4X tippet	.020" 23.5"+0.5"	.017" 18"	.015" 15"+0.25"	.013" 12"+0.25"	.010" 9"+0.25"-1.5"	n/a	n/a	.007" (4X) 24"+2"+ 0.25"	.007" (4X) 8"+2"+ 0.25"
8' (96") 5X tippet	.020" 23.5"+0.5"	.017" 18"	.015" 15"+0.25"	.012" 12"+0.25"	.009" 9"+0.25"-1.5"	n/a	.006" (5X) 24"+0.25"	n/a	n/a
8' (96") 5X tippet	.020" 23.5"+0.5"	.017" 18"	.015" 15"+0.25"	.012" 12"+0.25"	.009" 9"+0.25"-1.5"	n/a	n/a	.006" (5X) 24"+2"+ 0.25"	n/a
8' (96") 5X tippet	.020" 23.5"+0.5"	.017" 18"	.015" 15"+0.25"	.012" 12"+0.25"	.009" 9"+0.25"-1.5"	n/a	n/a	.006" (5X) 24"+2"+ 0.25"	.006" (5X) 8"+2"+ 0.25"

OAL = overall length   n/a = not applicable

Note: Leader design is not an exact science and, therefore, the dimensions specified in the table above do not have to be met precisely to assure maximum performance. A variance of an inch or less in length is acceptable. The overall length (OAL) of the leader and tippet sections specified in the table above does not include the connecting loops formed by the Chermanski Loop knot. Leader and tippet sections L3B, L4B, L5B, L6, T1 and T2 include various loop sizes, as specified in the table, for interconnection with other segments.

To assemble the system, leader sections L1 through L6, L1 through L3B, and L4B and L5B are joined together using a blood knot. A small loop of about 0.5 inches or less is formed using the Chermanski Loop knot at the end of semipermanent leader section L1 for interconnection to the PVC fly line loop. A small loop (about 0.25" long) is formed at the end of semipermanent leader sections L3B and L4B using a Chermanski Loop knot. A loop is also formed at the end of semipermanent leader sections L5B and L6 for connection to a tippet section. The size of the loop can be small (about 0.25" to 0.5" long) for interchanging tippet sections only or larger (about 1" to 1.5" long) for exchanging tippet sec-

tions pretied to flies.

It is recommended flies are pretied to tippet sections for quick and reliable substitution. The connecting loop in tippet sections T1 and T2 can be made as small as possible (0.25" to 0.5" long) using a Chermanski Loop knot. The loop in tippet section T2 should be formed from two lines created from a Bimini Twist. The tag end of the line used in tying the Bimini Twist can be applied as the lead section of a 2-fly tandem rig. A fly can be attached to tippet sections T1, T2 and T3 using either a Chermanski Loop knot or an improved clinch knot.

Type M: Compound Leader System for Clear, Shallow Saltwater Flats

The Type M leader system is specialized for sight-fishing marine species on clear, shallow flats where a shock trace is not required. The long leader, tapered by multiple sections, is necessary for pursing fish that ascend these shallow waters to feed. They seem to move across these calm, clear areas in a constant state of alarm.

Many of these marine species are easily spooked from shadows and the slightest disturbance. As a result, a long leader minimizes the impact of the fly line landing on the water. The multiple sections of the tapering compound leader reduce line shadow during the presentation and minimizes the disturbance on the water.

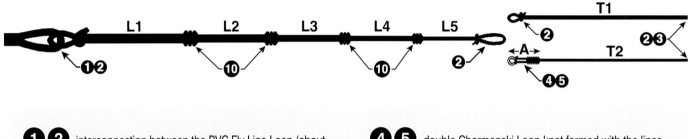

1 2 interconnection between the PVC Fly Line Loop (about 0.5 inches long) and the leader butt loop (about 0.5 inches long) formed by a Chermanski Loop knot.

3 Improved Clinch knot.

4 5 double Chermanski Loop knot formed with the lines created from a Bimini Twist.

10 Blood knot.

Type M Leader Specifications									
Fly Line	OAL	L1 + Loop	L2	L3	L4	L5 + Loop	T1 + Loop	A + Loop	T2
6-7 wt. F/I	10' (120")	.019"-.021" .019" HF 24"+0.5"	.017"-.019" 24"	.015"-.017" 18"	.013"-.015" 18"	.011"-.013" 12"+1.5"	n/a	≤2"+0.25"	24" 2-6 lb.
6-7 wt. F/I	10' (120")	.019"-.021" .019" HF 24"+0.5"	.017"-.019" 24"	.015"-.017" 18"	.013"-.015" 18"	.011"-.013" 12"+1.5"	24"-0.25" 8-12 lb.	n/a	n/a
6-7 wt. F/I	12' (144")	.019"-.021" .019" HF 30"+0.5"	.017"-.019" 30"	.015"-.017" 24"	.013"-.015" 18"	.011"-.013" 12"+1.5"	n/a	≤2"+0.25"	30" 2-6 lb.
6-7 wt. F/I	12' (144")	.019"-.021" .019" HF 30"+0.5"	.017"-.019" 30"	.015"-.017" 24"	.013"-.015" 18"	.011"-.013" 12"+1.5"	30"-0.25" 8-12 lb.	n/a	n/a
6-7 wt. F/I	15' (180")	.019"-.021" .019" HF 42"+0.5"	.017"-.019" 36"	.015"-.017" 30"	.013"-.015" 24"	.011"-.013" 12"+1.5"	n/a	≤2"+0.25"	36" 4-6 lb.
6-7 wt. F/I	15' (180")	.019"-.021" .019" HF 42"+0.5"	.017"-.019" 36"	.015"-.017" 30"	.013"-.015" 24"	.011"-.013" 12"+1.5"	36"-0.25" 8-12 lb.	n/a	n/a
8-9 wt. F/I	10' (120")	.021"-.023" .019" HF 24"+0.5"	.019"-.021" 24"	.017"-.019" 18"	.015"-.017" 18"	013"-.015" 12"+1.5"	n/a	≤2"+0.25"	24" 4-8 lb.

Type M Leader Specifications									
Fly Line	OAL	L1 + Loop	L2	L3	L4	L5 + Loop	T1 + Loop	A + Loop	T2
8-9 wt. F/I	10' (120")	.021"-.023" .019" HF 24"+0.5"	.019"-.021" 24"	.017"-.019" 18"	.015"-.017" 18"	013"-.015" 12"+1.5"	24"-0.25" 12-20 lb.	n/a	n/a
8-9 wt. F/I	12' (144")	.021"-.023" .019" HF 30"+0.5"	.019"-.021" 30"	.017"-.019" 24"	.015"-.017" 18"	013"-.015" 12"+1.5"	n/a	≤2"+0.25"	30" 4-8 lb.
8-9 wt. F/I	12' (144")	.021"-.023" .019" HF 30"+0.5"	.019"-.021" 30"	.017"-.019" 24"	.015"-.017" 18"	013"-.015" 12"+1.5"	30"-0.25" 12-20 lb.	n/a	n/a
8-9 wt. F/I	15' (180")	.021"-.023" .019" HF 42"+0.5"	.019"-.021" 36"	.017"-.019" 30"	.015"-.017" 24"	013"-.015" 12"+1.5"	n/a	≤2"+0.25"	36" 4-8 lb.
8-9 wt. F/I	15' (180")	.021"-.023" .019" HF 42"+0.5"	.019"-.021" 36"	.017"-.019" 30"	.015"-.017" 24"	013"-.015" 12"+1.5"	36"-0.25" 12-20 lb.	n/a	n/a
10-12 wt. F/I	10' (120")	.023"-.027" .021" HF 24"+0.5"	.021"-.023" 24"	.019"-.021" 18"	.017"-.019" 18"	015"-.017" 12"+1.5"	n/a	≤2"+0.25"	24" 6-12 lb.
10-12 wt. F/I	10' (120")	.023"-.027" .021" HF 24"+0.5"	.021"-.023" 24"	.019"-.021" 18"	.017"-.019" 18"	015"-.017" 12"+1.5"	24"-0.25" 12-20 lb.	n/a	n/a
10-12 wt. F/I	12' (144")	.023"-.027" .021" HF 30"+0.5"	.021"-.023" 30"	.019"-.021" 24"	.017"-.019" 18"	015"-.017" 12"+1.5"	n/a	≤2"+0.25"	30" 6-12 lb.
10-12 wt. F/I	12' (144")	.023"-.027" .021" HF 30"+0.5"	.021"-.023" 30"	.019"-.021" 24"	.017"-.019" 18"	013"-.015" 12"+1.5"	30"-0.25" 12-20 lb.	n/a	n/a

OAL = overall length   wt. = weight   F/I = floating or intermediate   HF = Orvis Hy-Flote   ≤ = less than or equal to   lb. = pound   n/a = not applicable

Note: Leader design is not an exact science and, therefore, the dimensions specified in the table above do not have to be met precisely to assure maximum performance. A variance of an inch or less in length is acceptable. The overall length (OAL) of the leader and tippet sections specified in the table above does not include the connecting loops formed by the Chermanski Loop knot. The L1 and L5 sections include loop sizes of 0.5 inches and 1.5 inches for interconnection with a PVC fly line loop and the tippet section respectively.

To assemble the system, leader sections L1 through L5 are joined together using a blood knot. A small loop of about 0.5 inches or less is formed using the Chermanski Loop knot for interconnection to the PVC fly line loop at the end of semipermanent leader section L1. A loop is formed at the end of semipermanent leader section L5. The size of the loop can be small (about 0.25" to

0.5" long) for interchanging tippet sections only or larger (about 1" to 1.5" long) for exchanging tippet sections pretied to flies. It is recommended flies are pretied to tippet sections for quick and reliable substitution. The connecting loop in tippet sections T1 and T2 can be made as small as possible (0.25" to 0.5" long) using a Chermanski Loop knot. The loop in tippet section T2 should be formed from two lines created from a Bimini Twist. A fly can be attached to tippet sections T1 and T2 using either a Chermanski Loop knot or an improved clinch knot.

Since I use this system exclusively for fishing flies on or near the surface of the water, I use Orvis Hy-Flote leader material for the semipermanent leader section L1. This line features six hollow chambers to provide permanent floatation at the tip section of a fly line. In addition, the fly line and leader can be lifted from the water more smoothly and efficiently with less disturbance and resistance.

Type N: Compound Leader System for 2-Fly Tandem Rigs

The type N leader system is designed for tandem configurations of dry flies, poppers and sinking flies for use in both freshwater and saltwater fishing situations. The tandem system can be used with the following fly combinations: popper/wet fly, dry fly/wet fly, two wet flies, two streamers or streamer/wet fly. The wet flies and steamers used in any of these combinations can be either weighted or unweighted. To minimize the two tippet sections from becoming fouled or tangled with wet fly or streamer setups, the fly attached to the lead section (L1 or L2) should be slightly heavier than the fly tied on the trailer section (T1 or T2) whenever possible. In most cases, a hook size larger or a fly slightly weighted on the lead section is usually sufficient to make the difference in preventing tangles. Even two weighted flies can be used effectively as long as the heavier of the two flies is attached to the lead section (L1 or L2).

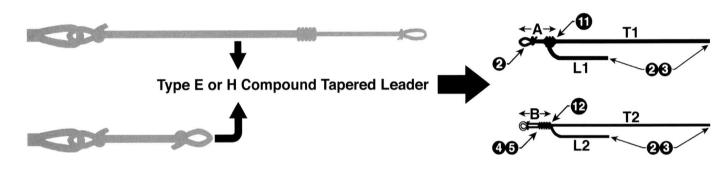

Type E or H Compound Tapered Leader

2 Chermanski Loop knot.

3 Improved Clinch knot.

4 5 double Chermanski Loop knot formed with the lines created from a Bimini Twist.

11 trailer section of a tandem rig created by a Blood knot.

12 lead section of a tandem rig produced by a Bimini Twist.

	2-Fly Tandem Rig Specifications					
Line Strength	A + Loop	B + Loop	L1 & L2	T1 & T2	OAL	Comments
12-20 lb.	≤2.5"+0.5"	n/a	8"	24"-26"	27"-29"	sinking flies
12-20 lb.	≤2.5"+0.5"	n/a	8.5"	15"-18"	18"-21"	popper or dry fly & sinking fly
4-12 lb.	n/a	≤3.5"+0.5"	8"	24"-26"	28"-30"	sinking flies
4-12 lb.	n/a	≤3.5"+0.5"	8"	15"-18"	19"-22"	popper or dry fly & sinking fly

OAL = overall length   ≤ = less than or equal to   n/a = not applicable

Note: Similar to leader systems, tippet design is not an exact science and, therefore, the dimensions specified in the table above do not have to be met precisely to assure maximum performance. A variance of an inch or less in length is acceptable. The overall length (OAL) of these tandem rigs does include the approximate length of the loops and extensions for interconnection to the semipermanent leader section of a Type E or H leader system.

To build a 2-fly tandem rig, lead section L1 is created from the tag end of joining two lines together to produce trailer section T1 using a blood knot. Lead section L2 is created from the tag end used in tying a Bimini Twist in trailer section T2. A small loop (about 0.5" long) is formed at the front end of the L1/T1 and L2/T2 tippet sections for connection to a Type E or H semipermanent leader section. It is recommended the tandem flies are pretied to the L1/T1 and L2/T2 tippet sections for quick and reliable substitution. The flies can be secured to the tippet sections using either Chermanski Loop or improved clinch knots.

Type O: Compound Leader System for 3-Fly Tandem Rigs

The type O leader system is designed for tandem configurations of three sinking flies of any design type. The 3-fly tandem system is effective in both freshwater and saltwater fishing situations. The wet flies and steamers used in any of these combinations can be either weighted or unweighted. To minimize the three tippet sections from becoming fouled or tangled, it is recommended the fly attached to the lead section (L1A or L2A) should be the heaviest of the flies used whenever possible. In most cases, a hook size larger or a fly slightly weighted on the lead section is usually sufficient to make the difference in preventing tangles.

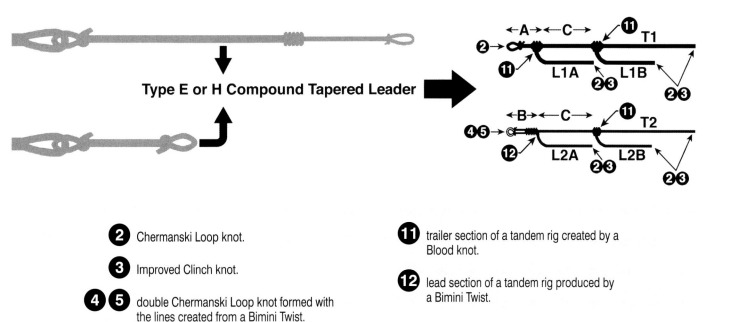

Type E or H Compound Tapered Leader

2 Chermanski Loop knot.

3 Improved Clinch knot.

4 5 double Chermanski Loop knot formed with the lines created from a Bimini Twist.

11 trailer section of a tandem rig created by a Blood knot.

12 lead section of a tandem rig produced by a Bimini Twist.

3-Fly Tandem Rig Specifications						
Line Strength	A + Loop	B + Loop	C	L1A & B L2A & B	T1 & T2	OAL
12-20 lb.	≤2.5" + 0.5"	n/a	6"-7"	8"	15"-18"	24"-28"
4-12 lb.	n/a	≤3.5" + 0.5"	6"-7"	8"	15"-18"	24"-28"

OAL = *overall length*   ≤ = *less than or equal to*   n/a = *not applicable*

Note: Similar to leader systems, tippet design is not an exact science and, therefore, the dimensions specified in the table above do not have to be met precisely to assure maximum performance. A variance of an inch or less in length is acceptable. The overall length (OAL) of these tandem rigs does include the approximate length of the loops and extensions for interconnection to the semipermanent leader section of a Type E or H leader system.

To build a 3-fly tandem rig, lead section L1A is created from the tag end of joining two lines together to produce trailer section T1 using a blood knot. Lead section L1B is created from the tag end of joining another line to trailer section T1 using a blood knot. The second blood knot is tied 6" to 7" from the first one. Lead section L2A is created from the tag end used in tying a Bimini Twist in trailer section T2. Lead section L2B is created from the tag end of joining two lines together to produce trailer section T2 using a blood knot. The distance between the Bimini Twist and the blood knot is 6" to 7". A small loop (about 0.5" long) is formed at the front end of the L1A/T1 and L2A/T2 tippet sections for connection to a Type E or H semipermanent leader section. It is recommended the tandem flies are pretied to the tippet sections for quick and reliable substitution. The flies can be secured to the tippet sections using either Chermanski Loop or improved clinch knots.

Type P: Tippet Systems for IGFA Record Pursuits

In the competitive and challenging nature of pursuing IGFA world records, any enhancements to fishing tactics and techniques or improvements to tackle performance can be critical to success. There are many subtleties that can be done with fly lines, leaders and tippets to increase the odds slightly in landing a large, powerful fish using a fine and fragile tippet. Success, however, ultimately relies on the construction and integrity of the tippet.

The Type P tippet systems are designed specifically for IGFA

world record pursuits when a shock trace is not required. It is a system I have been using successfully since 1971, although the use of an optional elasticity cord was incorporated many years later. These tippet systems are used with Type B, E and H semi-permanent leader sections. As a result, these specialized tippets are stored in a separate homemade wallet and they are available whenever the opportunity to pursue a world record avails itself.

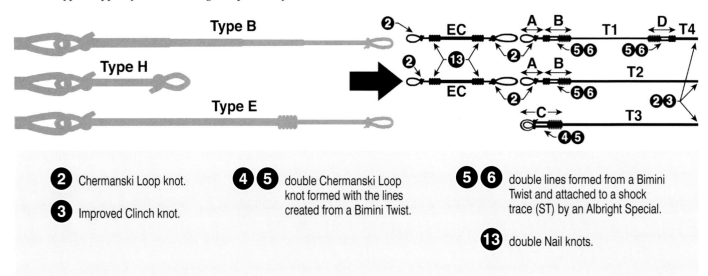

2 Chermanski Loop knot.

3 Improved Clinch knot.

4 **5** double Chermanski Loop knot formed with the lines created from a Bimini Twist.

5 **6** double lines formed from a Bimini Twist and attached to a shock trace (ST) by an Albright Special.

13 double Nail knots.

Type P Leader Specifications

IGFA Tippet Class	A + Loop	B (Optional)	C + Loop	D	T1	T2	T3	T4 (Optional)	EC
1 kg. (2.2 lb.)	0.25"-0.5"+0.25" 20 lb.	1"-1.25"	n/a	1"-1.25"	16"-20"	n/a	n/a	6"-10.5" 12-16 lb.	10"-12" 8-10 lb.
2 kg. (4.4 lb.)	0.25"-0.5"+0.25" 20 lb.	1"-1.25"	n/a	1"-1.25"	16"-20"	n/a	n/a	6"-10.5" 12-16 lb.	10"-12" 8-10 lb.
3 kg. (6.6 lb.)	0.25"-0.5"+0.25" 20 lb.	1"-1.25"	n/a	1"-1.25"	16"-20"	n/a	n/a	6"-10.5" 12-16 lb.	8"-10" 12-15 lb.
4 kg. (8.8 lb.)	0.25"-0.5"+0.25" 20 lb.	n/a	n/a	n/a	n/a	16"-24"	n/a	n/a	6"-8" 12-15 lb.
6 kg. (13.2 lb.)	n/a	n/a	≤2" OAL + 0.25"-0.5"	n/a	n/a	n/a	16"-24"	n/a	n/a
8 kg. (17.6 lb.)	n/a	n/a	≤2" OAL + 0.25"-0.5"	n/a	n/a	n/a	16"-24"	n/a	n/a
10 kg. (22 lb.)	n/a	n/a	≤2" OAL + 0.25"-0.5"	n/a	n/a	n/a	16"-24"	n/a	n/a

EC = elasticity cord   kg. = kilogram   lb. = pound   n/a = not applicable   ≤ = less than or equal to

Note: Similar to leader systems, tippet design is not an exact science and, therefore, the dimensions specified in the table above do not have to be met precisely to assure maximum performance. A variance of an inch or less in length is acceptable although the dimensions listed in the table above are more critical to the integrity of a tippet system. The overall length of the shock trace (ST) includes all the connecting knots at both ends in compliance with the rules regulated by the IGFA, which are discussed in Chapter 6.

To assemble the tippet systems, start with tying a Bimini Twist at one end of tippet sections T2 and T3, and at both ends of tippet section T1. The loop in tippet sections T1 and T2 are formed using a Chermanski Loop knot tied in a piece of semi-limp 20-pound nylon or fluorocarbon monofilament line. An Albright Special knot is then used to secure the loop to the two lines created from a Bimini Twist in tippet sections T1 and T2. The loop in tippet section T3 should be formed using a Chermanski Loop knot from the two lines created from a Bimini Twist. The size of the loop in all three tippet sections can be made as small as possible (0.25" to 0.5" long) using a Chermanski Loop knot. I pretie flies to tippet sections T2, T3 and T4 for quick and reliable substitution using a Chermanski Loop knot.

To protect the most fragile tippets from abrasion and to enhance knot strength at the eye of a hook, I use tippet section T4 between the T1 tippet and a fly. It is joined to the T1 tippet using an Albright Special knot. This section is considered as a shock trace by the IGFA and, therefore, can not exceed 12 inches in overall length, including all the connecting knots at both ends.

At times, the use of an optional elasticity cord (EC) is highly desirable, particularly with 2- and 4-pound class tippets. To build an EC, tie a 3- to 4-turn nail knot at both ends of the EC using semi-limp 30-pound nylon monofilament line. Do not cinch the nail knots too tightly on the EC. Using the tag ends of the EC, tie a 3- to 4-turn nail knot on the semi-limp 30-pound nylon

monofilament line and on the far side of the original nail knots. Do not cinch the nail knots too tightly on the monofilament line. Lubricate both lines near the first set of nail knots and slowly pull each knot tight then cinch tight both knots together. Repeat the process for the second set of nail knots. The step-by-step instructions for building an EC are illustrated in Chapter 6.

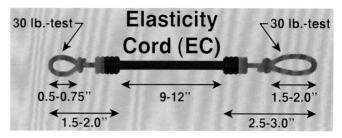

At one end of the elasticity cord (EC) form a small loop (about 0.25" to 0.5" long) in the semi-limp 30-pound nylon monofilament line using a Chermanski Loop knot for connection with the loop at the end of Type B, E or H semipermanent leader sections. At the opposite end of the EC, form a large loop (about 1.5" to 2" long) in the semi-limp 30-pound nylon monofilament line using a Chermanski Loop knot for exchanging tippet and shock trace sections pretied to flies. Refer to the previous drawing for the recommended lengths of the EC and nylon monofilament loop extensions.

Type Q: Tippet Systems with Interchangeable Shock Traces (ST) for IGFA Record Pursuits

The Type Q tippet systems are designed specifically for IGFA world record pursuits when a shock trace is required. It is a system I have been using successfully since 1990. These tippet systems are used with Type B, E and H semipermanent leader sections. These specialized tippets are stored in a separate home-made wallet and they are available whenever the opportunity to challenge an existing world record avails itself.

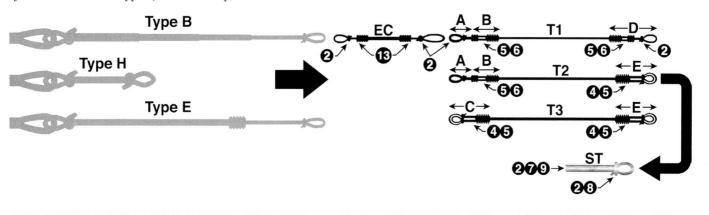

② Chermanski Loop knot.

④⑤ double Chermanski Loop knot formed with the lines created from a Bimini Twist.

⑤⑥ double lines formed from a Bimini Twist and attached to a shock trace (ST) by an Albright Special.

⑦ Haywire Twist.

⑧ Haywire Twist Loop.

⑨ twisted and burned plastic-coated stainless steel wire.

⑬ double Nail knots.

Type Q Leader Specifications

IGFA Tippet Class	A + Loop	B	C + Loop	D + Loop	E + Loop	T1	T2	T3	ST + Loop	EC
1 kg. (2.2 lb.)	0.25"-0.5" + 0.25" 20 lb.	1"-1.25"	n/a	1"-1.25" + .025"-.375"	n/a	16"-20"	n/a	n/a	9"-10.5" + 0.25"-0.375" 12-60 lb.	10"-12" 8-10 lb.
2 kg. (4.4 lb.)	0.25"-0.5" + 0.25" 20 lb.	1"-1.25"	n/a	1"-1.25" + .025"-.375"	n/a	16"-20"	n/a	n/a	9"-10.5" + 0.25"-0.375" 12-60 lb.	10"-12" 8-10 lb.
3 kg. (6.6 lb.)	0.25"-0.5" + 0.25" 20 lb.	1"-1.25"	n/a	1"-1.25" + .025"-.375"	n/a	16"-20"	n/a	n/a	9"-10.5" + 0.25"-0.375" 20-80 lb.	8"-10" 12-15 lb.
4 kg. (8.8 lb.)	0.25"-0.5" + 0.25" 20 lb.	n/a	n/a	n/a	1"-1.5" + .025"	n/a	16"-24"	n/a	9"-10.5" + 0.25"-0.375" 20-80 lb.	6"-8" 12-15 lb.
6 kg. (13.2 lb.)	n/a	n/a	≤2" OAL + 0.25"-0.5"	n/a	1"-1.5" + .025"	n/a	n/a	16"-24"	9"-10.5" + 0.25"-0.375" 25-100 lb.	n/a
8 kg. (17.6 lb.)	n/a	n/a	≤2" OAL + 0.25"-0.5"	n/a	1"-1.5" + .025"	n/a	n/a	16"-24"	9"-10.5" + 0.25"-0.375" 25-100 lb.	n/a
10 kg. (22 lb.)	n/a	n/a	≤2" OAL + 0.25"-0.5"	n/a	1"-1.5" + .025"	n/a	n/a	16"-24"	9"-10.5" + 0.25"-0.375" 25-100 lb.	n/a

ST = shock trace   EC = elasticity cord (optional)   kg. = kilogram   lb. = pound   ≤ = less than or equal to   n/a = not applicable

Note: Similar to leader systems, tippet design is not an exact science and, therefore, the dimensions specified in the table above do not have to be met precisely to assure maximum performance. A variance of an inch or less in length is acceptable although the dimensions listed in the table above are more critical to the integrity of a tippet system. The overall length of the shock trace (ST) includes all the connecting knots at both ends in compliance with the rules regulated by the IGFA.

To assemble the tippet systems, start with tying a Bimini Twist at both ends of tippet sections T1, T2 and T3. The loop in tippet sections T1 and T2 for connection to the loop at the end of Type B, E or H semipermanent leader sections or an optional elasticity cord (EC) are formed using a Chermanski Loop knot tied in a piece of semi-limp 20-pound nylon or fluorocarbon monofilament line. An Albright Special knot is then used to secure the loop to the two lines created from a Bimini Twist in tippet sections T1 and T2. The loop in tippet section T3 should be formed using a Chermanski Loop knot from the two lines created from a Bimini Twist. The size of the loops at both ends of all three tippet sections should be made as small as possible (0.25" to 0.5" long) using a Chermanski Loop knot. I pretie flies to shock trace sections for quick and reliable substitution using a Chermanski Loop, a Haywire Twist or plastic-coated stainless steel wire that is twisted and burned.

At times, the use of an optional elasticity cord (EC) is highly desirable, particularly with 2- and 4-pound class tippets. To build an EC, tie a 3- to 4-turn nail knot at both ends of the EC us-

ing semi-limp 30-pound nylon monofilament line. Do not cinch the nail knots too tightly on the EC. Using the tag ends of the EC, tie a 3- to 4-turn nail knot on the semi-limp 30-pound nylon monofilament line and on the far side of the original nail knots. Do not cinch the nail knots too tightly on the monofilament line. Lubricate both lines near the first set of nail knots and slowly pull each knot tight then cinch tight both knots together. Repeat the process for the second set of nail knots. The step-by-step instructions for building an EC are illustrated in Chapter 6.

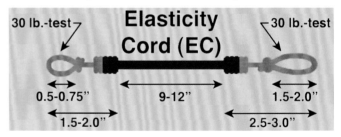

Elasticity Cord (EC)

30 lb.-test → 30 lb.-test ← 0.5-0.75"   9-12"   1.5-2.0"   1.5-2.0"   2.5-3.0"

At one end of the elasticity cord (EC) form a small loop (about 0.25" to 0.5" long) in the semi-limp 30-pound nylon monofilament line using a Chermanski Loop knot for connection with the loop at the end of Type B, E or H semipermanent leader sections. At the opposite end of the EC, form a large loop (about 1.5" to 2" long) in the semi-limp 30-pound nylon monofilament line using a Chermanski Loop knot for exchanging tippet and shock trace sections pretied to flies. Refer to the drawing on the previous page for the recommended lengths of the EC and nylon monofilament loop extensions.

Manufacturers & Suppliers

There are many manufacturers and suppliers of quality fly-fishing products. The products and materials mentioned in this book were purchased from many of the manufacturers and suppliers listed below. The sources highlighted in **bold face** pertain to the products I use and recommend.

Braided Nylon Monofilament

Cabela's: One Cabela Dr., Sidney, NE 69160; 800-237-4444; www.cabelas.com

Cortland Line Company: P.O. Box 5588, 3736 Kellogg Rd., Cortland, NY 13045-5588; 607-756-2851; www.cortlandline.com

Gudebrod: 274 Shoemaker Rd., Pottstown, PA 19464; 877-249-2211; www.gudebrod.com

Fly Line Backing

Cabela's: One Cabela Dr., Sidney, NE 69160; 800-237-4444; www.cabelas.com

Cascade/Crest Tools: 13290 Table Rock Rd., Central Point, OR 97502; 800-528-0001; flytying@cascadecrest.com

Cortland Line Company: P.O. Box 5588, 3736 Kellogg Rd., Cortland, NY 13045-5588; 607-756-2851; www.cortlandline.com

Gudebrod: 274 Shoemaker Rd., Pottstown, PA 19464; 877-249-2211; www.gudebrod.com

Orvis: Historic Route 7A, Manchester, VT 05254; 800-548-9548; www.orvis.com

Royal Wulff Products: 7 Main Street, Box 948, Livingston Manor, NY 12758; 800-328-3638; www.royalwulff.com

Scientific Anglers: 3M Center Bldg., 223-5N-03, St. Paul, MN 55144-1000; 888-364-3577; www.scientificanglers.com

The Hook & Hackle Company: 607 Ann Street Rear, Homestead, PA 15120; 412-476-8620; www.hookhack.com

U.S. Line Co.: 16 Union Ave., Westfield, MA 01086; 413-562-3629

Fly Lines

Cabela's: One Cabela Dr., Sidney, NE 69160; 800-237-4444; www.cabelas.com

Cortland Line Company: P.O. Box 5588, 3736 Kellogg Rd., Cortland, NY 13045-5588; 607-756-2851; www.cortlandline.com

Orvis: Historic Route 7A, Manchester, VT 05254; 800-548-9548; www.orvis.com

Rio Products: 5050 S. Yellowstone Hwy., Idaho Falls, Idaho 83402; 208-524-7760; www.rioproducts.com

Royal Wulff Products: 7 Main Street, Box 948, Livingston Manor, NY 12758; 800-328-3638; www.royalwulff.com

Scientific Anglers: 3M Center Bldg., 223-4NE-13, St. Paul, MN 55144-1000; 888-364-3577; www.scientificanglers.com

The Hook & Hackle Company: 607 Ann Street Rear, Homestead, PA 15120; 412-476-8620; www.hookhack.com

Leader & Tippet Material

Cabela's: One Cabela Dr., Sidney, NE 69160; 1-800-237-4444; www.cabelas.com

Cascade/Crest Tools: 13290 Table Rock Rd., Central Point, OR 97502; 800-528-0001; flytying@cascadecrest.com

Cortland Line Company: P.O. Box 5588, 3736 Kellogg Rd., Cortland, New York 13045-5588; 607-756-2851; www.cortlandline.com

Orvis: Historic Route 7A, Manchester, VT 05254; 800-548-9548; www.orvis.com

Mason Tackle Co.: P.O. Box 56, Otisville, MI 48463; 800-356-3640

Maxima America: 3211 S. Shannon St., Santa Ana, CA 92704; 714-850-5966; usa@maxima-lines.com

Rajeff Sports: 7113 N.W. 25th Ave., Vancouver, WA 98665; 866-347-4359; www.rajeffsports.com

Rio Products: 5050 S. Yellowstone Hwy., Idaho Falls, Idaho 83402; 208-524-7760; www.rioproducts.com

Royal Wulff Products: 7 Main Street, Box 948, Livingston Manor, NY 12758; 800-328-3638; www.royalwulff.com

Scientific Anglers: 3M Center Bldg., 223-4NE-13, St. Paul, MN 55144-1000; 888-364-3577; www.scientificanglers.com

The Hook & Hackle Company: 607 Ann Street Rear, Homestead, PA 15120; 412-476-8620; www.hookhack.com

Miscellaneous Tools, Glues & Accessories

Bimini Twist Knotmaker: www.chermanski.com

Cabela's: One Cabela Dr., Sidney, NE 69160; 800-237-4444; www.cabelas.com

Cortland Line Company: P.O. Box 5588, 3736 Kellogg Rd., Cortland, New York 13045-5588; 607-756-2851; www.cortlandline.com

Knot Assistant: www.chermanski.com

Loon Outdoors: 2728 S. Cole Rd. #110, Boise, Idaho 83709; 800-580-3811; www.loonoutdoors.com

Orvis: Historic Route 7A, Manchester, VT 05254; 800-548-9548; www.orvis.com

The Hook & Hackle Company: 607 Ann Street Rear, Homestead, PA 15120; 412-476-8620; www.hookhack.com

U.S. Line Co.: 16 Union Ave., Westfield, MA 01086; 413-562-3629

Shock Trace Material

American Fishing Wire: 205 Carter Dr., West Chester, PA 19382; 800-824-WIRE; sales@americanfishingwire.com

Cabela's: One Cabela Dr., Sidney, NE 69160; 800-237-4444; www.cabelas.com

Malin Co.: 5400 Smith Rd., Cleveland, Ohio 44142; 800-967-9697; www.malinco.com

Mason Tackle Co.: P.O. Box 56, Otisville, MI 48463; 800-356-3640;

Maxima America: 3211 S. Shannon St., Santa Ana, CA 92704; 714-850-5966; usa@maxima-lincs.com

Orvis: Historic Route 7A, Manchester, VT 05254; 800-548-9548; www.orvis.com

To Receive a FREE sample copy of
Flyfishing & Tying Journal magazine

call 1-800-541-9498 or email
customerservice@amatobooks.com
and make a request

(This offer applies only to non-subscribers)